THE RACETRACK GANGS

DICK KIRBY

has also written:
Rough Justice: Memoirs of a Flying Squad officer

The Real Sweeney

You're Nicked!

Villains

The Guv'nors: Ten of Scotland Yard's Greatest Detectives

The Sweeney: The First Sixty Years of Scotland Yard's Crimebusting
Flying Squad 1919–1978

Scotland Yard's Ghost Squad
The Secret Weapon against Post-War Crime

The Brave Blue Line
100 Years of Metropolitan Police Gallantry

Death on the Beat
Police Officers killed in the Line of Duty

The Scourge of Soho
The Controversial Career of SAS Hero
Detective Sergeant Harry Challenor, MM

Whitechapel's Sherlock Holmes
The Casebook of Fred Wensley OBE, KPM
Victorian Crimebuster

The Wrong Man
The Shooting of Steven Waldorf and
The Hunt for David Martin

Laid Bare
The Nude Murders and
The Hunt for 'Jack the Stripper'

London's Gangs at War

Operation Countryman
The Flawed Enquiry into London Police Corruption

Scotland Yard's Gangbuster
Bert Wickstead's Most Celebrated Cases

The Mayfair Mafia
The Lives and Crimes of the Messina Brothers

Scotland Yard's Flying Squad
100 Years of Crime Fighting

Scotland Yard's Murder Squad

The Racetrack Gangs

Four Decades of Doping, Intimidation and Violent Crime

DICK KIRBY

PEN & SWORD
TRUE CRIME

First published in Great Britain in 2020 by
Pen & Sword True Crime
An imprint of
Pen & Sword Books Ltd
Yorkshire – Philadelphia

Printed and bound in the UK by CPI Group (UK) Ltd, Croydon, CR0 4YY.

Pen & Sword Books Limited incorporates the imprints of Atlas, Archaeology, Aviation, Discovery, Family History, Fiction, History, Maritime, Military, Military Classics, Politics, Select, Transport, True Crime, Air World, Frontline Publishing, Leo Cooper, Remember When, Seaforth Publishing, The Praetorian Press, Wharncliffe Local History, Wharncliffe Transport, Wharncliffe True Crime and White Owl.

For a complete list of Pen & Sword titles please contact

PEN & SWORD BOOKS LIMITED
47 Church Street, Barnsley, South Yorkshire, S70 2AS, England
E-mail: enquiries@pen-and-sword.co.uk
Website: www.pen-and-sword.co.uk

Or
PEN AND SWORD BOOKS
1950 Lawrence Rd, Havertown, PA 19083, USA
E-mail: Uspen-and-sword@casematepublishers.com
Website: www.penandswordbooks.com

To Ann

This maiden she lived with no other thought
Than to love and be loved by me.

Edgar Allan Poe (1809–49) – *Annabel Lee*

Praise for Dick Kirby's Books

'His style of writing pulls no punches and he tells it the way it is. Highly recommended.' *POLICE HISTORY SOCIETY MAGAZINE*

'These are the real-life accounts of a tough London cop.' *DAILY EXPRESS*

'All of the stories are told with Dick Kirby's acerbic black humour in a compelling style, by a detective who was there.' *AMERICAN POLICE BEAT*

'New Scotland Yard legends are vividly brought to life by a man who had walked the walk, the Flying Squad's own Dick Kirby.' JOSEPH WAMBAUGH, AUTHOR OF *THE CHOIRBOYS*

'It's a rollercoaster ride; detectives who took crime by the scruff of its neck and wouldn't let go.' *EAST ANGLIAN DAILY TIMES*

'I am delighted that Dick Kirby has written this book. I am sure those who read it will realize how very hazardous the life of a policeman is.' MICHAEL WINNER

'Kirby looks to untangle facts from speculation and questions everything.' *GET WEST LONDON*

'Ex-cop Dick Kirby has now laid bare the Krays' empire.' *DAILY STAR*

'A vivid and fascinating account of policing some of the era's most serious crimes, written by an experienced and retired police officer.' *THE LAW SOCIETY GAZETTE*

'Real *Boys Own* stuff, this. Tinged with a wry sense of humour which makes this an excellent read.' METROPOLITAN POLICE HISTORY SOCIETY

'This is a fast-paced, riveting read, made even more enjoyable by Kirby's trademark humour.' *TANGLED WEB*

'This is simply the best book about police gallantry ever written and arguably the best book about any sort of gallantry awards. It comes with our highest possible recommendation.' *HISTORY BY THE YARD*

'A sensational and gripping account'. *PEGASUS YEARBOOK*

'Dick Kirby pulls no punches as he looks in depth at some of the most infamous names from the criminal underworld.' *MEDIA DRUMWORLD*

'Murder, torture and extortion all feature prominently as Mr Kirby investigates some of the most famous incidents of the post-war era.' *DAILY MAIL*

'Old-school, but effective – how the Met took the fight to the underworld.' *THE SCOTSMAN*

Contents

About the Author   ix

Acknowledgements   xi

Introduction   xiii

Chapter 1   The Sport of Kings   1

Chapter 2   The Main Contenders   9

Chapter 3   Enter the Flying Squad   17

Chapter 4   A Case of Mistaken Identity   29

Chapter 5   Slashings and Shootings   39

Chapter 6   Blackmail and Intimidation   45

Chapter 7   Gunfight at the Fratellanza   57

Chapter 8   The Misadventures of Alf White   63

Chapter 9   When Nothing's Quite Like It Seems   69

Chapter 10   Death at the Eden Social Club   73

Chapter 11   Widespread Gang Warfare   79

Chapter 12   Questions in Parliament   87

Chapter 13   Preventative Measures   91

Chapter 14   Alf Solomon Needs Help   101

Chapter 15   A Cowardly Attack   107

Chapter 16   Dirty Work at Croydon   111

Chapter 17   Death between Friends   115

Chapter 18   The Battle of Lewes Racetrack   123

Chapter 19   Downfall of the Sabinis   137

Chapter 20   Demise of the 'Tecs   145

Chapter 21   Death and Resurrection   149

Chapter 22   Jack Spot and Billy Hill   159

Chapter 23   The Francasal Affair   167

Chapter 24   The Dopers   175

Chapter 25   'A Beautiful French Blonde'   181

Chapter 26   Intimidation and Retribution   187

Chapter 27   The Fall and Rise of Dimes   195

Chapter 28   Dimes Triumphant?   199

Chapter 29   A Question of Murder   203

Epilogue   207

Bibliography   209

Index   213

About the Author

Dick Kirby was born in 1943 in the East End of London and joined the Metropolitan Police in 1967. Half of his twenty-six years' service as a detective was spent with the Yard's Serious Crime Squad and the Flying Squad.

Married, with four children and five grandchildren, Kirby lives in a Suffolk village with his wife. He appears on television and radio and can be relied upon to provide his forthright views on spineless senior police officers and other politicians, with their insipid, absurd and mendacious claims on how they intend to defeat serious crime and reclaim the streets.

He contributes regularly to newspapers and magazines, acts as a consultant to film and television companies, reviews books, films and music and writes memoirs, biographies and true crime books, which are widely quoted – this is his twentieth.

Kirby can be visited on his website: www.dickkirby.com.

Acknowledgements

First and foremost, I must thank my friends and fellow writers, Michael Nesbitt and David Rowland, for their kindness and generosity in supplying me with and permitting me to use their material to assist in the compilation of this book; I am most grateful to both of them. They are followed by the staff of Pen & Sword Books, especially Brigadier Henry Wilson, Matt Jones, Tara Moran, the skilled and inventive illustrator, Jon Wilkinson and my lynx-eyed editor, George Chamier. My thanks to them all.

Robert Bartlett MA Cantab, CF; Bob Fenton QGM, President of the Ex-CID Officers' Association; Susi Rogol, editor of the *London Police Pensioner Magazine*; Alan Moss, author and originator of the History of the Yard website; Cullum Fraser of the *Islington Gazette*; Jonathan Burcham and Zoltan Szentpeteri of the Grand Hotel, Brighton; and Mick Carter of the ReCIDivists' Luncheon Club. All of these successfully conspired to assist me. My thanks to you all.

I gratefully received wise words of assistance from: Michael Gwinnell; the late Bob Higgins; 'Maria'; the late Terry O'Connell QPM: Hugh Parker; Tim Phillips; the late George Sharp; Sue Summerbell; Ken Wood and Sharon Wood. And I have to thank Robert Bartlett, Mick Gray, Michael Nesbitt, Terry O'Connell and David Rowland for the use of photos. Others are from the author's collection, and while every effort has been made to trace other copyright holders, the publishers and I apologise for any inadvertent omissions.

My thanks as always go to my daughter, Sue Cowper, and her husband Steve for guiding me through the minefield of computer-land, my daughter Barbara Jerreat and her husband Rich and my grandchildren: Emma Cowper B. Mus; Jessica Cowper B. Mus; Harry Cowper; Samuel Jerreat and Annie Grace Jerreat. All of them, plus my sons, Mark and Robert Kirby, have provided love and support for me during my scribblings. Most of all, my thanks go to my dear wife Ann who, for almost sixty years has managed the rudder on my sometimes erratic ship.

Dick Kirby
Suffolk, 2020

Introduction

'Remember', said the lady in a very no-nonsense fashion who was sitting opposite me at a table in the Savoy Hotel's River Room, 'I don't want my name mentioned in any of your books!'

I nodded my assent, for three reasons: first, I can be relied upon to keep my word; second, she was paying for luncheon; and third, she possesses a very fiery temperament. Therefore, using a modicum of subterfuge, I shall refer to my friend as 'Maria', and the reason for my mentioning her at all by this *nom de plume* is because she really is responsible for the writing of this book.

Maria was the daughter of Italian immigrants who were so successful in their line of business that they were able to send her to the prestigious St Paul's Girls' School, from where she emerged with an British accent which is only slightly less cut-glass than the enunciation of the Princess Royal.

That – and her fierce disposition – were put to good use with stunning style as she was walking home one evening, when she encountered a couple struggling in the middle of the road. At first glance, Maria thought that the man was punching the woman.

'I say!' she said (in the way that Old Paulinas do), 'I say! Would you mind awfully not hitting that lady?'

But Maria suddenly realized that the man was not punching the woman at all; he was repeatedly stabbing her with a rather large kitchen knife.

'You bastard!' screamed Maria, and with that, she smashed the stabber over the head with her umbrella, which at least diverted his attention from the stabbee. Not content with that, her temper now thoroughly roused, Maria bashed the assailant over the head several more times, shrieking, 'You – filthy – *BASTARD*!' the final epithet coinciding with a resounding blow from her brolly, which by now had started to resemble a pretzel.

Fortunately – for everybody concerned – a neighbour had witnessed the man's initial attack and had telephoned the police, and they, plus an ambulance, arrived pretty well simultaneously.

'All right, Miss', said one of the two grinning constables. 'We'll take it from here!'

The unfortunate victim was carted off to hospital, where fortunately she eventually made a full recovery, the battered perpetrator later commenced a three-year prison sentence and Maria was presented with a bravery award, together with a new umbrella, at the local police station. I mention that story simply to let the reader know that it's *extremely* unwise to cross Maria.

Back to the luncheon, where she (a pillar of her local Catholic Church) and I were talking about crime in London in general, and in her area of the capital in particular.

'Huh!' she snorted. 'There *is* no law and order any more!' and then she added, 'What we need is another Pasqualino Papa!'

'Pasqualino Papa?' I echoed. The name rang a distant bell. 'Isn't he dead?'

'Dead? Of course he's dead!' said Maria impatiently. 'Him, and the Sabinis and the Cortesis. Of course, they were gangsters but they did have a code of conduct and they never messed with people not involved with them. *That's* what we need! A few more Bert Marshes around and the streets would be safe – they're not now!'

After lunch, I strolled through the Victoria Embankment Gardens to the Tube station to return home, but as I did so, those names were going round and round in my head. I didn't know then that Pasqualino Papa and Bert Marsh were one and the same, that he had boxed professionally as a bantamweight between 1917 and 1925, winning forty out of his sixty-one bouts, nineteen of them by knockouts. Similarly, I didn't know that he and Darby Sabini (at one time also, allegedly, a middleweight boxer) were devoted to each other, or that Papa would later stand trial for murder. The Sabini/Papa partnership was a formidable one.

And the Cortesis – well, I didn't know their name at all. No more than I knew the names of Alf Solomon, Fred Gilbert, George 'Brummie' Sage or Billy Kimber.

But now, of course, I do – and although a very small percentage of Clerkenwell's population saw some of them as Robin Hood-type folk heroes, what a black-hearted bunch they, and many others, were, being responsible over a period of approximately thirty years for some of the worst gang warfare – blackmail, woundings and murders – ever seen in this country during the twentieth century.

And the mayhem was not confined to the racetracks; violence spilled out into the streets, railway platforms, buses, pubs, clubs and cafés. The gangs shot, slashed, clubbed and hacked at each other anywhere they pleased, often in plain view of the police, many of whom reacted with exemplary bravery. Others did not; some did nothing at all, some took the part of one gang against another and some took bribes.

In practically every case, these gangsters had no compunction in bribing and terrifying witnesses and employing lawyers as crooked as they were, in order to bamboozle juries. And yet, although much of this book deals with horrendous violence between the gangs, there's more: the gangs who doped horses, to go either faster or slower, and those who introduced 'ringers' on to the racetrack. But to those readers who demand a fair share of snot and gore, never fear; violence and death often featured in those cases.

It's taken a long time (and a lot of research) since that delicious luncheon at the Savoy for that story to be told – but here it is.

CHAPTER 1

The Sport of Kings

Horseracing – 'The Sport of Kings' – has for centuries found favour with the British public. There was a lull during the First World War for obvious reasons, but at the war's conclusion, the racecourses to be found all over England – Aintree, Epsom, Greenford, Newmarket, Goodwood, Lewes – slowly came back into operation. They were soon flooded with punters eager to watch the racing, steeplechasing and point-to-points; every meeting had at least five or six races each day. Despite the pandemic known as 'Spanish 'flu' which swept the world, claiming the lives of 50 million people, and the virtual collapse of world trade, plus the fact that unemployment was about to hit an all-time high, ordinary folk wanted to forget the four terrible years of war and enjoy themselves.

Half a million copies of the racing editions of evening papers, as well as 100,000 copies of the *Sporting Life*, were sold daily to cater for the needs of the four million people who bet every week.

No doubt about it, racing was big business, contributing heavily to the economy in the form of saddlers, blacksmiths and veterinary surgeons, plus the farmers who supplied forage for the horses. In addition, huge profits from betting by post, telegrams and telephone were generated for the Post Office.

On-course betting was permitted; off-course was not. A gentleman could place a bet by telephone to his bookmaker from his London club, but thanks to the Street Betting Act of 1906, those less fortunate relied on unlawful street bookmakers. A case in question involved a girl who, for some reason unknown, was referred to as 'Nelly with the cast-iron belly' and was a classmate of my wife's. Habitually late in returning from lunch, her teacher frostily demanded the reason for her tardiness.

'I 'ad to put a bet on for me Dad, miss', explained Nelly, adding earnestly, 'If I 'adn't and the 'orse 'ad won, 'e'd 'ave bleedin' killed me!'

Hopefully, Nelly survived to live a full and an un-bashed life, but the policing of street bookmakers was a farce. Local inspectors of divisions would appoint police constables in plain clothes to carry out observations and make arrests. Unfortunately, to officers who possessed a streak of venality this was a golden opportunity to work alongside the bookies, who would put up a series of 'mugs', men with no previous convictions, to be arrested; thanks to their clean records, they would be fined a risible amount at court which would then be paid by the bookie; the arresting officer would also receive a bursary for his trouble.

It was a way of 'keeping up the figures' for the local inspector and providing not very compelling evidence that he and his men were doing a great job of keeping the streets clear of ne'er-do-wells, who were not doing any great harm in any event and, indeed, some good, by preventing the likes of 'Nelly' from getting a pasting. It was not until 1960 that legislation in the form of the Betting and Gaming Act altered this state of affairs.

⋆　⋆　⋆

At the Epsom Derby, attendance might run to half a million; at Doncaster and Aintree, rather less, with crowds of 200–300,000. To add to the crowd's enjoyment at Epsom, ice cream and fish and chips were on sale, as well as entertainment provided by roundabouts, swings and fortune-tellers. Gypsies, who traditionally attended races, provided the latter amusement, as well as offering, for a fee, to find parking places for vehicles. Some found the gypsies' presence annoying, although generally they were well behaved.

In 1920, railway strikes caused some meetings to be abandoned, and the following year, the coal strike brought out the railway and transport workers in sympathy, which resulted in the Government banning horseracing. But this was a temporary measure, just a blip, and before long, business was booming once more.

In some rural areas, punters arrived on horseback, but the vast majority travelled to the races by train; race day specials and cheap day excursions were laid on by the railway companies. In 1930, Aintree saw forty-three special trains arrive on Grand National Day; by 1935 this had increased to sixty, and often included in these race track specials were two or three horseboxes per carriage.

In addition to the trains, racegoers arrived in cars, charabancs, buses and coaches. It was not unusual for 200 buses to apply for parking permits at the Epsom Derby, and racecourses would charge anything from 2s 0d to £1 for these facilities. Later, the mode of transport progressed to private aeroplanes chartered to fly racegoers to Aintree and Chepstow; at Goodwood, a special landing strip was constructed. It is estimated that between the two World Wars the turnover in racing circles amounted to £500 million.

Tipsters abounded at the racetracks ('I 'ad a word with the owner this morning, Guv'nor . . .'), many of whom were worthless, although some were actually cheeky enough to offer to place the punters' cash on for them! Some, in an attempt to provide authenticity for their tips (which would be offered to the punter for anything between 6d and 2s 6d), would purport to be stable boys or former jockeys; some could be relied upon to dress themselves accordingly. However, Ras Prince Monolulu (aka Peter Carl McKay) was probably the most famous, especially for his cry, 'I gotta horse!' occasionally alternated with 'Black man for luck!' He commenced his business as a tipster in 1903, but when he picked Spion Kop out of nineteen runners at the 1920 Derby, at long odds of 100-6 which netted him the enormous sum of £8,000, people began to take him much more seriously.

In the midst of this carnival atmosphere, tic-tac men ostentatiously signalled their information to the bookies in order to lay off heavy bets or even up the betting, and the punters flooded in; but so did a large number of criminals, who mingled with them on the trains and at the races.

One group of four travelled to a race meeting by train without obtaining tickets. Upon arrival, one of the gang posed as a ticket collector and, after he had acquired four tickets, mingled with the crowds, joined his companions and distributed the tickets, they all successfully passed through the barrier. Even easier was the practice of conmen at the racetracks who, pointing to a small tent, shouted, ''Ere you are – public convenience!' Those who wished to divest themselves of their bodily wastes hurriedly handed over the penny demanded for entry to the tent, only to discover that the facility therein amounted to no more than a noisome hole in the ground. From a criminal point of few, these cheeky antics were very small beer indeed.

Smooth-talking card-sharps and three-card tricksters on board the racing specials fleeced gullible punters who erroneously saw the fraudsters' machinations as an easy way of earning a few quid. At the tracks there was the game of 'Find the Pea' under the three thimbles, although the mugs seldom did. Rather more impossible was the 'Spinning Jenny'; a spring underneath the board, when pressed, ensured that the pointer stopped at the spot where no money – or failing that, the least amount – had been placed. Other tricks to divest the mugs of their money were 'Pricking the Garter' and 'Box-and-Ball' – which were all as crooked as their operators.

Additionally, criminality was starting to emerge from within the racetracks themselves: crooked gatemen would allow gangs in for free, and dodgy ring officials were involved in the corrupt selling of bookmakers' pitches.

More serious were the gangs of pickpockets from all over the world who infested the racetracks, the railway stations and the racecourse car parks – the Hoxton Mob and the Titanics were two of the best known from London – and they enjoyed rich pickings. Often, when the fraudsters saw a mug extract a couple of pounds from a bulging wallet, they would tip off the pickpockets (aka the 'dippers' or the 'whizz mob') to the presence of a potential target, for a dividend of the profits, of course. The dippers usually worked in groups of four or five, although some, such as the Titanics, preferred the 'steaming' approach and would rush into a crowd, pinching whatever they could.

But the most serious of all were the race gangs – teams of criminals who intimidated bookmakers and took over the best pitches, or demanded protection money from them. To allow bookies to continue their trade, the gangs rented them stools (at a rate of 10s 0d per day) and made them purchase chalk (it was referred to as 'chalk money') for their blackboards, even though the bookmakers already possessed these commodities. To wipe the chalked-up odds on the blackboards between races cost the bookmakers half-a-crown (2s 6d) a time, which was chucked into (and collected from) their water buckets. The gangs also sold the bookies the required race cards, containing a printed list of the runners, which cost one farthing ($\frac{1}{4}$d) to manufacture and half-a-crown to buy, and demanded bogus subscription-list collections or non-returnable 'loans' of between £5 to £10. In these and other ways, the gangs could clear £4,000 at Brighton and £15,000 on Derby Day. There were various ways of dealing with defaulters: a bookmaker might be beaten up at the end of a meeting, or a fight would be engineered close to his pitch over a claim for a non-existent bet, so that no regular punters could get near enough to place a bet – not that they would wish to. Nor would they wish to intervene when a bookmaker refused to pay protection and the cry went up, 'A dirty welsher!',[1] whereupon he would be mercilessly attacked by the gang.

The bookmakers appealed to rival gangs for protection, and so the scene was set for internecine warfare. To focus the bookmakers' attention, gangsters held open their jackets to reveal

---

[1] One who refused to pay winning bets.

hammers thrust into their waistbands; if the implied threat failed to work, bookmakers' stands were trashed, their owners attacked and their money stolen. Hammers were just one weapon; iron bars, bottles, hatchets, coshes, knives and cut-throat razors were others. Testifying in court against an aggressor was considered to be highly inadvisable.

But upsets at racetracks were nothing new. There was an optimistic report in Surrey's *Globe* newspaper, dated 7 July 1898, which described Lingfield Park as having a racecourse police of its own, made up of Metropolitan Police pensioners and Army Reserve men, in the belief that they would work 'in perfect harmony' with the Surrey County Constabulary; when not required at Lingfield, they would be much in demand at Windsor and Gatwick racetracks.

Exactly one year later, on 7 July 1899, the attention of the racecourse police at the Lingfield meeting was drawn to the behaviour of a bookmaker who gave his name as 'John Smith' – it's possible that this may not have been true – and who after welshing on bets, attempted to escape from the ring. George Hewitt of the racecourse police detained him and after a violent struggle forced Smith to cough up the money owed to his clients. There was a disturbance, and a bottle and a glass were thrown at Hewitt and his companions, although no injuries were inflicted.

Smith was allowed to go on his way, but when the officials left the park to go home and entered a footway on their way to the railway station, they were confronted by a mob who had armed themselves with bottles as well as stakes torn from a fence. Smith, in the front row and armed with a rail, hit Walter Coburn, one of the racecourse police officers, knocking him to the ground. He then tried to hit Police Constable Hornett of the Surrey Constabulary with a heavy post; Hornett managed to evade the blow, but then Smith used the same post to hit George Hewitt (against whom he obviously felt he had a grievance) a terrific blow across the head, causing deep lacerations and knocking him unconscious.

In the middle of all this excitement Smith managed to escape, but he was arrested a week later in London's Newington Causeway, having in the meantime divested himself of the moustache which had adorned his upper lip at the time of the assaults.

Believing this to have been sufficient to make a case of mistaken identity, Smith put up an alibi when he first appeared at Oxted Police Court, but at the next remand, he decided that this defence might be more trouble than it was worth and discarded it. Charged with assaulting and obstructing police, inflicting grievous bodily harm and damaging a fence to the tune of £2, Smith – or whatever his name was – was committed to the November assizes.

Some eighteen months before the First World War temporarily shut down Gatwick racecourse, Police Constable Cadman of the racecourse police had a surprise when he discovered George Bray trespassing inside a horse loose box, followed by a nasty shock when Bray charged at him wielding a stable fork, the prongs of which pierced PC Cadman's tunic, the outer case of his watch and his spectacles case. The Bench at Reigate Police Court took a dim view of matters on 26 May 1913 and sent Bray to hard labour for one month.[2]

⋆   ⋆   ⋆

Known criminals could be refused admission to the enclosures, but at courses on common land – Epsom and Doncaster were two prime examples – the enclosures were only partially fenced off. As early as 1903, at the Epsom Derby, the Executive engaged the following (to ensure 'order and comfort to the public') to attend the meeting: fourteen detectives, fifteen more detectives from Scotland Yard, seven police inspectors and nine police sergeants, as well as what was described as 'seventy-six police and a supernumerary contingent of specially selected men from the army reserve and the Corps of Commissionaires'. It seemed the Executive took their duties seriously, since this workforce was committed to maintaining order and excluding bad characters; in addition, they intended to have a sizeable number of the Surrey Constabulary in attendance.

At Epsom racetrack, no organization had jurisdiction over bookmakers' pitches, and although members of the Grandstand Committee were still buying up the Downs in 1925 to obtain control, these sites were goldmines for the gangs who made the bookmakers pay heavily for the purpose of making a book.

By the 1920s, there were 14,625 bookmakers in business – there might, of course, have been a few more whose details were not recorded – who could be charged as much as 50 per cent of their earnings by the gangs. By 1925, the situation was so bad that no bookmaker could operate unless he paid up a minimum of £25 per day – in return, his 'protectors' could be relied to frighten

---

[2] Hard labour was an additional form of punishment for sentences of up to two years' imprisonment. It included industrial work, oakum-picking and using a treadmill. Like penal servitude, it was abolished in 1948.

away punters possessing winning tickets, which they confiscated, and welshing thus became commonplace. In other cases, gangs might completely take over a bookmaker's stand, and a variation on this particular theme was practised by a gang known as 'The Lightning Bookmakers'; four smartly dressed men would take up a position between two well-known and respectable bookies, and while the course officials were otherwise engaged, the men would jump up and offer two points over the market prices. Punters – especially inexperienced ones – would rush to them and hand over substantial sums of money to get longer odds; and that was the last they saw of both their money and 'The Lightning Bookmakers'.

They might have been detected, because due to the traffic congestion caused by vehicles leaving the racetracks, someone at Scotland Yard came up with the bright idea of putting up balloons, an airship and an aeroplane to report on the confusion down below. It was a good idea which should have worked, but it didn't; due to their lack of radio, those Argonauts of the air had to land before passing on any information, by which time the traffic would have sorted itself out and 'The Lightning Bookmakers' would be several counties away. Matters would not improve until 1934, when a Scotland Yard autogyro was launched, from which the observer could transmit useful information by means of a Morse key strapped to his leg. By this time, with regard to the racetrack gang wars, it was a case of too little, too late.

So that was the unhappy scenario of the racetracks – Epsom and Ascot were considered the most lawless – in the 1920s. Racing costs increased considerably during this period, and payments for the attendance of police, as well as gatemen and paddock supervisors, rose significantly, as did the cost of the Entertainment Tax, advertising and Income Tax schedules A and D. Horse racing income started to drop during the 1920s; this was put down to the General Strike, the Betting Tax and just plain bad luck. Although it was seldom mentioned at the time, the proliferation of gangs was also a contributory factor.

The criminals who infested the racetracks were collectively referred to as 'pests'. Some, however, were far more pestilential than others, and it's time to take a look at who was behind this organized banditry.

Chapter 2

The Main Contenders

Billy Kimber is first, mainly because of the two chief contenders it appears that he was the first to become involved in gang warfare.

Aston, near Bordersley, Birmingham, is the home of Aston Villa football club, and the area, developed during the nineteenth century, was a mixture of workers' housing, small factories and shops. Nearby larger factories gave the area its industrial character, the River Tame's water provided power for the mills, and water from artesian wells helped establish breweries. It was a tough area – infant mortality rates were high – and born in 1882, good-looking, smartly dressed Kimber grew up amongst the gangs of the area. He became a member of a group known as 'The Peaky Blinders' (now the subject of a hugely popular television series of the same name), so called because of their unattractive habit of inserting razor blades in the peaks of their caps, which were used with often devastating effect, it was said, to swipe their adversaries across the face. This (and similar associations) led Kimber to a period of imprisonment in 1901 for assault, and following his release, shortly afterwards in August, to two months' hard labour for assaulting two police officers. He was living a life of general lawlessness, picking pockets, fighting and indulging in rowdyism; in 1906 he was one of four youths fined one guinea (with the alternative of one month's imprisonment) for evading his fare on a London to Birmingham train.

He had already met up with George 'Brummie' Sage, who was five years his senior and who introduced him to the niceties of racetrack gangsterism. Although Sage hailed from Stoke Newington, London, due to his friendship with Kimber he became an honorary Midlander, hence the sobriquet 'Brummie'. Wishing to expand his business and take complete control of the racetracks in the south of England, Kimber formed an alliance with Charles 'Wag' McDonald. The latter was the head of the Elephant and Castle Gang, who were at daggers drawn with the West End Gang headed by two Irish-born brothers, Matt and Mike McCausland; they, in turn, teamed up with Alf White and his King's Cross Boys.

Hostilities opened in 1909, when two of the Elephant Gang attacked two King's Cross bookies; that was followed on 10 July 1910 in Berwick Street, Soho, when members of the Elephant Gang (which included Kimber and Henry Byfield) suddenly encountered the McCausland brothers, one of whom was heard to say, 'There's Byfield'. Mike McCausland pulled out a revolver and fired four shots at Byfield's legs which missed, and Kimber made himself scarce, unlike Byfield, who should have done. During the ensuing melée Byfield returned fire with a revolver of his own and was then hit with an iron bar wielded by Matt, who in turn was coshed by Byfield. Mike fired another inaccurate shot at Byfield, who stabbed him in the hand with a dagger, then inflicted several more incisions in Mike's neck. Police Constable Robbins, lustily blowing his whistle, made the crowd disperse and brought an end to the fracas.

At the Old Bailey on 8 September, Mathew, who perhaps surprisingly was of good character, received twelve months' hard labour, and Mike, who had previously been convicted of assault, was sentenced to eighteen months' hard labour. Byfield, who had a string of convictions, mainly for violence, received five years' penal servitude, with Mr Justice Hamilton remarking that he was 'quite an intelligent, primitive ruffian' (which was rather a contradiction in terms) but adding, 'It must be perfectly manifest that anything in the nature of leniency in dealing with faction riots and affrays of this sort would be a public mistake.'

Billy may or may not have been the William Kimber who was sentenced to seven days' imprisonment for begging in Coventry in 1910, but he was certainly the William Kimber who appeared at Lambeth Police Court in 1914, together with three others, charged with being drunk and disorderly and assaulting the police, following their return from Towcester races. Having pleaded guilty, they were most fortunate to be collectively fined a total of £8 6s 0d. By now, the Peaky Blinders had all but died out, so Kimber was looking for fresh horizons to fuel his dishonest lifestyle.

Returning to his native Birmingham, Kimber formed alliances with gangs in Leeds and Uttoxeter and established himself as head of 'The Birmingham Boys', also known as 'The Brummagem Hammers', although not all members of the gang were from that part of England. Some were part of the Elephant Gang, others from different gangs in Cardiff and Hoxton, and some were simply thugs who attached themselves to the gang that they thought most likely to become top dogs. Allegiance was not a strong suit amongst the members; some quit to join a different (often, an opposing) group, taking with them much useful information regarding their former associates' strengths and weaknesses, others became police informants, and there were some who dropped out following a prison sentence or through lack of interest.

But once more, Kimber's greedy eyes swivelled to the lucrative racetracks of the south; and Alf White, sensing trouble, decided to make a fresh alliance of his own. He found it, 117 miles south-east of Bordersley, at Clerkenwell, North London – and just one mile away from his own headquarters.

*   *   *

In Dickensian times, Clerkenwell had a terrible reputation for dishonesty and squalor, inhabited as it was by thieves and the poorest of the poor. The area was contained within the boundaries of Clerkenwell Road, Farringdon Road and Roseberry Avenue. Saffron Hill, a through road south of the Clerkenwell Road, was narrow, muddy and filthy; little wonder Dickens chose that thoroughfare as being the lair of his arch-villain, Fagin. But conditions had improved, and in the late nineteenth century the area became home to many Italian immigrants from the south of that country – those from the north appeared to favour Soho – and 2,000 of them melded in with the local Clerkenwell population of 12,000 to inhabit the 1,105 homes there. The majority of the immigrants were hard workers and brought with them their skills, food and language. Understandably, the area became known as 'Little Italy', and the focus of its attention, erected in 1845, was St Peter's Church.

The name 'Sabini' became known even before the better known members of the family were regarded as terrors of the racetrack. The father of the person who would become known as 'Darby' Sabini was named Octavio Sabini; he may have been born in Italy in 1856, and sometime prior to 1880 he arrived in England. He also called himself Octavia, Joseph or Charles Sabini, providing different names on each of his children's birth certificates; he could be said to have been a stranger to the truth.

In December 1883, an Italian named Antonio Barzo appeared at Clerkenwell Police Court charged with attacking Octavio (his name was also spelt Ottavio) Sabini in a public house, hitting him with the leg of an iron bedstead and knocking out some of his teeth. The constable who was called to the pub stated that some fifty Italians, all of whom had too much to drink, were fighting in the bar, armed with a variety of weapons, including knives and pokers. Prior to that, it appeared that Giulio O. Stachini was attacked

outside the pub by Sabini and another man named Leonardo –
all three were ice cream sellers – and while Sabini hit the victim
with a piece of hose with an iron ring on the end of it, Leonardo
stabbed him three times in the back with a large knife. None of
the weapons used were found. It would be a foretaste of things to
come with the Sabinis.

The following year, there was more trouble when Sabini had
a confrontation with a Tomasso Cassella, who was charged with
wounding Sabini with intent to murder him outside a restaurant
in Eyre Street Hill. On 19 November 1894 at the Old Bailey,
the jury took a more lenient view of matters and found Signor
Cassella guilty of the lesser charge of unlawful wounding, for
which he was sentenced to eight months' hard labour.

Six years later, Sabini appeared in yet another bloody interlude,
this time as an onlooker. Marzielli Valli stabbed a fellow Italian,
one Ugo Milandi, and Sabini assisted Police Constable 218
'G' Walter Selby in taking the victim to the Royal Free Hospital,
where he expired; Sabini was a witness in the case held at the
Old Bailey, where on 8 September 1890 Valli was convicted of
manslaughter and sentenced to ten years' penal servitude.[1]

A witness to the attack on Sabini in 1883 was a young woman
named Eliza Handley, who described him as being 'her young
man'; the only matter that one can be sure of regarding Darby
Sabini's parentage is that Eliza – or perhaps Elizabeth Eliza
Handley – was his mother's name and that she was an illiterate
Englishwoman. Darby was born on 11 July 1888 at 4 Little
Bath Street, Saffron Hill, Clerkenwell. His father was probably
Ottavio Sabini, who by then had relinquished the selling of ice
cream as a profession and was now a carman (the driver of a
horse and van), but it was difficult to be sure, since at the time
of Darby's birth Miss Handley was unmarried. Nevertheless,
Darby was christened Ottavio Handley, although he was also
known as Octavius, Charles and Fred Sabini, as well as Fred
and Frank Handley. Miss Handley and Ottavio Sabini rectified
their previous oversight – it was likely that the older Ottavio was
serving a sentence for wounding which delayed their nuptials – and

---

[1] The Penal Servitude Act 1857 replaced transportation; its sole purpose
was not to try to reform, but to punish the prisoner. It covered terms
of imprisonment from three years to life; for the first nine months of
their sentence prisoners were kept in solitary confinement and were then
employed on public works or for private contractors, often in quarries.
Leg-irons were often used on the prisoners; hence penal servitude was
often known as a 'lagging', a corruption of leg-irons. Penal servitude
was abolished in 1948.

eventually married eighteen months after her second son's birth. Young Ottavio became known as 'Darby' Sabini, which is how he will be referred to throughout this narrative. He was preceded by Fred (born 1881) and succeeded by Mary (1890), Joseph (1893), George (1895) and Harry (known as Harryboy) in 1900.

Now living at Mount Pleasant, Darby attended the Drury Lane Industrial School; opened in 1895, this was an institution designed for 200 boys and girls who were considered neglected or at a risk of becoming delinquents. It provided all meals for the children and employed such revolutionary ideas as forgoing corporal punishment for the girls; the boys, of course, continued to be caned or birched whenever the necessity arose. There Darby stayed until the age of eleven, when he moved to Laystall Street Elementary School in Holborn. He left at the age of thirteen, which coincided with the death of Ottavio Sr., and therefore he became one of the family's breadwinners. Eliza, the matriarch of the family, was employed in the coal business, as were her daughter and, with the exception of Fred, her other four sons. Nor was that all. On 9 July 1911, Eliza's coal and wood shed in Bowling Green Lane, Clerkenwell was raided by preventative officers from the Inland Revenue, who discovered crates of beer for sale. A number of people were summoned to appear at Clerkenwell Police Court on 2 October 1911, but in the event, only Eliza, Fred and George Sabini turned up before the Magistrate, Mr d'Eynecourt.

It is highly likely that the 'Fred' who appeared in the dock was, in fact, Darby, who denied any involvement with the illicit sale of beer and whose case was dismissed after Eliza and George took the blame. Eliza was fined the (then) enormous sum of £60 with 4s 0d costs, and George was fined £10.

As previously mentioned, name-swapping was something Darby specialized in; when he was bound over not to visit gaming houses at Marylebone Police Court on 17 May 1920, he used the name Frederick Handley.

It was said that Darby boxed professionally as a middleweight (the name 'Darby' has boxing origins), but if he did, it was under an alias, and his bouts might well have been held at fairground booths. It was also said he boxed under the name of Charles Sullivan, but the only record of such a boxer is of one who was far younger than Darby. Darby would later claim that he boxed under the name of Fred Handley, and a record exists of a fighter using that name who lived in Clerkenwell and who between 1905 and 1912 fought thirty-one bouts as a flyweight, winning fourteen of them. It might have been Darby, but who knows? For someone who used as many aliases as he did, it's difficult to say.

But whatever his pugilistic record, he certainly possessed a hard punch, and he was employed by boxing promoter Dan Sullivan as a bouncer at Hoxton Baths. No more than 5 feet 8 inches tall, Darby possessed a formidable physique, being broad-shouldered with a barrel chest; but for someone who would become known as a top gangster, he had none of Billy Kimber's sartorial elegance. Darby's habitual clothing was a flat cap, a collarless shirt and a rather grubby waistcoat and dark suit. Around his neck he wore a knotted muffler or scarf with both ends tucked into his jacket; neckties were seldom worn by the working classes, except on special occasions. No matter how much money he accrued – and at the height of his career, he was said to have a yearly income of £20–30,000 – his dress sense never varied, and he resembled a rather unsuccessful mafioso. Whilst he may or may not have been half-Italian, he spoke only English, sprinkled with Italian vowels from his possibly half-native habitat.

In 1913, under the name of Ottavio, he married Annie Emma Potter – also spelled 'Porter' – who was four years his junior, and they later had three children. It's told as part of the Darby Sabini legend that he came to notice in the Saffron Hill area of Clerkenwell when in the Griffin public house he knocked out a tough named Tommy Bennyworth (also known as 'Monkey' and 'The Trimmer'), who had insulted an Italian barmaid. It might be true; potential gang-leaders need a modicum of Robin Hood spirit to boost their charisma and to elevate them above common or garden thuggery. Darby, plus some of his brothers, drifted into the racetrack scene at the behest of Eddie Emanuel, a tough, heavily built Jewish bookmaker, who in 1909 had not only survived being shot in the chest at point-blank range but had chased after his attacker. No slouch at fisticuffs himself, Emanuel needed help against the hostile attentions of Billy Kimber and he enlisted the aid of Alf Solomon (a great deal more will be heard about this consummate villain throughout this book). Solomon summoned the help of the Sabini brothers, and it therefore suited Alf White (head of the King's Cross Boys) to throw his lot in with Darby as well. This was now a formidable partnership, especially since Solomon had been at odds with Jack 'Dodger' Mullins and his Bethnal Green Mob.

This is the general picture – slightly confusing though it may be – of the dramatis personae of the racetrack gangs set to enter the scene following the end of the First World War, although in the pages that follow more space will be given to them and to those who accompanied and fought with them.

* * *

But since the cessation of hostilities in the 'war to end all wars' and the resumption of hostilities on the racetracks, it's only fair to ask: what were the police doing about all this? Well, not a great deal. At that time, police conditions were pretty bad, and with a force of 18,200, the Metropolitan Police were chronically 4,000 men under-strength; their wages had been so poor that many of them (and their families) were suffering from malnutrition. In August 1919, the police went on strike for the fourth time in less than half a century – and 1,056 constables were immediately dismissed. Even more worrying for the politicians was that crime went through the roof, with armed holdups, masked burglars and smash and grabs. The racetrack gangs were just part of the mayhem.

Evidence of this appeared on 14 September 1919, when 24-year-old Thomas Wilson, a commission agent, a Russian named Barnet Dutchen, also twenty-four, and Simon Defries, a 32-year-old Dutchman, who had been among a party of some fifteen others returning from Alexandra Park races, were arrested for being suspected persons at King's Cross railway station. Their peccadilloes had been spotted by two Scotland Yard officers, Detective Sergeant David Goodwillie and Detective Wilkins, who had accompanied them on the train, but with the superior numbers of the gang's associates, the arrests were not going to be easy. The crowd, identified as a racetrack gang from Sheffield, turned on the detectives, who were kicked, punched and struck with walking sticks and umbrellas.

'Who has a shooter?' shouted Wilson, as he punched Wilkins in the face. 'Let 'em have one!'

When Wilkins punched him back, there were cries of 'Shoot 'em, boys!' from the mob.

Wilkins was knocked down to the platform, where again he was struck with sticks, but as he tried to get to his feet there was a shout of 'Throw him over!' and he was pushed violently on to the track, pulling with him Wilson, whose head came into smart contact with the rail. Wilson was undeniably dazed, but still full of fight.

'Give him another one!' he shouted to the crowd. 'That'll just about do him!'

As a train approached, railwaymen jumped down on to the track with considerable courage and pulled both men to safety. With modest understatement, a railway official described the confrontation as 'a brutal affair'. Wilkins, who was bleeding freely from cuts to his head, was conveyed to the Royal Free Hospital, where he was detained for several days. Assistance had arrived, and three more men were detained, also on a charge of being suspected persons.

At the prisoners' first appearance at Clerkenwell Police Court, Wilkins was still detained in hospital, but on 22 September he was able to give evidence before the Magistrate, Mr Bros, as did Sergeant Goodwillie.

Wilson stated in his defence that he was a 'tic-tac' man to a bookmaker and was unaware that Wilkins was a police officer. 'I might have struck him, but only after he hit me', he told the court, and denied that he had called upon the crowd to shoot or strike Wilkins.

Defries said he approached the crowd to see what was going on and suddenly realized that out of the market tickets valued at £50 that he had had in his possession £42 was missing, so he rushed into the crowd to find the man who had robbed him. He denied hitting anybody. Unfortunately for him, when Dutchen gave evidence, he said that he saw Defries hit Detective Wilkins with his umbrella.

'It upset me inside', Dutchen told the court, and he believed that Wilkins was 'absolutely dead'; when he saw Wilson punching Wilkins, he lashed out at Wilson with his umbrella, but unfortunately it hit Wilkins instead. He was punched by Sergeant Goodwillie and, believing the officer to be a member of the gang, he ran away; this was quite an imaginative defence, but even after telling the court, 'I was so upset at seeing this murder, I have not slept since', he was found guilty, and he and Defries went to hard labour for two months, with Wilson receiving six months.

Even though Detective Wilkins had survived being thrown on to the railway track (many thought that a charge of attempted murder should have been preferred), this type of behaviour was thought to be extremely demoralizing for the police. Something had to be done to rectify this state of affairs. Within precisely one month of the appearance at Clerkenwell Police Court, something was.

CHAPTER 3

Enter the Flying Squad

Fred Wensley was, by any stretch of the imagination, a remarkable copper. Having joined the Metropolitan Police in 1887, much of the first twenty-five years of his forty-two years' service was spent in London's East End, where he nailed strips of bicycle tyre on to the soles of his boots in an unsuccessful effort to creep up on and apprehend 'Jack the Ripper', arrested a double murderer whilst he was off-duty and went on to arrest murderers by the dozen, robbers by the score and burglars and receivers in their hundreds. By the time he was promoted to chief inspector he had smashed up the gangs who had terrorized East London – the Bessarabians, the Odessians and the Vendettas – survived the Siege of Sidney Street and been punched, kicked, clubbed, shot and stabbed at, and on one auspicious occasion, whipped. At the time of his promotion he had been commended on 242 occasions (the final figure would exceed 300), and when the first King's Police Medal was struck in 1909 it was awarded to Wensley. He was appointed MBE and later advanced to OBE – but this is the most important point: Wensley was a brilliant thief-taker and, moreover, completely unorthodox; there was never any question (at any stage of his career) of obeying the strict rules which then governed the Metropolitan Police, of requesting permission from the superintendents of divisions to enter their area to make arrests, or of handing over prisoners when they had committed offences in areas other than his own. He and his men went out in disguise, using covered wagons to follow thieves anywhere, and after they had been observed stealing property, he let them continue on their way until they had led him and his men to their receivers, whereupon the detectives would step straight in, arrest the thieves and receivers and recover the stolen goods.

So when he was asked by the Assistant Commissioner (Crime) in 1916 whether it would be possible to form a group of detectives who were 'more fluid', to be relieved of the restrictions which governed them, to go where and when they were needed, Wensley agreed that it could, simply because he had been doing that for years.

But there was a war on; it would take another three years, by which time Wensley had been promoted to the rank of superintendent, for this concept to be realized. On 20 October 1919, the Metropolitan Police District was split into four areas with a detective superintendent in charge of each (Wensley, naturally, was one of them) and two days later, two horse-drawn wagons, leased from the Great Western Railway, emerged from Scotland Yard and clip-clopped into Whitehall, indistinguishable from the thousands of other wagons in the capital. However, under their canvas hoods were a dozen detectives from all over London, hand-picked by Wensley personally for their abilities as thief-takers and informant runners – as well as for their courage. As they peered through spyholes cut in the canvas, on the look-out for villainy, these twelve detectives would soon swap the horse-drawn wagons for Crossley Tenders, purchased from the Royal Flying Corps. Number plates were regularly changed and posters advertising products, concerts or railway excursions were pasted on the sides of the vehicles. They could receive Morse transmissions but not – at that stage – transmit their responses. Messages had to be telephoned from public call boxes or police stations to Central at the Yard; there would be no Police boxes to telephone from until 1929, and until 1934 no Information Room to receive the messages. The office used by the men was so small that if four officers entered it at any one time it would become distinctly crowded – but from these inauspicious beginnings arose what would be known as the Flying Squad.[1]

* * *

Ten years had passed since Billy Kimber's spirited flight from the homicidal McCausland brothers in Soho; but death caught up with him once more on the evening of 5 December 1919, when he and his wife were drinking in the King Alfred public house in Lissom Grove. It is not possible to confirm the Kimbers' marital status. He and his wife Maude, whom he married in 1902, had long since divorced. When he remarried in 1926 he described himself as a widower, so perhaps the lady in question, that night

---

[1] For further details of this extraordinary detective, see *Whitechapel's Sherlock Holmes: The Casebook of Fred Wensley OBE, KPM, Victorian Crime Buster*, Pen & Sword Books, 2014 – also *The Sweeney: The First Sixty Years of Scotland Yard's Crimebusting Flying Squad 1919–1978*, Pen & Sword Books, 2011 and *Scotland Yard's Flying Squad: 100 Years of Crime Fighting*, Pen & Sword Books, 2019.

in Lissom Grove, was the one who called herself Anna Kimber, Kimber's co-defendant at the time of their conviction at Lambeth Police Court, when evidence was given that after verbally and physically attacking one of the police officers she screamed, 'I'll blow your fucking brains out when I get out – I'll know you again!'

If that was so, 'Mrs Kimber', now aged forty-eight – who, if she did not become the late Mrs Kimber, thereby justifying her husband's claim seven years later to be a widower, would otherwise be referred to as his 'common law wife' – complained that a certain Ernest Westaway Shobrook, a local furniture dealer also drinking in the bar, had 'grossly insulted' her. The nature of the insult was never made quite clear to the public but it was to Kimber, and it was sufficient for him to invite Shobrook outside.

Shobrook told him, 'I apologise if I have said such a thing to your wife, but I doubt whether I have.'

This apology seemed to satisfy Kimber, and the two men shook hands and parted. But shortly afterwards, Shobrook returned (apparently 'in an excited state') having heard that Kimber had spoken of his apology to others, and he struck Kimber. In what he described as self defence, Kimber pushed his adversary away, who fell, striking his head against a wall, then the pavement, fracturing his skull, and although he was conveyed to the Marylebone Infirmary he died there eight days later due to extensive damage to his brain.

An inquest had returned a verdict of excusable homicide, but the police thought this too good an opportunity to miss, and Kimber appeared at Marylebone Police Court on 23 December charged with Shobrook's manslaughter with a view to committing him for trial. Mr C. V. Hill for the defence asked Detective Sergeant Pinnock if, given the jury's verdict, they intended to proceed with the charge, but the Magistrate, Sir Chartres Biron stated, 'Oh, yes. We are not in any way affected by the Coroner's jury.' However, having heard the facts of the case, Sir Chartres was obliged to say, 'I do not think that any jury would convict on these facts', and Kimber once more was a free man.

But when Jewish bookmakers refused to pay up, one of them, Moey Levy, was attacked by Kimber and his brother Joe at San-down Park's Military Meeting on 12 March 1921, and they were all bound over to keep the peace. Joe was three years younger than his brother; he was an accomplished pickpocket and between 1902 and 1906 notched up seven convictions for larceny from the person or loitering with intent to do so, incurring sentences of imprisonment of between one and six months, with and without hard labour.

The Kimber brothers were not the only Brummagem hard-nuts to cause trouble at Sandown Park that day. Thomas Samuel John Armstrong, a 47-year-old bookmaker from Birmingham, was also there and he was looking for trouble. First, he attacked Abraham Joel; this was witnessed by Joel's brother-in-law, Samuel Hirschowitz who, together with his friend, 52-year-old Philip Jacobs, a Whitechapel bookmaker – he was also known as Phil Oker – tried to separate the two men. Hirschowitz was knocked to the ground by Armstrong and kicked, and when Jacobs went to assist his friend, Armstrong struck him on the head with the racetrack gangster's favourite tool, a hammer, and Jacobs fell to the ground, hitting his head on a stone.

This attack was also witnessed by another bookmaker named Maurice Forman, although he stated the blow was struck by Armstrong wielding field glasses. Additionally, Forman said that Armstrong surrounded him with four or five other toughs and demanded money from him; and because, he said, 'I was afraid of my life', he handed over £2.

But when Jacobs attended another race meeting at Goodwood on 30 July he became unwell and died at Guy's Hospital the same day as a result of apoplexy and Bright's Disease – possibly aggravated by that blow on the head.

The inquest was opened at Southwark Coroner's Court on 1 August, and Jacobs' widow told the court, 'Everybody knows Armstrong. He's a big and desperate man. My husband told me that after he had been assaulted, Armstrong said to him, "I'm very sorry, Phil; I didn't know it was you".'

'At present, I have no knowledge of the man Armstrong', Detective Inspector Webber told the court, but there were those there who did; having given his evidence, Forman was threatened by men outside the Coroner's Court, which prompted him to ask for police protection.

Inspector Webber lost no time in identifying the killer, and when Armstrong was detained at Birmingham police station he said:

> I know I had a fight with two men in the small ring at Sandown on that day, and I know I hit one of them and knocked him down. I didn't hit him with a hammer, because if I had, I should have killed him, then . . . I had been drinking all that day and didn't know what I did . . . I got laid out at Brighton after the last meeting there, and they nearly did me in. I was unconscious and was in Brighton Hospital two or three days.

He appeared at Tower Bridge Police Court charged with the wilful murder of Jacobs on 3 August, but on his next appearance, eight days later, the murder charge was dropped and a charge of manslaughter was substituted. He was committed to the Old Bailey, but despite the compelling evidence (including Forman telling the court, 'I had been threatened with my life') Armstrong denied hitting Jacobs, and on 9 September he was acquitted.

★   ★   ★

However, matters were hotting up, and eleven days after the attacks on Levy and Jacobs, on 23 March 1921 at Greenford Park trotting track, elements from the Elephant gang and George 'Brummie' Sage's amalgamation with the Kentish Town Mob under the direction of Billy Kimber were waiting for Darby Sabini to arrive.

It has been mentioned previously how gang members could fall out, and what happened next was a classic example of it. Fred Gilbert's professional boxing career, comprising sixty-eight bouts between 1909 and 1919, came to an abrupt halt after he was jailed that year for a racecourse riot. He had been affiliated to the West End Gang and Alf White's King's Cross Boys, and the amalgamation between them and the Sabinis was solid. But Gilbert hated Jews, and when the Sabinis joined up with Eddie Emanuel and Alf Solomon, Gilbert's allegiance changed quite sharply in favour of Billy Kimber.

Joe Sabini had patriotically enlisted in the Army in March 1916, seeing active service with the British Expeditionary Force and the Royal Welch Fusiliers, before he was wounded while serving in France. Invalided out with a character assessed as 'good', he was awarded a weekly pension of 12s 0d.

So whilst it was Joe's brother Darby whom the Kentish Town Mob were seeking, it was Joe they spotted first, and he was attacked by a crowd wielding clubs and bottles. But then Darby arrived. He would later say that an unknown benefactor threw a revolver to him, although this is extremely unlikely; it was known that he inevitably carried a loaded revolver with him. In any case, he fired a shot in the air, then another into the ground. As Inspector Heaps ran up, he saw Darby waving the revolver at the crowd from left to right and shouting, 'I'll shoot!'

'Shoot the bastard!' shouted one of the crowd, and as Darby started to run backwards, a police sergeant flung his arms around him and the inspector shouted at Darby to drop the weapon. It was a fraught moment; men were hitting Darby with bottles and pieces of wood and one of them shouted, 'I'll murder him!' There was a struggle to relieve Darby of the revolver, but it was eventually taken from him by a constable. Two men in particular, Sandy Rice (also known as Alex Tomaso) and Fred Gilbert, were urging the crowd to attack Darby, shouting, 'Come on, now – we've got them on the run! Let's go for the bastard – the police are frightened of us!'

Both men adopted fighting attitudes when arrested, with Gilbert shouting, 'I'll kill the lot, the police included!'

It was slightly amazing, given the weight of evidence, with Gilbert saying he was knocked down and Rice improbably saying that he had gone to Darby's assistance, that charges of disturbing the peace were dismissed in court.

Meanwhile, in an effort to calm the inflamed situation, Darby had been hustled away to Greenford police station; when he was charged with shooting at persons unknown, he replied, 'I had the revolver given to me today when I looked like getting murdered; I don't know by whom. About twenty of those Birmingham racecourse pests got hold of me. I did not shoot at anyone. I did it to frighten them.'

When he appeared at Ealing police court, the police stated that Darby had 'been in fear of his life' and that they had saved him – this might have been true. It's also possible that money changed hands, because the charge of shooting at persons unknown was dismissed, although Darby was later fined £10 for being in possession of a firearm without a certificate.

But before that happened, while Darby was remanded on his own recognizance of £200, plus two sureties of £100 each, and waiting to appear at court, on 26 March, Robert Harvey, one of the Birmingham Boys, was one of two men slashed at London Bridge Station; he had been accused of welshing at Greenford. It appeared to be a tit-for-tat reprisal for the attack on Darby.

The very next day, Billy Kimber arrived at Darby's house, which he rented for the sum of £2 6s 6d per week, at 70 Collier Street. Walter Beresford, a distinctly dodgy bookmaker, had promoted the meeting between Darby and Kimber, ostensibly in an effort to pour oil on troubled waters. In fact, his motives were far more self-serving since, in his own words, he wanted to push out 'the low-class Birmingham men'.

A large number of people attended what was described as 'a merry party' at Darby's house, and at 10.00 pm the women left. But at about midnight, the singing and laughter stopped; half a dozen men emerged from the house appearing to try to eject one of their number, but the man – it was Kimber – struggled free and got back inside. This fracas was due to the fact that negotiations appeared to have broken down: Kimber's idea was that the Sabinis should relinquish their hold on the racecourses at Ascot and Epsom; Darby's counter-proposal was that Kimber and his gang should go straight back to Birmingham. Moments later, a shot was heard, there was shouting, the door again opened and Kimber was ejected, unconscious, into the roadway. The police arrived, and Kimber was conveyed to the Royal Free Hospital, where he was detained suffering from a gunshot wound to his side and injuries to his head.

He later allegedly said, 'I never come copper on anyone and I ain't starting now' – although it seems unlikely that this type of phraseology would have been used by a Brummagem.

On Monday 28 March, at 2.45 pm, Alf Solomon walked into King's Cross police station, where he saw Divisional Detective Inspector William Smith and said, 'I hear you're making enquiries about that man Kimber who was shot in the street this morning?'

Smith replied, 'Yes. The man is now detained in the Royal Free Hospital, Gray's Inn Road, suffering from a bullet wound.'

'I wish to tell you all about it', said Solomon, who was asked if he wanted his statement to be taken down in writing. 'I do', said Solomon. 'It was me that shot him. It was an accident.'

His statement was to the effect that Kimber had been drunk, had threatened Solomon with a revolver and that during the struggle which ensued, the gun went off. Charged with shooting Kimber with intent to cause him grievous bodily harm, Solomon made a brief appearance at court before being granted bail – since there was 'nothing against his character' – in the sum of £20.

On 5 March at Clerkenwell Police Court, Mr Barker appeared on behalf of the Commissioner of Police and told the magistrate, Mr Bros:

> Although the case is a serious one, the evidence I have is of the slenderest and such as it is, comes from witnesses some of whom I would be sorry to put in the box. The facts were that on March 27, there seemed to have been a drunken orgy at a house in Collier Street, King's Cross. It ended in Kimber being shot. Kimber now refuses absolutely to say anything about the occurrence and I shall have to ask for a remand for him to appear and see if he will say anything when he gets here.

Nevertheless, Solomon was committed to the Old Bailey, where on 27 April 1921 he was discharged after Mr Justice Darling told the jury, 'In the absence of other evidence I must decide there is no case against the defendant.'

There are different versions of what happened: one was that Solomon used his own gun to shoot Kimber and another was that it was Darby who had fired the shot with *his* own gun. Be that as it may, between Kimber being shot and Solomon being acquitted, violence was still being perpetrated, this time at Alexandra Park.

On 2 April, police were fully aware that there was going to be a massive confrontation at the racetrack between the gangs, and the area was flooded with officers, both uniform and plain clothes. But despite that, and in full view of the police, fighting broke out in the Silver Ring (the enclosure cheaper than Tattersalls and usually sited next to it). Joseph Best from Bethnal Green was shot in the head, Thomas Joyce from Lambeth suffered severe lacerations when he was hit on the head with a hammer, and a notice was inserted in the number frame requesting the attendance of a doctor in the weighing room. Mr Davies, a friend of Best's, said that they were standing with race cards in their hands watching the numbers board and ticking off the runners, when men approached saying, 'You're two of them', whereupon he was kicked and Best was shot. Other shots were fired, but the police found that the large crowd made their movements difficult. Former Detective Chief Inspector Tom Divall, who was employed by the racing authorities, with the assistance of the one-time professional boxer, Dutch-born Moss Deyong, cleared out first the Sabini faction, then the Birmingham Boys from the course. Antonio 'Anthony' Martin from Birmingham was arrested and charged with shooting Best with intent to murder him, after Police Constable Hunter saw Martin shoot Best as he lay on the ground, then throw the revolver away. However, Martin was bailed from Wood Green Police Court after Detective Inspector Gibbon stated that the revolver which had been found had not recently been fired, since the barrel was rusty. Although there is the possibility that money changed hands, and the retrieved gun might not have been the same one which had been in Martin's possession, it seemed to back up his assertion that 'I've never had a revolver in my possession in my life.'

Best gave evidence at the Police Court saying that he and Davies had been in the Silver Ring and that after they were approached by a mob of men, he walked away, then ran. 'They came after me and after being pushed and knocked about, I found myself on the ground, bleeding.'

He added that he had heard a loud report. Answering Mr Keeves for the defence, Best said that he was not a frequenter of racecourses, he had never seen Martin in his life, he had no grudge against him and, as far as he knew, Martin had no grudge against him. Although the defence suggested that the case was one of mistaken identity, Martin was committed to the Old Bailey, for trial. After Best refused to identify Martin as his assailant, there was the same depressing outcome: before Mr Justice Shearman, on 5 July, Martin was acquitted of all charges.

The court did not hear the whole story, because Best was being less than frank; a taxi driver, he had arrived to convey Darby from the grounds. When Kimber's mentor, George 'Brummie' Sage, went to attack Darby, Best stepped in and Sage knocked him to the ground. As he lay there, Martin, a Birmingham Boy enforcer, stepped in and shot him. If that was indeed the case, Darby did nothing to help Best.

*   *   *

As well as at Alexandra Park, trouble was brewing at Kempton Park racecourse on Easter Monday 1921, but on that occasion the Flying Squad nipped it neatly in the bud. Detective Sergeant Selby had kept John Carpenter, a 47-year-old fruiterer, William Barney Cook, a fishmonger aged 45 and 41-year-old greengrocer, George Moss under observation – they were all described as being 'men of large stature' – and saw them approach several bookmakers and demand money with menaces. When one demurred, Cook brandished a hammer in his face, whereupon the bookmaker handed over cash from his satchel. This was repeated at the stands of other bookmakers, some of whom gave the men money. When they were arrested, Moss had an empty beer bottle in his possession.

But when Detective Sergeant Tongue asked the bookmakers to give evidence at Feltham Police Court, not only did they all refuse, saying they were too frightened of the consequences if they did so, but they also refused to give their correct names and addresses.

The prisoners, all of whom pleaded not guilty to being suspected persons (Moss was additionally charged with being a person subject to the Prevention of Crimes Act), gave evidence, with Cook stating that he was a number runner and only went to the bookmakers to collect his wages.

Mr Knight, who prosecuted in this case, told the Bench that he would like them to hear from a police officer about the blackmailing and bullying that was going on at racecourses. Step forward Detective Inspector Grosse, who told the Bench:

> This so-called number running and what follows from it is a very serious matter at the present time. Serious disturbances have arisen on various racecourses in connection with it. A number of men have banded themselves together and called

themselves number runners and used this as a means of blackmailing bookmakers whose lives were endangered if they did not pay; and not only them, but innocent racegoers. If a man is big enough and bully enough, the bookmaker must pay up and he dare not come forward to prosecute. The Commissioner of Police has been compelled to take action in this matter.

The Bench dished out hard labour: twelve months to Moss, one-time leader of the Elephant Gang and known to the denizens of South London as 'Mad Mossy', and three months each to Carpenter and Cook.[2]

⋆   ⋆   ⋆

Within weeks, the Birmingham Boys beat up Jewish bookmakers in the Silver Ring at Bath, and on 20 April two groups, one from Birmingham, the other from King's Cross, left the Southampton Arms by Mornington Crescent Tube station, and an argument commenced at a nearby coffee stall. A fight broke out, a shot was fired and when three of the men tried to escape in a taxi, an enterprising constable jumped on to the taxi's footboard and directed the driver to Albany Street police station, where the three passengers were detained. One of them was found to be in possession of a bludgeon made out of a German grenade affixed to a short stick. Later, several of the mens' associates arrived at the police station in a taxi; this was a common tactic – to bluster, demand to know on what grounds their associates were being held and demand their release, all done in an attempt to display that they, and not the police, were in charge. However, in this case their plan backfired, because whilst they were inside making their bellicose representations, an officer found a loaded revolver on the taxi's seat, which resulted in their being detained rather longer than they might have expected.

On 1 June 1921, David Levy, a Bethnal Green bookmaker (and the possessor of eighteen previous convictions) was arrested at Epsom in possession of a revolver and ammunition, together

---

[2] Moss was extremely fortunate; being subject to the Prevention of Crime Act 1908 meant that, being a person over the age of sixteen who had been convicted of crime on three occasions and was leading a dishonest life, he was classed as 'a habitual criminal', and that having been sentenced to penal servitude, he could be sentenced to a further period of preventative detention not exceeding ten years and not less than five, for the protection of the public.

with his brother Moses, and both were sentenced to three months' imprisonment. Being Sabini associates, it is highly likely that they were fingered by one of the opposing factions; it was common practice for a rival gang member to be jocularly clapped on the back, leaving a tell-tale chalk mark on their jacket, a sure sign to any detective so inclined that this was someone worth nicking.

Others considered worth nicking were five men who travelled down from Birmingham in the hope and expectation of attending the Derby but who neglected to pay the train fare required; they appeared at Willesden Police Court, and for what on the face of it appeared to be a fairly trivial offence, they were all remanded in custody.

It was a mild piece of excitement that day at the Derby – a bigger thrill was Steve Donoghue, with the first of three consecutive wins, romping home on Humourist at odds of 6-1, presenting the winner with £6,450, a feat which was about to be eclipsed by acts of utter barbarity.

CHAPTER 4

A Case of Mistaken Identity

On the day after the Derby, the Birmingham Boys were at Epsom in force. Three of them were Ernest Mack, William Darby and Charles Franklin, and they were kept under observation by the police as they pushed through the crowds. Approaching bookmakers, and with Darby holding out his hand, Franklin told them, 'Give us a quid, come on', and most did hand over some silver. Those who refused were threatened by Darby, who told them, 'Come on, we're four-handed.'

The sentences were surprising; William Darby, who appeared to be the prime mover, was fined £25, and while Mack was sentenced to three months' imprisonment, so was Franklin, who had only just been released from a sentence of ten years' penal servitude for shooting with intent to murder.

So that was a hiccup for the Birmingham Boys but not one of monumental importance because there were still plenty of them left, and they decided that the Levy brothers' arrests of the previous day would be only the *hors d'oeuvre* to the *plat du jour* of the Italian Mob. Both opposing factions were at Epsom; so was the Flying Squad under the direction of Detective Inspector Stevens, who had sorted out Franklin and Co. Therefore the Birmingham Boys left the race meeting early and set off back towards London in vehicles which included a charabanc and a taxi. At 4.30 pm, at Ewell, Surrey, near the Brick Kiln public house, they hid the vehicles, and for half an hour lookouts using field glasses were posted to keep watch for their adversaries; suddenly, a tender – ironically, a converted Crossley, as used by the Flying Squad – was spotted travelling from the direction of Epsom. It chugged lugubriously up the incline to the London Road, and since a Crossley's top speed in that situation was no more than 10 mph, the gang had plenty of time to ready themselves. The Crossley had almost reached the Brick Kiln pub when one of the gang shouted, 'Here come the Italian bastards – kill the bloody lot of them!' and the hidden taxi drove out of a side turning, blocking its passage. Approximately forty of the Birmingham Boys then rushed out of the bushes armed with axes, hammers, bottles, guns and housebricks. There was a shout of

'This is the Brummagem Gang!', and they pulled the luckless ten bookmakers and their assistants out of the vehicle and set about them, breaking arms, smashing teeth and slashing heads open in front of horrified residents, who screamed in terror at the sheer ferocity of the attack.

And ferocious it was; the Birmingham Boys appeared to be in the grip of a bloodlust, wildly hacking and slashing; when Lazarus Green, one of the occupants of the tender (none of whom were members of the Italian faction) whose arm had been fractured, suddenly recognized one of the Birmingham Boys chasing him as being an ally and shouted, 'You've made a bloomer – we're Leeds men!', it made no difference at all.

His pursuer, who was wielding a hammer, replied, 'I hope not! Anyway, get into the field and lie behind the trees – or else they'll kill you!' It was only by a gracious dispensation of providence that they didn't.

Many of the bookmakers were kicked into insensibility, then the majority of the Birmingham Boys got back into their vehicles and headed off towards London; others ran off across the fields. Charles 'Woolf' Schwarz was hit by someone wielding a chopper but managed to escape into the lavatory of the Brick Kiln pub. Schwartz (a deserter from the 28th Middlesex Regiment with a string of convictions for larceny to his name) later identified some of the attackers but refused to do so in court. 'If I did, I wouldn't be able to go racing again', he told the investigating officers.

Some of the wounded, still conscious and bleeding heavily, staggered into the house of a Mrs Martin in Kiln Passage, and while she and her husband rendered first aid, their son jumped on his bicycle and went for a doctor and the police. A garbled report (probably from Master Martin) that there had been a Sinn Féin riot at Ewell was received at 5.45 pm by Inspector Stevens at Epsom police station, and he and his officers made their way there through the race-going crowds. Even he was sickened at the shocking sight of the injuries; one man had had three fingers severed. Apart from Schwarz and Green, Joseph Cohen, David Robinson, Solomon Levison, Michael and Isaac Lewis, Herbert Whiteley, Sam Barnett and Jack Morris had received injuries of varying severity. They were taken to Epsom's Cottage Hospital, where their wounds were treated; due to the gravity of their injuries, five of the bookmakers were detained. Two vehicles at the scene of the attack were badly damaged; the driver of one of them, Walter Giles, was sitting by the side of the road, and Inspector Stevens informed him that he should consider himself under arrest.

The rumour that there had been a Sinn Féin riot gathered momentum – they were particularly active at the time – and many of the race-goers either turned around and returned to Epsom or took alternative routes home.

A description of the attackers and their vehicle (it was a rather distinctive light blue colour) was sent out on an 'All Stations' message, and a little later, at 7.30 pm, Police Constable Shoesmith spotted the charabanc outside the George and Dragon public house on Kingston Hill. He contacted his station, and upon arrival at the pub, Police Sergeant 63 'V' Merritt lifted the bonnet and, to prevent the gang's escape, ripped the leads off the sparking plugs. Police Sergeant 110 'V' Joseph Dawson's superintendent, still believing that there had been an outrage by the IRA, had armed him with a revolver, and he walked into the pub's garden, where twenty-eight members of the Birmingham Boys – others had returned to London, one of whom may have been 'Dodger' Mullins – were refreshing themselves after their exertions. They were well able to do so; the previous day, they had obtained £140 (all in silver) by blackmailing the bookmakers. Having ascertained that they had originated from Birmingham (their charabanc's licence had been issued by the Birmingham licensing authorities), Sergeant Dawson politely asked the group to consider themselves under arrest. All twenty-eight rose as one, but before they could rush him, Dawson drew his revolver, informed them, 'I shall shoot the first man who tries to escape!' and held them there. Sub-divisional Inspector Hooper had surrounded the area with fifty officers, whereupon it was discovered that one of the Birmingham Boys, Thomas Eivers, was carrying a fish basket; it was found to contain two hammers and a loaded Mauser pistol. Another of the gang, Henry Tuckey, tried to hide a loaded Webley revolver, and other weapons were found concealed under the seats in the pub's garden. Using the gang's charabanc, the prisoners were taken to Kingston police station in two shifts. It was considered the largest number of criminals ever arrested simultaneously in Kingston.

The investigation was overseen by Divisional Detective Inspector James Berrett ('the bearded detective'), and the following day, all but two of the gang were identified by witnesses to the attack.

On the morning of 3 June a large crowd gathered at the police station to see the men leave for court; in fact, some of the crowd had been waiting for six hours. By noon, the numbers had increased massively to 1,500, and although it had been initially decided to use the gang's charabanc to convey them to Epsom

Police Court, common sense prevailed and tenders were brought from the Yard, plus forty extra officers.

The prisoners were rightly considered so dangerous that when they were taken to court in seven motor vans they were handcuffed and chained together, and cars and motorcycles accompanied the armed officers to and from court. By the time the convoy set off at 1.30 pm the crowd had all but disappeared, leaving just one or two interested folk, to whom the prisoners put on a show of defiance, smoking and acting with nonchalance. Some tried to cross-examine Inspector Stevens at their initial appearance; those who asked for bail were refused. Threats were continually made against Berrett's life, and he told the court that some of the bookmakers were so badly injured that they could not immediately assist in identifying the perpetrators. When the accused were committed for trial at the Surrey Sessions in Guildford, the dock had to be specially enlarged to contain them, and the charges – conspiracy to commit bodily harm to ten persons, committing grievous bodily harm and possessing firearms and ammunition – filled twelve pages of the indictment. Five were found not guilty, but the rest were told by the Trial Judge, Mr Justice Rowlatt, 'This sort of blackguardism in charabancs by numbers of ruffians descending on the county and committing outrages will be stamped out', and those with no previous convictions were weighed off first: Arthur Vincent, Thomas Conway, Ernest Hughes, William Goulding and Thomas Tuckey each received nine months' hard labour.

Berrett informed the court of the rest of the prisoners' past misdeeds; William Stringer with eighteen previous convictions had managed to be convicted as an incorrigible rogue on the third occasion when he was on the run from the Army and was now sentenced to eighteen months' hard labour. As Berrett later remarked, 'one or two had very bad records'. They included Joseph Whitton who, since the age of thirteen had been convicted on thirteen occasions and at the age of twenty-one had been sentenced to four years' penal servitude together with fifteen strokes of the cat for robbery with violence. During the First World War he had deserted from the Worcestershire Regiment on two occasions and had been dishonourably discharged after being convicted of shopbreaking in 1918. Berrett described him as being 'a violent, vicious and dangerous man'.

Whitton was sentenced to three years' penal servitude, as was John Lee. It is difficult to imagine a more repellent pedigree than Lee's: in 1899 he had been convicted of manslaughter, for which he received a sentence of eighteen months; in 1903 came a three-year sentence for wounding and attempted murder; and at the time of his arrest, he was a convict on licence, having been convicted of unlawfully and maliciously wounding a woman at Leeds Assizes in 1916.

John Allard had been convicted of manslaughter in 1911. Having quarrelled with a man and threatened to 'bodge out his eyes', Allard ambushed him, knocked him down, continued to punch him and then made good his promise by thrusting the ferrule of his umbrella into the eye of his victim, who died the following day. Charged with murder, the jury accepted Allard's (and his witnesses') explanation that his victim had been the aggressor, but Allard notched up his twelfth conviction. After hearing that amongst his many transgressions eleven were for various assaults, the judge sentenced Allard to seven years' penal servitude. Therefore, Allard could probably consider himself fortunate to have received eighteen months' hard labour on this occasion; Edward Banks, who the previous year had shot at Darby Sabini, was sentenced to fifteen months' hard labour. The same sentence was imposed on 34-year-old Edward Tuckey, and his brother, Henry, four years older, received eighteen months.

As for the rest, it was imprisonment with hard labour for William Hayden (ten months), William Bayliss and William O'Brien (twelve months each) and Thomas Eivers (fourteen months).

Amongst those acquitted was the deeply unpleasant William 'Cockney Bill' Graham, a pimp who had served a five-year sentence for wounding.

Two more of those who walked free were Walter Giles, the taxi driver, and Frank Lane, the driver of the charabanc; both claimed to have been coerced by the gang. Lane had very sensibly put his defence forward at the earliest opportunity at the lower court. The coach driver from Birmingham told the bench that strangers had joined his party at the start of the return journey from Epsom and had 'threatened him with chastisement' if he refused to allow them on board. This had been reinforced by one of them holding a pistol to his head. At Ewell, he had parked in a side turning, a taxicab drew across the road and the tender ran into it. He had later received orders to drive as quickly as possible to Kingston, but since the occurrence he had been threatened and in Birmingham, on the evening of Sunday, 12 June, he had been offered £100 not to give evidence; these persons, Lane told the court, 'were strangers to me'.

Mr Justice Rowlatt commended the plucky and resourceful Sergeant Dawson, as did the jury and the police commissioner; highly commending him (as he did both Stevens and Berrett), the commissioner also awarded Dawson the princely sum of £5.

Since his weekly wages at that time amounted to £3 5s 0d, Dawson was delighted, as were the Italian Mob; less so the Birmingham Boys, whose numbers had been somewhat depleted.

★   ★   ★

On 5 July 1921, an attack was carried out at Salisbury railway station by the Elephant Boys on members of the Yiddisher Gang, who were on their way to the races. James Ford was arrested, and when the rest of his gang tried to free him, the police were seriously assaulted. A taxi knocked down one of the gang and the driver was assaulted by Ford and Frank Sundock; they were later sentenced to two months' hard labour each. Jack Levene, a fruiterer, was sentenced to four months' imprisonment for assaulting the police, and Herbert Less and Harry Lewis were each sentenced to six months' imprisonment for assaulting police officers so violently that they were hospitalized. The Salisbury Magistrates sat late into the evening of 18 July deliberating the fate of the prisoners; after weighing off the first five defendants, the Bench decided that the most suitable punishment for Jack Berman, Samuel Hatter, Israel Cohen and Thomas Mack (the nephew of Ernest Mack who had been convicted the previous month) was to bind them over in what would turn out to be the forlorn hope that they would be of good behaviour.

The case provoked a furious article in *The Times* demanding that the Jockey Club take action and saying, 'They cannot be ignorant of what is happening.' The Jockey Club hit back, saying that the disturbances had taken place outside the enclosures, that there was practically no rowdyism at the meeting and suggesting that the disturbance was partly caused by the police for having the impudence to break up games of chance.

There were a couple more skirmishes in July and August 1921.

There had been bad blood between Billy Fowles, a member of the Camden Mob, and Leonard Mitchell, who was affiliated to the King's Cross Boys. Apparently, Fowles with two companions had gone to Mitchell's house at Albert Street, Camden Town in February 1921 and, without warning, had attacked Mitchell, blacking his eyes and breaking his ankle. As Mitchell later told Detective Sergeant Waldron, 'I thought an explanation was necessary and a promise of no more threats.'

This was achieved by Mitchell, together with James Foy, Norman Gill and also William Gale (who was probably there simply to make up the numbers since he was described as being a blind paralytic) waiting for Fowles to return home at North Street,

Edgware Road from his employment as a porter at the Regent Palace Hotel.

When he did arrive, at 1.40 am on Sunday, 7 August, Mitchell seized Fowles by his coat, said, 'Just a minute; this is the man I want' and punched him on the nose, causing him to fall into the gutter. As he scrambled to his feet, a revolver was fired, and the men were charged with shooting at Fowles with intent to murder him.

Mr d'Eynecourt, the magistrate at Marylebone Police Court, thought there was sufficient evidence to commit the men for trial, but alas, the jury thought there was an insufficiency of it to convict them.

We now come to 17 August at Bath, when Billy Kimber sought to extract a suitable revenge for being shot some five months previously. The bullet which had hit him passed right through him, ricocheted around the room and allegedly ended up on Darby Sabini's mantelpiece; and Kimber discharged himself from hospital days later. Now he appeared fully recovered and, with the humiliating events of two months previously, when the ranks of his gang had been seriously reduced due to their embarrassing blunder in mistaking the Leeds Mob for the Italians still fresh in his memory, he led the gang into the attack.

Prior to the race meeting, the drivers of three charabancs containing the Birmingham Boys were told to stop outside St Stephen's church, whereupon the occupants swarmed out and attacked a number of Sabini-affiliated bookmakers. One was Frank Heath, a clerk to a bookmaker, who was walking up the hill when he was attacked from behind, knocked to the ground and kicked. It appeared he had been hit with a hammer; taken to the Royal United Hospital, his injuries consisted of a broken finger, cuts to his hand and scalp wounds.

The other (and more serious) attacks came at 10.30 am outside the Grand Pump Room Hotel, and this time the victims were Alf Solomon and his clerk, Charles Bild. Solomon could – apparently – recall little of the attack, saying that he was struck from behind with a heavy weapon and knocked to the ground, whereupon he was hit with other weapons and kicked violently. Bild was more voluble, saying that he had just emerged from a shop in Stall Street when a large man grabbed him by the lapel.

'First, a man hit me with a large lump of iron, and finally I was hit by a sandbag and knocked nearly unconscious', he said, adding, 'Solomon was also knocked down and I managed to crawl to the Grand Pump Room Hotel.'

He described a mob of 100–150 around him – this may have been an exaggeration, since onlookers put the likely number at fifty – and when he and Solomon were taken to the same hospital as Heath they looked a sorry sight, their shirts and waistcoats covered in blood. The house physician, Dr Hosford, dressed their injuries – abrasions to their knees, lacerations to their scalps – and Bild stated that his attackers were part of the Birmingham Boys who had attacked the Leeds bookmakers some six weeks previously; in fact, he provided the names of two of them 'who I know well'.

The charabancs continued to the racetrack, where one of the drivers reported seeing what he described as a policeman's truncheon lined with lead and studded with horse nails on one of the seats; then, half an hour after the attack in the town, police saw a sudden rush of men enter the two shilling ring and attack Alf Solomon's brother, Henry, who drew a loaded, six-chambered revolver from his pocket; but before he could use it, it was grabbed by one of the mob. George Riley of Brighton was in the two shilling ring at the time, saw Henry with the revolver and also heard a shout of 'Put that revolver down!' Police Constable Stevens disarmed the man, then saw another man hit Henry with a hammer as he lay on the ground. The officer grabbed hold of the attacker, but four or five of the crowd pushed him against the rails, forcing him to release his captive. An associate was given assistance when he climbed over a fence crying out, 'They'll kill me if they get me!' and ran off at a great pace. The police moved in to stop further assaults, and Henry was treated by the St John Ambulance Brigade for a severe head wound. He refused all particulars and was found to be in possession of an open razor and a life preserver.

Several other witnesses apart from police officers gave evidence at Weston County Police Court (with Riley being one of several who was threatened with violence for doing so), and although Henry had denied having the revolver, he pleaded guilty to possession of a firearm without a certificate, and the more serious charge of possessing it with intent to endanger life was dismissed. Mr Charles Crank Sharman, his rather excitable lawyer, suggested that the matter might be best disposed of by means of a bind-over, but the Chairman of the Bench took a different view and sentenced Henry to hard labour for one month, ordering him to pay special costs.

The attack on Bild was heard at Bath City Police Court with Philip Thomas in the dock.

'I'm innocent', he told the police. 'I don't know why they picked on me for this, I don't mix up with them.'

The case dragged on and on, with the prosecution stating that Bild was too unwell to attend the proceedings. Thomas was later joined in the dock by Edward Joyce and Billy Kimber, who was now living at 18 Warren Street, Islington. They had appeared at Bath's central police station accompanied by a Mr Bradbury, who told Detective Inspector Marshfield, 'These are the men you want to see.'

On 8 October Mr Sharman, who prosecuted in this case – in other words, he had previously defended a Sabini man and now prosecuted the Birmingham Boys – failed to appear at court; so did Bild. A successful application was made that in the absence of the prosecutor and no evidence having been given against the three accused, the case would be dismissed.

'Of course', said the magistrates' clerk, Mr E. Newton Fuller, 'the matter will go to the Director of Public Prosecutions', but in the event, no further action was taken.

CHAPTER 5

Slashings and Shootings

M atters had become so grave that in August 1921 the Racecourse Bookmakers' and Backers Association (RBBA) was formed to protect southern punters and bookmakers from attacks. It appeared to be a step in the right direction, but neither the Jockey Club nor the police could provide adequate assistance, and Walter Beresford, the Club's president, employed the worst racecourse scoundrels to staff the association. His vice-president was Eddie Emanuel, and Emanuel's son, Philip, was one of the eight stewards, hired at £6 per week. Others were Darby Sabini, Alf White and Fred Gilbert. Harryboy Sabini had already been employed as Beresford's clerk. Incredibly, they were seen by the senior Jockey Club supervisor as being 'men of integrity and fair dealing'.

★   ★   ★

Aaron Jacobs, a 36-year-old bookmaker's clerk, was seen by Flying Squad officers passing through the turnstile at Hurst Park racecourse and was fortuitously overheard by Detective Dawkins to say to his companions, 'If any of the fuckers are here today, they'll catch it.' Dawkins noticed that Jacobs had a hatchet concealed in his coat pocket and followed him into the crowd. Jacobs was looking up and down a line of bookmakers as though searching for someone, but then realized that he was being watched and ran away. He was later seen to speak to a bookmaker, who shook his head, after which Jacobs picked up an old newspaper, wrapped it around the hatchet and tried to hide the weapon in the pocket of a bookmaker's car. He was allowed to leave the course because Dawkins had received information that the men who had accompanied him there were armed, and it was his intention to arrest them all; unfortunately, the others escaped and Jacobs was arrested for being a suspected person. Asked what he was doing with the hatchet by the car, Jacobs replied, 'I'm not mixed up in this turf trouble; I'm going to work for a bookmaker named Crawford.'

This was Alexander Crawford, who appeared as a witness for Jacobs at Kingston-upon-Thames County Police Court on 22 August 1921, saying that Jacobs had worked for him and had been entrusted with sums of money.

'You employed him as a terror?' asked Detective Inspector Grosse, to which Crawford answered somewhat evasively, 'Not exactly, but I know he can take his own part.'

When Jacobs gave evidence and told the Bench that he used the hatchet for pointing the wooden stakes used by bookmakers in fixing up their boards, Grosse pointed out that the hatchet was brand new and still bore its price label.

Asked by the Chairman of the Bench, Lieutenant Colonel Hepworth, if anything was known to Jacobs' detriment, Grosse was able to read out a long list of previous convictions dating back to 1901 which included robbery with violence and two cases of living on immoral earnings; his sentences included one of twenty-one months' hard labour and another of nine months, together with twelve lashes of the cat o'nine tails. This was sufficient for the Chairman to impose a sentence of three months' hard labour.

On 23 February 1922, two of the Birmingham Boys, Michael Sullivan and Archie Douglas, were razor-slashed in Soho's Coventry Street by a gang including Alf White, Alf Solomon and his brother Henry (now looking for a little action, plus revenge for the attack on him and the one month's imprisonment), and although they were arrested, they were also bailed. Alf Solomon was again arrested shortly afterwards following a savage razor-slashing on Fred Gilbert. He was formally a Sabini man, but there had been a falling out with the Italian and Jewish factions, and now Gilbert's Camden Town Gang had affiliated itself with 'Brummie' Sage's gang. A mob led by Alf Solomon on Good Friday had treated Gilbert to an appalling attack with knives, razors and a machete which required the insertion of sixty-nine stitches. In both cases, proceedings were dropped due to lack of evidence.

Darby was dropped as well, from stewardship of the Bookmakers and Backers Association, as were several other racecourse thugs in September 1922, since they had started to impose unauthorized charges of their own. During a court case that followed, the judge stated that the sooner the association was dissolved, the better.

On 24 July 1922, John Thomas Phillips – he had taken the stand of Fred Gilbert – was attacked following a meeting at the Chatfield Hotel, Brighton, the night before the Goodwood races. The persons responsible were said to be Harry Sabini, Alf and

Henry Solomon and Alf White, although the only two charged were 28-year-old James Ford and George Langham, aged thirty-four. Both had boxed professionally, and Langham (whose real name was Angelo Gianicoli), having returned home on leave during the war, had promptly gone on the run and, changing his name, had boxed as a flyweight, being referred to as 'Bill Shelton's Unknown'. He had previously been sentenced to six months' hard labour at the Old Bailey for wounding, and not only had he been recruited at a very early stage as one of Darby Sabini's principal thugs, he was also one of the 'stewards' employed by the RBBA. Ford had already been jailed for two months following a fight at a railway station the previous year, and on this occasion he and Langham had demanded the 'loan' of £2 from Phillips. The men had left the hotel, and Phillips, apparently too frightened to refuse, handed over the money. While Langham punched and kicked Phillips, Ford slashed him with a razor, causing injuries which necessitated fourteen stitches in his face and his ear, which was almost completely severed.

Phillips went to the local police station, where Sergeant Swannell saw that he was suffering from a severe cut to his neck and that his shirt and chest were covered in blood. He gave a written statement, but the paper upon which it was written was covered with so much blood that it had to be destroyed, and only a copy could be produced.

Following their appearance at Brighton Police Court, the prisoners' defence was a total denial of the offence; yes, Langham had drunk with Phillips at the hotel on the night of the attack, but Phillips had left, and when Langham walked out of the hotel, there was the poor fellow on the ground; not wanting to be attacked as Phillips had been, Langham walked smartly away. Harry Weston, a commercial traveller, corroborated Langham's account, as did Harry Cohen, a bookmaker. Ford said that he knew nothing of the affair until the following day at Goodwood races, when he heard that the police were looking for him, at which point he immediately went to Brighton police station to state that he knew nothing about the matter. He denied being in the hotel on the night of the attack – Solomon Cohen, a bookmaker corroborated this – and Ford further stated, 'A friend of Phillips, named Gilbert, is an enemy of mine and he got Phillips to frame the case up against me and Langham.'

But Fred Gilbert had been in Phillips' company at the time of the attack – he was an important prosecution witness, so where was he? Mr J. Arthur Davis, prosecuting the case, provided the answer when he asked the court for an adjournment, saying,

'My principal witness was shot at in Camden Town on Saturday night.'

*   *   *

There had indeed been a shooting in Camden Town, but much more had happened prior to that dramatic announcement in court. Four days after John Phillips' wounding, John, his brother Arthur, together with Fred Gilbert, Joseph Jackson, William Edwards, George Baker – he was also known as Lawrence Tobin – and a number of others went in search not only of John Phillips' attackers, but of anyone associated with them.

They were a desperate bunch: 40-year-old Edwards, from Hoxton – he was later described as being 'a Sabini man', although this seemed extremely unlikely – possessed eighteen convictions for larceny and assaulting the police. Enlisting in the 5th Royal Fusiliers in 1915, he was sentenced to twelve months' imprisonment in 1918 for attempting to pick pockets; and when he was released on 15 February 1919, he was handed to a military escort. He escaped the same day and at the time of this punitive expedition he was shown on his Army records as being a deserter.

Jackson's record was no better: aged thirty-four, a father to five children under the age of eleven, he had enlisted in the Army in 1906 and within two years had a record consisting of indiscipline, striking an officer, committing a felony and repeatedly deserting; and whilst he was receiving treatment in a military hospital for shell-shock and neurasthenia, he had found it beneficial to his rehabilitation to demand money from shopkeepers and coster-mongers in the Bermondsey area.

On the evening of 24 July 1922, the gang homed in on the Red Bull public house in Gray's Inn Road. Darby Sabini was there, as was Alf White. Also in their company was Detective John Rutherford of the Flying Squad who, according to differing accounts, was either off-duty, keeping observation, obtaining information or on annual leave.

There was a confrontation between the two groups, who then left the pub; in the street, the crowd increased to about thirty in number.

'I was in the public house at about 10.15 pm when I heard a shot', said a Mrs Baker. 'I looked out the door and saw a man dressed in a dark suit with a big revolver in his hand taking deliberate aim at someone I could not see in Gray's Inn Road; he fired twice.'

James Cann, a barman, also witnessed the incident, seeing a man walking backwards down Portpool Lane and firing a revolver as he went. 'The firing frightened our customers', he said, 'and some of the women fainted.'

William Beland, hearing the sound of shots, went towards the scene but was stopped by Fred Gilbert, who produced a revolver. 'Go the other way', he told this curious passer-by, adding, 'or I shall blow your fucking brains out.'

Another witness was none other than George Langham, on bail from Brighton Police Court; seeing Arthur Phillips (who, he said, was holding a revolver) and four other men enter the pub, he prudently hid behind the counter. He later followed the group outside, but when the shooting started, he ran straight back into the pub; later, he untruthfully told the jury at the Old Bailey that he was not a member of the Sabini Gang.

Out in the street, it was pandemonium. Shooting had started, and Rutherford ran out into the street, saw the men brandishing firearms and heard Baker, who had recognized Rutherford, shout, 'Shoot them!'; at a distance of 15 yards he fired at him, at the same time shouting, 'Let him have one!'

Detective Herbert Cory (he was Chief Constable Wensley's son-in-law) ran up and told Rutherford, 'I'm with you, Jack', and the two officers, blowing their whistles, followed the men through various streets, with uniform officers joining in the chase. Both Edwards and Phillips pointed their revolvers at the officers and Phillips shouted, 'Go back, Rutherford!', after which both fired at the officers. In Hatton Wall, Rutherford caught up with Jackson, who told him, 'Go away or I'll do you in', whereupon Rutherford knocked him to the ground and disarmed him. George Fagioli (who was a Sabini man, and nothing to do with Jackson and Co) tripped up an officer before being arrested in Way Street, Clerkenwell Road; upon arrival at the police station, he dropped a small revolver which had been in his pocket. Phillips and Edwards got away, the latter being arrested in his bed.

None of the shots fired resulted in anyone being injured, although one of the bullets hit a tramcar in Gray's Inn Road, entering one side of the car and burying itself in a panel at the rear; it had missed one of the passengers by just 12 inches.

Detective Inspector David Goodwillie was the senior CID officer in charge at King's Cross police station when Arthur Phillips was brought into his office and made a statement in which he admitted being at the pub with two girls on the night in question and which read, in part:

> We were having a drink when I saw Darby Sabini, Alf White and another man outside the public house with razors. Inside was

the Camden Town Gang. Long Jim was there and I could see there was going to be trouble. When the shooting commenced the two girls ran away. All this trouble is through my brother Johnnie being slashed at Brighton. They tried to do him in and now they are trying it on me.

At the Old Bailey, Rutherford stated that at the pub he had noticed Alf White, Darby Sabini, Alf Solomon and George Langham (as well he might have, since he had been drinking with them) and was asked the cause of rivalry between the gangs. 'It started with racing', replied Rutherford, 'but I believe the cause that night was the "razoring" of Phillips' brother at Brighton.'

In his defence, Jackson said that he had seen a man firing a revolver but had taken away his weapon and fired it into the ground until it was empty. It was true, he said, that he had pointed the revolver at some men who had chased after him, but he was unaware that they were police officers and, in any event, he had not taken deliberate aim at Rutherford. Jackson, Fagioli and Baker were found guilty of possessing firearms, with Jackson and Baker additionally being found guilty of possessing firearms with intent to endanger life and shooting at Rutherford with intent to cause him grievous bodily harm.

Both William Edwards and Arthur Phillips denied having anything to do with the affray, and surprisingly, given the weight of evidence against them, they were both cleared of all charges. John Phillips, who had allegedly accompanied the vengeful mob, didn't feature at all in the proceedings.

Chief Inspector Brown castigated Jackson, and when his barrister, Mr J. D. Cassels, pointed out that Rutherford had previously stated that his client was not connected with any of the racing parties (which was quite untrue), Brown stated quite emphatically that Jackson was 'a confirmed and dangerous thief'.

Sentence was postponed until other matters were concluded.

CHAPTER 6

Blackmail and Intimidation

There was plenty going on regarding the Sabinis and Fred Gilbert, but we can take a break from them for the moment, because it's time to mention Pasqualino Papa, Darby Sabini's right hand man, who was born in 1894.

His first serious brush with the law came six days after the thrilling events in Gray's Inn Road, not a million miles away in Roseberry Avenue, after Joseph Dasher had boarded a tramcar. Dasher suddenly felt a blow on the back of his head and a pain in his left hip; he had been struck with a hammer and stabbed with a knife. Turning, he saw that Papa had been responsible for his injuries, and Papa struck out with the hammer again before running off. Dasher was taken to the Royal Free Hospital, where he was seen by Detective Sergeant Woods from 'E' Division and provided him with a statement. Papa was arrested, denied any knowledge of the attack, was put up for identification, charged and released on bail; this was rather unfortunate, because on 14 August, Dasher was threatened by Papa and two associates as to his likely fate if he gave evidence. On 17 August, Mr Bingley, the Magistrate at Clerkenwell Police Court, committed Papa in custody to stand his trial at the Old Bailey, where on 12 September 1922 he was sentenced to six months' hard labour.

Precisely what had triggered the attack was unclear; Papa was, of course, a Sabini man, and although Dasher denied that he was one of the Holloway Gang, it's quite possible that he was. The two men knew each other from boxing circles, so apart from the animosity between the two factions, it could well be that Papa, seeing Dasher boarding the tramcar, thought that this was a heaven-sent opportunity to disable one of the enemy.

Papa was released in time to win with a technical knockout a match at the Walham Green Baths, Fulham against Georges Pessieto on 28 March 1923 and to go on to box in eleven more contests. Perhaps his licence wasn't pulled because the National Sporting Club, the precursor of the Boxing Board of Control, knew him as Bert Marsh, instead of by his baptismal name.

But while Papa was on remand, Dasher had problems of his own. By 27 August he had recovered sufficiently from the injuries inflicted upon him one month previously, because in Brooksby Street, Islington, he accosted Arthur Pobjoy, a bookmaker's clerk, and said, 'Give me a pound.' When Pobjoy stated that he had no money, Dasher punched him in the eye, knocking him to the ground and kicking him in the shoulder, before putting his hand inside his pocket. Pobjoy pushed the hand away, and Dasher dashed off.

Detective Sergeant Appleby told Mr Gill, the Magistrate at Clerkenwell Police Court, that the whole matter was mixed up because Dasher was prosecuting one of the Sabini gang, and while Dasher protested once more that he was nothing to do with the Holloway Gang, he was committed to the Old Bailey to stand his trial for assault with intent to rob.

*   *   *

Back now to the trials and tribulations of Fred Gilbert and Co. Gilbert had not been arrested for the affray in Gray's Inn Road; but on 1 August, he and Fred Brett met Harry Margolis, a bookmaker's clerk, who was walking home across Claremont Square.

Gilbert asked, 'Are you Harry Margolis?' to which Margolis replied, 'If you know who I am, you have heard I have just got out of serious trouble.'

The 'trouble' referred to was this: Margolis, a professional thief, had been convicted of shopbreaking and sentenced to three years' penal servitude; but at the Court of Appeal, Mr Justice Darling and others agreed there was insufficient evidence to support his conviction and quashed it.

Now, one week after Margolis' providential release, Gilbert produced a revolver and said, 'I'll blow your brains out, you've got to stop this cutting business' (a direct reference to the assault which had been carried out on him), and Brett chimed in by saying to Gilbert, 'Give him one.' Pushing the revolver in Margolis' face, Gilbert said, 'Give me a tenner and I'll let you go.'

'Don't shoot, for the sake of my wife and kiddies', pleaded Margolis, and when the men momentarily stood aside, he seized the opportunity to escape. But not for long. He was again threatened on 14 August at Nottingham by the same men, plus George 'Brummie' Sage, Billy Kimber's mentor. Sage had first been convicted of larceny when he was seventeen; two years later, he was sentenced to nine months' hard labour, and in 1906 he was convicted in the name of William Johnson for shopbreaking and sent to penal servitude for five years. Now, in Nottingham, he was present when Gilbert drew a revolver from his pocket and told Margolis, 'Give me that tenner. I've got you on our manor, now. We're fifty-handed tonight and we mean to fight to the finish.'

Gilbert then saw him again, five days later, at the Rising Sun public house at Waterloo. On this occasion, Margolis was accompanied by Jack Delew, a bookmaker, and while Brett took a butcher's knife from his sleeve and held it against Delew's throat, saying, 'Shall I do him?', Sage grabbed hold of Margolis and said, 'This is one of the bastards; do him, Fred, through the guts.'

Gilbert again demanded 'a tenner' from Margolis and, pulling out a revolver, said, 'This is for Alf White, Sabini and "Spider". We're going to be top dogs tonight.'

At the same time and place, Samuel Samuels, a commission agent, was returning from the races when he was confronted by 'Brummie' Sage, who said, 'You Jew bastard. You're one of the cunts we're going to do. You're a fucking bastard Jew and we're going to do you and the Italians and stop you going racing. Did you win any money? Give me some.'

When Samuels replied that he hadn't any, he noticed that Gilbert had a hand in his pocket with the butt end of a revolver protruding from it. Then Michael Sullivan, one of the Birmingham Boys who had been razor-slashed six months previously, entered the pub, saying, 'Leave them alone; they'll do later', and Sage told the bookmakers, 'If you don't want to get done, you'd better get out of it as quick as you can.'

When the three men were arrested, Inspector Goodwillie stated that when charged, Sage replied, 'What I have to say, I will say to my solicitor.' At Clerkenwell Police Court, the officer told the Magistrate that he was instructed to oppose bail very strongly; in turn, the Magistrate stated that he would require a very good reason for *not* granting bail.

'We look upon these men as very violent characters', said Goodwillie. 'They have been engaged in assaulting others and going about with revolvers and other weapons for some time.'

But the Magistrate had other ideas, saying that he thought that substantial bail would meet the case, and he fixed a surety of £50 for each of the defendants.

However, on the same day that Margolis and Co. reported these matters to the police, this happened.

⋆   ⋆   ⋆

On the evening of 19 August 1922, a number of people, including Fred Gilbert and George Sage and their wives, left the Southampton Arms public house in Mornington Crescent at about 10.15

pm. The Italian faction must have had good intelligence, because right at that moment, three taxis screeched to a halt and a dozen men emerged brandishing weapons and firearms and opened fire. None of the shots hit Sage or Gilbert, and not all of the gang were caught, or even identified, but six were: Joseph Sabini, Alf White, George West, Simon Nyberg, Paul Boffa and Thomas Mack.

One of the gang had a coat on his arm; underneath it was concealed a pistol, which he fired, shouting, 'Take that!' West also opened fire, shouting, 'Take that, and all!' while Joseph Sabini also shot at Gilbert, shouting, 'That's for you!'

The weapon that Sabini had used had a handle resembling a walking stick, but it was a combined six-chambered revolver and stiletto which, when recovered, had traces of Gilbert's blood on the point. The attackers scattered; after running 50 yards, Sabini, having dropped his weapon in the gutter, was caught by Police Constable Robert Clark, who had witnessed him fire at Gilbert.

Sabini said, 'I'm innocent, Guv'nor. I've not got any firearms.'

A Browning pistol was also discarded, and a life preserver was tossed into a garden; Nyberg was seen to drop a heavy hammer, then ran slap-bang into the side of a tram and put his shoulder out; and Mack, who was chased by Gilbert, boarded a tramcar, where he struggled with a young woman named Amy Kemp who was screaming – Mack had knifed her in the arm, and Police Constable Archer, who was travelling on a bus, hearing whistles blown as well as the commotion, stopped the bus and boarded the tram. A crowd had gathered, and when they saw Mack there was a shout of, 'There he is – let's kill him!'; for the first time in his life, Mack was probably grateful to the police for arresting him and saving him from the depredations of the mob, even though his helpers found a closed knife in his pocket.

One by one, the men were brought into Albany Street police station, where Nyberg said, 'When I was arrested I was absolutely drunk; I didn't know what I was taken to the station for. I had nothing in my possession. I'm not guilty. I know nothing about it.'

Sabini said, 'I'm being defended', and Boffa told the officer, 'I had nothing in my possession, at all.'

West told Detective Inspector William Boothey, 'I wasn't there. I never had a firearm in my life, except the one I took away from Gilbert. This is all a concocted tale against us.' He then made a written statement in which he denied taking any part in the affray, saying in part:

> On returning from Hurst Park races, I was warned that a gang of thirty were looking for me and meant to 'do me in'. Friends

smuggled me into a taxi cab and I drove to the Strand, where I
gave information to Inspector Grosse.

What West did not mention in the statement was that when he got
into the taxi at the scene, a police constable jumped on to the cab's
running board and told the driver to disregard the address that
West had given him and drive direct to Albany Street police station.

When the six men appeared at Marylebone Police Court on
22 August to be remanded, the matter was considered so serious
that as well as Inspector Boothey appearing for the police, one of
the big guns was also in attendance. Detective Chief Inspector
Arthur Neil – known as 'Drooper Neil' because of his lugubrious
expression – was a very fine officer who had charge of Central and
North London. When Boothey opposed bail for the men, saying
that if they were liberated they would be in danger from people
of their own class, it caused Mr Sharman (who had previously
defended the Sabini faction and prosecuted the Birmingham
Boys) to sneer:

> That is an extraordinary reason for opposing bail. There are
> many thousands of police in London and yet they could not
> protect these men from persons who may attack them?

Neil – who had been responsible for sending Severin Klosowski to
the gallows for three murders and to his dying day believed him
to be 'Jack the Ripper' – stepped into the breach and firmly told
the magistrate that definite evidence would be forthcoming that
Sabini and West had fired shots at Gilbert and Sage, and the six
men were remanded in custody. So were Gilbert and Sage, now
charged with blackmailing Margolis.

A new charge was added to the former one of shooting with
intent to murder Gilbert and Sage; it was 'being concerned together
in riotously and tumultuously assembling together, to the terror of
people in Mornington Crescent', and when Gilbert was asked by
the Magistrate, Mr Symmons, 'Were you hit when Sabini fired?'
Gilbert took the opportunity to reply, 'No. I've been wounded by
these men before, though, and had to have seventeen stitches.'
He took the opportunity to add that when he had gone to Brighton
on 2 August to give evidence in the case of John Phillips, he was
threatened by Darby and Harry Sabini.

'Did you prosecute then?' asked Sharman (knowing full well
he had not), but it provided an opening for Gilbert to reply, 'No.
I didn't even prosecute on Good Friday when they cut me about
so that I had to have seventeen stitches.' (It is unclear whether

Gilbert had seventeen or sixty-nine stitches inserted on that occasion.)

Harry Sabini had also been arrested, charged with assaulting Fred Gilbert by pointing an automatic pistol at him and threatening to murder him at Paddington Station on 29 August, ten days after the shooting; he was remanded on bail. This matter will be left for now; otherwise, details which are already complicated enough might well become even more perplexing.

But now, matters started to become unglued in the prosecution's case, which was led by Mr Percival Clarke for the Director of Public Prosecutions. George Sage, who admitted he had several convictions (although, as he told the court, the last was fifteen years ago), was in the witness box and described how four or five men got out of a taxi and shots were fired. Two of the men in the taxi were White and West – or so he initially thought. Now he was not so sure.

'Were the shots fired by anybody who got out of the taxi?' asked the Magistrate, to which Sage replied, 'I can't tell you that.'

'Did you make a statement to the police the next day?' asked Mr Clarke, and Sage replied, 'Yes, but I have to withdraw that statement and am now giving evidence in reply to what you're asking me.'

'When you made that statement', asked the Magistrate, 'were the facts fresh in your mind?'

'No', replied Sage. 'I'd been drinking.'

'Can you recall who fired the shot?' asked Mr Clarke.

'I was given to understand it was two North Country people.'

'Who at the time did you think it was: White and West?'

'Yes, until I was told.'

The questions came thick and fast, with Sage saying that what he'd said in his statement was true, according to his beliefs then, and the Magistrate telling him he was obviously trying to mislead the court and giving the prosecution permission to treat him as a hostile witness. The solicitor, Mr J. A. Davis, who had been keeping a watching brief on behalf of Gilbert and Sage, realized, as had the whole court, that business definitely of the monkey variety was being conducted, and he withdrew – as far as Sage was concerned – from the case. However, that was just the start of the shenanigans.

Police Constable William Watmore had given evidence that on the night of the affray he had seen Joseph Sabini take the pistol from his inside pocket; he agreed that the jacket that Sabini was wearing in court was similar to the one he was wearing on that night. Sabini's counsel, Mr Myers, challenged the constable to find the jacket's inside pocket and then pointed out that there was none; the officer was obliged to agree. An investigation was swiftly carried out by a former Flying Squad stalwart, Detective Inspector Walter Hambrook, who in the court's waiting room accused Harry Sabini of exchanging jackets and waistcoats with his brother Joseph.

'I'm sorry, Mr Hambrook', replied Harry. 'I hope it won't get any of the men into trouble. We exchanged clothes in the lavatory.'

Joseph Sabini told Hambrook, 'What the boy [Harry] says is right, but we didn't mean any harm.'

It was now revealed that inside the coat that Harry was now wearing was a pocket exactly as Watmore had described. For once, the prisoners had scored an own goal, because it enabled Mr Clarke to say:

> You may recall that he was wearing a grey suit and that his brother, Harry Sabini who has just been bound over on another charge was present in court waiting for his sureties. That is an illustration of the craft to which a person may take refuge, in the position of Sabini.

In those circumstances, given the amount of chicanery going on (plus the further amount which would soon materialize) it is somewhat surprising that the brothers Sabini were not charged with conspiracy to pervert the course of justice. Perhaps this was because that would have necessitated them being joined them in the dock by the slimy Mr Harry Myers, who was quick to inform the court that when he was cross-examining PC Watmore he had not the slightest idea that the jackets had been changed. If the Magistrate, Mr Symmons, thought that Myers was as bent as a nine-bob note, he gave no indication of it.

Next came Peter McNeil, an electrician, who stated that he had made a mistake in his statement to police in which he identified Alf White as firing a shot. Mr Clarke said he would like to treat him as a hostile witness.

'You *can* treat him as a hostile witness', snapped the Magistrate, telling McNeil, 'Have a little pluck. Do your duty as a citizen. You shall be protected in every possible way.'

Another witness, James Camp (who could not remember how many convictions were recorded against him), declined to give his address, then gave evidence which, when he was cross-examined, proved to be entirely different from his police statement, and the Magistrate said that he would not treat him as a hostile witness; that would be a question to be decided at the trial.

Mr Clarke produced the statement made by George Sage's wife, Ellen, and made several attempts to determine whether or not it was true, until the exasperated Magistrate told her he would send her to prison for contempt if she refused to answer. Eventually, she said it was true. But when Mr Clarke quoted from her statement, 'A man I know as Thomas [an alias for West] and White fired shots at my husband and Gilbert', she said that she hadn't seen White fire, and when Mr Clarke asked, 'Was the statement true or not?' she replied, 'It was not true.'

Cross-examined, she said that West was not one of the men who got out of the taxi, and the Magistrate accused her of being a person who was totally careless with the truth and saying something that someone had asked her to say. Just to make his meaning unequivocally clear, he added, 'You are an absolutely untrustworthy witness.'

'Have you been offered any money to alter your story?' asked Mr Clarke, and she replied, 'No, not by anybody', but it did not sound particularly convincing, any more than her answer did after he asked, 'How have you got your living since your husband has been in prison?' and she replied, 'Pawning and selling things'.

★　★　★

So far, this incident has been a shocking tale of attempts to pervert the course of justice on a grand scale, not only by the prisoners in the dock but by prosecution witnesses as well – and never fear, there'll be much more of the same when we reach the trial at the Old Bailey. But not only that, we have the lawyer, Myers, attempting to deliberately mislead the court (whilst fulsomely denying it) in the matter of the jacket that Joseph Sabini was wearing; and there is also the matter of the tricky Mr Sharman, who inevitably appeared on behalf of the Sabinis and their associates.

Sharman was born in 1850 and obtained a little more than articles as a solicitor: in 1888 he was acquitted of misappropriation of funds but was suspended by the Law Society for two years. This, by the way, is a bit of a spoiler; you can guess what's coming next. Sharman, from his offices in Stratford, as well as concocting defences for his clients, was a full-time fence. In addition, he was in cahoots with another highly dodgy solicitor (or perhaps a solicitor's clerk) named William Cooper Hobbs, a blackmailer and forger who in 1920 was sentenced to two years' hard labour for conspiracy, in 1925 to a further two years for blackmail and finally, in 1938, to five years' penal servitude for forgery.

In 1922, some of the contents of a mailbag which had been stolen on a train between Liverpool and London were cashed by Sharman. Despite being identified by a bank clerk, Sharman walked free. One month later, another mailbag was stolen from a train, this time between Birmingham and London, and a Quebec railway stock certificate for $900 was found in Sharman's office. Once more, like so many of his clients, he walked free.

But two years later, matters changed dramatically. There was no change in the modus operandi of the crooks; once more, a mailbag was stolen, from a Bristol to Paddington train, and when a £50 Mexican share certificate was sold by someone matching his description in Manchester, Sharman provided an alibi that on the day in question he was at home all day. But when war bonds from the same mailbag were sold in Canada, nine people identified Sharman as the seller, and he duly appeared at the Old Bailey in 1925 charged with conspiracy to steal and receive mailbags. Sharman was then aged seventy-five, and as Mr Justice Salter told him, 'If you were a younger man, I would have sent you to penal servitude for seven years'; instead, Sharman went down for three years. Being sent to penal servitude aged seventy-five in Sharman's case and seventy-four in Hobbs' can't have been too pleasant, given the rocks that had to be broken up in the Dartmoor quarries, but both, incredibly, survived their sentences.

*　*　*

Back now to the more common or garden criminals who were committed in custody to the Old Bailey (with the exception of Paul Boffa, who was discharged by the Magistrate). It was made quite clear to the jury by Mr Clarke that some witnesses, perhaps through fear, might be somewhat nervous about giving their evidence. What he did not say was that others would be lying their heads off, although that was how Mr Justice Roach interpreted matters when he said that Ellen Sage and Fred Gilbert were 'hostile to the prosecution', meaning that the statements which they had made to the police could be read in court.

'Has anybody frightened you?' asked Mr Cassel, who defended White.

'No, Sir,' dutifully replied Ellen Sage. 'I have not seen a soul.'

'And your evidence today is freely given, it's true?'

'Yes.'

After the statement of William Wye (who had been one of those in the pub with Gilbert and Sage) was read – he too was a hostile witness, having materially altered his testimony – Mr Fulton, appearing for West, asked, 'How come you said what you said?'

'I was so bitter against these people firing at us that I would have said anything that night', he replied.

'When did you cease to be bitter towards them?'

'I realized next morning what lies I had told.'

James Camp denied that he had been threatened by anybody, but during cross-examination he stated that he was 'not comfortable'. This caused general hilarity in court, mainly because those who were amused were aware that Peter and Jimmy McNeil had already been acquitted of attacking Camp to ensure that his memory would be even more unreliable than before. The Judge was less than amused, saying, 'This is no laughing matter. It is a matter of the gravest possible import when witness after witness comes in here, obviously afraid; obviously uncomfortable.'

Summing up, Mr Justice Roach said that George West had put up an alibi which had been completely made out and he should be acquitted. Sabini and White were found guilty of shooting with intent to cause grievous bodily harm, unlawful possession of firearms and riotous assembly. Nyberg was found guilty of riotous assembly as was Mack, plus unlawfully wounding Amy Kent on the tramcar.

The judge then deferred sentence; he was going to deal with the affrays in Gray's Inn Road and Mornington Crescent together, and on 3 November 1922 he did so, stating:

> I am going to teach these people to act through the police, and to rely on them for protection and, as far as I can, to stop people taking the law into their own hands.

Dealing with the Gray's Inn Road case first, he sentenced Baker – who with Jackson had been convicted of possessing firearms with intent to endanger life, plus shooting at Rutherford – to five years' penal servitude (whereupon a woman shrieked, 'My God!' collapsed, and had to be carried out of court), Jackson to seven years' penal servitude and Fagioli, convicted of the lesser charge of possessing a firearm, to nine months' hard labour.

The Judge commended the police officers, particularly Rutherford who, he said, 'had acted with great courage'. He was later awarded the King's Police Medal for gallantry.

Next, it was the turn of those convicted of the Mornington Crescent affray. White, the court was told by Chief Inspector Brown, had on several occasions given information to the police regarding racing matters and dangerous criminals frequenting racetracks, as well as being a steward for the Bookmakers Protection Association, the object of which, Mr Cassels for White suggested, 'was to take steps to prevent ruffianism on racecourses, and those steps were not violent'. To this the crusty Mr Justice Roach declared, 'I am not going to investigate the merits or demerits of the Bookmakers Protection Association.'

Before he could pass sentence on White, a woman came to the front of the dock and cried, 'Have mercy upon him, my Lord!' The Judge asked that she be 'gently removed' – this was probably Mrs White, who had previously and piteously asked the magistrate to grant her husband bail because he had a business and eight children to care for; but whilst White obtained freedom on that occasion, he was unlucky this time. Told he would go to penal servitude for five years, with a concurrent sentence of two years' hard labour, he groaned, 'My God!' and placed his head in his hands.

Joseph Sabini did little better, despite Chief Inspector Brown telling the court that he had 'never been in contact with the police before', had given information to the police and had assisted them 'as much as he could'; he was sent to penal servitude for three years.

Nyberg (who, in the past ten years had notched up sixteen convictions) was sentenced to twenty-one months' hard labour, and Mack to hard labour for concurrent terms of eighteen and six months.

However, there are still matters to be cleared up. The case against Fred Gilbert, Brett and Sage for demanding £10 from Harry Margolis came to a grinding halt, the Judge telling the jury:

> You have lived for two days in an indescribable atmosphere of knavery, lies and human folly, which might have astonished you, much as you might know about the world.

The men were acquitted after Gilbert's barrister, Ronald Oliver, said that his client 'was merely asking for repayment of a loan'. Mind you, the acquittal had been aided and abetted by George Moore, John Gilbert, Tommy Ackroyd and Joseph Smith, who told Margolis and Samuels the likely effect on their health if they persisted in giving evidence. Moore and Co were arrested; their case was chucked out as well.

As for George Langham and James Ford, they were acquitted at Sussex Assizes on 11 December 1922 of unlawfully wounding John Thomas Phillips.

Then there was the matter of Harry Sabini threatening Fred Gilbert with a pistol; having heard that there was a warrant in existence for him, Sabini went along to Paddington police station, where he saw Detective Sergeant Copley who read him the warrant. Sabini replied:

> What a liar! I never said a word to him! He was supposed to go to Brighton on a job – that's why he got bail. But he turned up at Paddington with a crowd. Alfie Solomon asked him why he was going and whether he was going to make trouble. He told him to mind his own business. The train started and we rushed to get in. We only got out in case Gilbert's crowd set about Alfie. I never carry a gun or anything. I don't like trouble of any kind.

Gilbert did give evidence at Marylebone police court, saying that Sabini had pointed the pistol at his head and had told him, 'I'll blow your brains out.' Sabini in turn stated, 'I had no pistol in my possession that day.' But the Magistrate disagreed, and although he described Sabini as 'a dangerous man' he imposed the surprisingly lenient penalty of binding him over to keep the peace for a period of twelve months in the sum of £200, with a surety in the same sum – otherwise Sabini would go to prison for six weeks.

It was a leniency that was misplaced; within weeks Sabini was summoned to show cause why he should not estreat that amount, owing to the fact that he had been earlier fined for assaulting one of the Cortesi family. In fact, he was ordered to forfeit just £3, as was his surety, one Edward Emanuel. But never fear, the brothers Sabini and Cortesi will surface again very shortly in stunning style.

CHAPTER 7

Gunfight at the Fratellanza

The Cortesi brothers had once been allies of the Sabinis, but after the latter sided with the Jewish gang in the early 1920s, the Cortesis found allies elsewhere. The member of the Cortesi family referred to in the previous chapter was George Cortesi, who was assaulted by Harry Sabini, together with a worthy named 'Jumbo' Esposito and some other Italians. That had taken place in the Fratellanza Social Club, a workingmen's club in Great Bath Street, Clerkenwell, on 2 October, and the assault was almost certainly the catalyst for what happened at the same club on the night of 19 November 1922.

Shortly before midnight, there were 8–10 people present in the bar, two of whom were Darby and Harry Sabini. Time had just been called and the members were preparing to leave, when the door opened and 39-year-old Harry 'Enrico' Cortesi, who also lived in Great Bath Street, five doors away from the club, walked in and demanded coffee. Accompanying him were his brothers, Augustus Cortesi aged thirty-six, George Cortesi, thirty-three and Paul Cortesi, as well as Alexander Tomaso (also known as Sandy Rice), the latter two both thirty-one years of age. It was Sandy Rice who with Fred Gilbert had launched an attack on Darby Sabini at Greenford Park some eighteen months earlier.

Louisa Doralli, the daughter of the club's secretary, Antonio, started to tell Augustus that only members could be served, but as Darby went to leave, Augustus turned to him and said, 'Oh, here you are, you bastard; now is the time to fight.' Someone threw a cup of hot coffee over Harry Sabini, and Augustus then pulled a pistol from his hip pocket; with great bravery, Louisa grabbed hold of his hand, and he dropped the pistol and pushed her aside. Augustus and Rice advanced towards Darby, and Rice threw a soda water bottle at him which knocked him to the floor. This attack rather dispelled the belief of some biographers that Darby possessed a mouthful of gold teeth, since the only teeth he possessed were false ones which were broken by the impact of the bottle. Augustus fired two shots from a distance of three yards which missed Darby and went through a window pane. Harry Cortesi then pointed his gun at Harry Sabini, and Louisa stepped in front of him (for which she was later highly commended in court), but he pushed her to one side, whereupon Harry Cortesi fired, hitting him in the right side of his abdomen. Harry Sabini gasped, 'They have hit me!', and he was tended by Louisa until he was taken to the Royal Free Hospital, where he was treated by the resident house surgeon, Dr Geraldine Barry, and the police were called.

Arrests were quickly carried out. George Cortesi told the arresting officer, 'All right, I don't remember what happened', whereas Paul said, 'I was not there.'

Sandy Rice told the police, 'I've not been out all night. We had a party.' Later, he changed his mind, admitted that he had gone out and, referring to Harry Cortesi as 'Harry Frenchie', said that he gone to a public house with him where they saw Darby Sabini but did not speak to him. When he enquired as to 'Harryboy's' condition and was told, he replied, 'I'm going to say no more. I'm going to leave it to my solicitor.'

Harry Cortesi initially managed to escape, which resulted in this rather histrionic description of him in the *Daily Express*:

> He is sharp-featured, five foot eight inches tall, with sallow complexion, brown hair, grey eyes and a pronounced Roman nose. He walks with a Charlie Chaplin step, the result of flat feet and knock-knees but is said to be able to disguise not only his walk or his features. Detectives believe that he took refuge in a house, not a hundred yards from the Fratellanza Club and emerged in the disguise of an old woman.

When Harry Cortesi walked into the police station and saw Detective Inspector Grosse he offered a rather different explanation:

> You know, Mr Grosse, I don't get mixed up in these things. It's not my game; but on Sunday night I was at my mother's house about midnight, which is a few doors from the club. I heard there was a row. When I went into the club, everybody was struggling somewhere on the floor. I had no gun. I heard a shot fired and walked out. I went to the Turkish baths; I often go there. The next morning, I went to the City to see my employer and at about one o'clock my employer rang me up on the phone. He told me that you had been making enquiries about me, so I thought I had better come and see you.

It wasn't quite convincing enough, and all five men were charged with attempting to murder both Darby and Harry Sabini. George Cortesi replied, 'Yes, I was there, I don't remember what happened', while Rice reverted to his original statement and said, 'I wasn't there.'

In addition to the charges of attempted murder, the five defendants were also charged with possession of firearms and riotous assembly, and they appeared at Clerkenwell Police Court, where they were remanded in custody, Inspector Grosse telling the magistrate, 'This man may die, yet.'

On the remand appearance, as usual Mr Percival Clarke appeared for the prosecution. Darby Sabini took the oath, giving his name as Charles Sabini although, paradoxically, he later stated that 'Charles' was not his name. He – and the other prosecution witnesses – were fiercely cross-examined by the prisoners' defence counsel, Ronald Oliver. Darby denied starting the quarrel which led to the shooting and denied that it was his revolver that had been used. Did he know a man named William Kimber who was shot at his house, asked Mr Oliver, to which Darby untruthfully replied that Kimber had been shot in the street outside his house.

'I'm a quiet, peaceful man', he told the court. 'I never begin a fight. I've only once been attacked; I've never attacked anyone . . .' He said that only once had he carried a gun and that was at Greenford Park, when he was attacked. He had never carried a gun since and was not carrying one now; in the witness box he ostentatiously turned out his pockets to prove the point.

Within a month, Harry Sabini had recovered sufficiently to appear at the Police Court, where he told Mr Arnold Baker (now appearing for the defence) that he was a peaceful, law-abiding citizen who never attacked people. This was stretching credulity just a tad too far, and he was obliged to admit his conviction for hitting George Cortesi, but he added that he bore him no enmity and had not been in possession of a revolver on that occasion or, indeed, on the night of the shooting at the Fratellanza Club. He did state that his brother, Darby, had been drunk that night, and although that assertion was denied by the next witness, the bookmaker Harry Cohen (who had been so helpful in establishing fellow Sabini member George Langham's innocence), he did agree that it was Harry Cortesi who had shot Harry Sabini. He also refuted the suggestion that it was the Sabinis rather than the Cortesis who were in possession of the revolvers, saying, 'It is a lie, Sir. The Sabinis were inoffensive.'

There was also another witness named Alzapiede, who told the court that after the shooting he had been talking to three police officers outside the club, when about twenty men came out of a French café led by Augustus Cortesi, who punched him in the face, then kicked him. Astonished, the Magistrate asked, 'Was that in the presence of the constables?'

'Yes', replied Alzapiede, adding, 'I think the constables were afraid.'

Police Constable Cole shed a slightly different light on the matter by saying that when he tried to arrest Harry Cortesi after the shooting he was obstructed by Augustus Cortesi, who was leading a group of about twenty men.

There was a sufficiency of evidence to commit the five men to the Old Bailey, where they appeared before Mr Justice Darling.

Mr Travers Humphreys appeared for the defence and suggested to Louisa Doralli that the affray was staged by the Sabinis in retaliation for Harry Sabini's conviction for threatening George Cortesi; she denied this, although she did admit that Pasqualino Papa and Thomas Mack were members of what was referred to as 'The Sabini Fraternity'.

Darby Sabini stated that he, Rice and Augustus and George Cortesi had been stewards of the Bookmakers Protection Association but had quarrelled with Rice when he wanted him to do 'blackmailing work'. This, coming from Darby, was a bit rich.

Harry Sabini admitted changing jackets with his brother Joseph at the police Court, and when Mr Justice Darling asked why, he replied that he wanted to because his own smelled – which caused a great deal of amusement in court.

But there was rather less amusement when on 17 January 1923, Augustus and Harry Cortesi were found guilty of shooting with intent to murder the Sabini brothers; Rice, Paul and George Cortesi were found not guilty and were discharged, charges of unlawful assembly having already been withdrawn.

Detective Inspector Grosse told the Judge that for eighteen months he had done little else than look after the gangs at race meetings. There had been numerous fights, many people were injured and some forty Birmingham men (a slight exaggeration) had been arrested in Epsom for assaulting Jews and some had been sent to penal servitude. With respect to Augustus Cortesi, Grosse stated that he had been born in Paris of Italian parents and had arrived in England in 1895. He lived in the Italian quarter of Saffron Hill and had worked as an interpreter at Clerkenwell Coroner's Court. However, during the war he had deserted, his character was described by the Army as 'indifferent' and he was regarded as a very violent man, especially when in drink, and had been convicted on several occasions for gambling, drunkenness and assaults on members of the public as well as the police.

Harry Cortesi, said Grosse, was a man of different character, and he admitted that he was surprised to find him mixed up in this affair. Also born in Paris, Harry had at one time been in partnership with a bookmaker, was married to an English woman and had seven children.

Passing sentence, Mr Justice Darling said:

> You appear to be two lawless bands – the Sabini and the Cortesi. Sometimes you are employed together against the Birmingham people and sometimes you are employed against each other. On this occasion, you were carrying out a feud between you and the Sabini. I do not think there is much to choose between you, but the Sabini are within the King's Peace while in England, and people must not be allowed to shoot them or at them.

He then sentenced the brothers each to three years' penal servitude but then called the prisoners back, because the Grand Jury[1] had recommended deportation in the event that any alien was convicted. This, the Judge declined to do but thought it respectful to explain why. He said:

> The whole Italian colony should know of the Grand Jury's recommendation, and I wish to say to you all that if this band of lawless conduct goes on, the Judges and the Ministers of the Crown who administer this particular law will take care that those who get convicted in future will be turned out of this country with their wives and children. Let it be a warning to you all, to lay aside these lawless practices and settle down to observe the law peaceably.

It seemed, however, that there was little chance of that. Nevertheless, the Cortesi brothers drifted from the scene and the Sabinis reasserted control.

---

[1] A Grand Jury consisted of at least fourteen, but no more than twenty-three members of the public who were sworn at courts of Quarter Sessions and Assizes to determine whether there was sufficient evidence to put a person on trial. This was gradually made redundant by the development of committal proceedings from the Police Courts under the Justices Protection Act, 1848, and it ceased to function after the introduction of the Administration of Justice (Miscellaneous Provisions) Act, 1933.

CHAPTER 8

The Misadventures of Alf White

Everybody who was convicted in the Gray's Inn Road and Mornington Crescent affrays appealed; only Alf White was successful. He had called the professional boxer, Ted 'Kid' Lewis, as an alibi witness.[1] On 19 December 1922, after the Lord Chief Justice admitted that the Court of Appeal had come to its decision 'with the greatest reluctance', he walked free; but unfortunately, as will be seen, he failed to profit from this show of clemency.

Alf White was now aged thirty-five and the head of the King's Cross Boys; also a staunch supporter of the Sabinis. This was displayed on 15 February 1923, when White, together with a George Drake (whose previous convictions included slashing a prostitute in the face after she was late paying her dues), met a prison warder named Matthew Fright from Maidstone Prison, where Joseph Sabini had started his three-year sentence of penal servitude. Fright was on his way to the local Post Office when he saw four men, one of whom he recognized as Drake; the two had met previously, when they served together in the Royal Artillery during the war.

Drake asked if he knew Sabini.

'Yes', replied Fright. 'I remember his case.'

'We're down here to do him a bit of good', said Drake. 'It'll be worth £2 per week to any man to look after him and get a note in and out occasionally.'

Drake then introduced the warder to White, who with astonishing arrogance told Fright, 'I'm the Alf White that got off on appeal.'

Fright said, 'According to the Judge's remarks, you were lucky', to which White replied, 'Yes, damned lucky.'

White then asked, 'Can anything be done for Sabini?'

To his credit, Fright replied, 'Yes. You can do a bit of good for Sabini and go straight back to London and leave him alone. If

---

[1] Lewis would go on to better things: being acquitted, fifteen years later of conspiracy to pervert the course of justice, and later still, becoming a chum of the Kray twins.

the authorities get to hear you are trying to get a word into him, they'll transfer him to Dartmoor.'

This was a possibility. At Dartmoor prison there was a quarry just waiting for prisoners serving penal servitude to come and break its rocks.

But Drake and White refused to give up. Next on their list was Warder Ernest Frederick Ludlow, whom they met the same day; Ludlow recognized Drake as being a former prisoner, and when he said he wanted to get some information about Sabini, the warder told him to see the prison governor. Drake insisted to Ludlow that if he could get a note into Sabini 'it would be worth his while', but Ludlow told him he wanted nothing to do with it. In fact, he reported the matter to the governor, as did Fright and several other prison officials, one repeating an overheard conversation in which White, on a visit to Sabini, had said, 'Well, old man, how are you getting on? We've been down here for about a week and had no luck, but we'll try again.'

They didn't. White was arrested by Chief Inspector Brown of Scotland Yard at Kempton Park races on Saturday, 24 February on a warrant alleging conspiracy with others to solicit warders to convey documents to Sabini, whereupon he replied, 'I was at Maidstone. I went down there to see a man named Walters about buying a shop. I saw a warder and asked him if there was a chance of getting a special visit to see Joe. He told me to see the governor. That was all I said to him.'

The same afternoon, Brown saw Drake at Cannon Row Police station and read the warrant to him. He replied, 'Yes. I'm George Drake. That's all I have to say.'

Of the other two men who accompanied White and Drake to Maidstone, it was said that one was Joseph's brother, George Sabini, but if it was (and for whatever reason), he was never prosecuted. The men appeared at Maidstone Police Court on 26 February, when an application for bail was made. Brown said that he would have no objection, providing there were substantial sureties, but the bench thought otherwise and remanded them in custody. But on their next appearance, on 3 March, when the men were committed for trial, the Magistrates did allow bail in the sum of £300 each. White's freedom permitted him, once more, to indulge in a little bloodletting.

On 13 May, at the Brecknock Arms public house, Camden Road, Steve Griffin was attacked by a William Kimberley, who struck him with a broken glass, severing the tendons of his right wrist and cutting his left wrist and his head.

As well as Kimberley, it was thought that William Homer, a bookmaker, who had boxed forty bouts as a flyweight under the name of Tancy Lee, was responsible. James Harper told Homer, 'Griffin has been done by Bill Kimberley, so we're going to do you. I'll get Alf White and his mob to do you, if it costs me £1,000.'

On 20 May, Harper went to Homer's house at Brecknock Road together with Matthew McCausland, who said, 'What about coming to terms with the Griffin case?' to which Homer replied, 'I don't know anything about it.'

At that, Alf White and Alf Solomon pushed forward, telling Homer, 'We've come to knock you out', and McCausland hit Homer on the forehead with a hammer, while the others kicked him, pointed a revolver at his head and demanded £20.

Detective Inspector John Gillan saw Harper and McCausland at Kentish Town police station on 26 May. McCausland said, 'Yes, I admit belting him. Harper had nothing to do with it.'

Harper said, 'I know nothing about it. I admit having seen Homer on the evening he was thrashed. I told him I would get him thrashed but I didn't mean what I said. I was foolish and excited.'

Gillan also saw White and Solomon at Wood Green and told them he was going to take them to Kentish Town police station where, if they wished, they would be put up for identification.

White replied, 'We don't want that. We've come here to give ourselves up. We were there. I never slashed Homer.'

Solomon said, 'I was there in the fight. Steve Griffin is an old pal of mine and it grieved me to see his hands nearly cut off.'

At Marylebone Police Court, on 28 May, Kimberley and McCausland were remanded in custody and the others were given bail, although after the Magistrate was told that difficulty had been experienced in obtaining statements from witnesses, he said in open court, 'If the police hear that any pressure has been brought on any outside people, bail will be refused at the next hearing.'

Pressure was certainly brought, on both Homer and Griffin. On 6 June at Marylebone Police Court, the Magistrate, Mr Symmons, exploded with rage. 'Look, he's in absolute terror!' he snapped, pointing to Griffin who, having originally identified Kimberley as his attacker, was now unable to do so and was treated as a hostile witness, as well as to an excess of bile from Mr Symmons:

> Listen to me. We are here to protect you. You have a duty to
> the state, as well as we. You are not doing it. If further danger
> comes to you, you will thoroughly deserve it. You are on your

oath now and you are not trying to speak the truth. Whether it is
the fear of further violence or not, I do not know but your best
chance of avoiding further danger is to tell the truth.

Having told the Magistrate that he really did not know who had
attacked him, Griffin was very coldly informed, 'It is very cowardly
of you.'

Dealing with the Homer case, the Magistrate fared little better,
asking the victim, 'Do you now go in fear?'

'No, certainly not', replied Homer, adding, 'if they come one
at a time.'

'We cannot protect you if you do not tell the truth', said
Mr Symmons, and although Homer, in stating he was unable to
identify his assailants, replied, 'I have', he was being less than
frank.

Perhaps it was surprising that William Kimberley was convicted
at the Old Bailey of wounding Griffin; and after hearing him
described by DI Gillan as 'a racecourse pest', the Judge sent
Kimberley to hard labour for twelve months. His career of
lawlessness continued: twelve years later, as a member of a pickpocket team at London's Adelphi Theatre, he received four more
months' hard labour.

Much more predictable was the outcome at the same court a
day or two later, when McCausland was found guilty of common
assault on Homer and was bound over to keep the peace.
White and Solomon, charged with conspiracy to cause bodily
harm, were acquitted. There were outrageous (and nonsensical)
comments from DI Gillan, who told the trial Judge, Mr Justice
Swift, 'The feuds between race gangs are now more or less wiped
out and they have all become friends again.'

Even more unfortunate was Homer, who on 2 April 1926
fought his forty-first (and final) fight after a five-year lay-off; he
was disqualified.

A week prior to McCausland's sentence, also at the Old Bailey,
it's refreshing to report that Alf White and Drake were convicted
of attempting to corrupt warders. White had told the jury that
when he was overheard saying to Joseph Sabini, 'We've had no
luck', he was of course referring to not backing any winners
at the racetrack, but for once he was disbelieved. Mr Justice
Avory said that the warders deserved commendation 'for the
promptitude with which they reported the matter' and sentenced
Drake who, he said, 'had a very bad record' to two years' hard
labour, and White, who despite his many court appearances had
only three convictions, to eighteen months' hard labour.

Naturally, both men appealed, White not on the grounds that he was innocent but because the Attorney-General's fiat[2] had not been obtained to bring one of the charges. However, it was pointed out that the Attorney had given his consent for the prosecution; there was no necessity that his fiat should specifically refer to each particular count in the indictment. Probably realizing the Court of Appeal's mistaken judgement in previously releasing White, the Lord Chief Justice's ruling was:

> If he was rightly convicted, is eighteen months a day too much for a man who interfered with the good faith of a prison warder? Think of the cruelty of what is being done. If he were to succeed, nobody could foretell the consequences; it is perfectly certain that, if it came to be known, the prison warder would be dismissed from the public service.

Drake appealed on the grounds that his sentence was too long, his barrister telling the court that 'it was evident he was a tool in the hands of others'. He had served in the army from the age of fourteen, he had been described as having a 'good record' and he had been employed as batman to a Regimental Sergeant Major. But as Mr Justice Swift remarked:

> If prisoners are to be allowed, at the will of a warder to communicate with their friends outside, what becomes of punishment by imprisonment, at all? They will simply remain in prison until it is convenient for them, with the assistance of their friends outside, to walk out.
>
> It is clear that society is not safe unless Drake is in the army or in prison and as the court cannot send him into the army, what are we to do? One thing is certain. If the sentence stands, he will not be able to bribe another warder from outside.

Because his appeal centred on a point of law, White lost none of his remission. Because Drake's appeal failed, too, on the grounds that he was whining, it meant that his remission went straight out of the window and his sentence recommenced from 30 July 1923, the date of his appeal. Nor was that the end of his run of bad luck. Twenty years later, he had an unfortunate run-in with Jack Spot at a pub in Paddington. At the age of sixty, it was unwise of Drake to risk a confrontation with such a very tough customer, who was exactly half his age and who very nearly killed him.

---

[2] Permission

A day at the races.

Ras Prince Monolulu.

Gangsters preparing to visit a racetrack.

Above left: Darby Sabini.

Above right: Darby Sabini, wife and family.

Darby Sabini in
later years.

Above left: Joseph Sabini.

Above right: Harryboy Sabini.

Below: Bert Marsh.

Above left: Augustus Cortesi.

Above middle: Luisa Doralli.

Above right: Paul Cortesi.

Below left: Harry Enrico Cortesi.

Below right: George Cortesi.

Above left: Billy Kimber.

Above right: Sir Edward Marshall Hall KC.

Below left: Angelo Gianicoli.

Below right: Alf Solomon.

Above left: Bert Marsh (having been acquitted of murder).

Above right: George 'Brummie' Sage.

Below left: Alf White (hand to face) and George Drake (in bowler hat).

Below right: Arthur Harding.

CHAPTER 9

When Nothing's Quite Like It Seems

It's never a good idea to suggest that you're something you're not; when it comes to the crunch and explanations are demanded, you're bound to be found out. I recall a fellow who had never served in any of the armed services but who insisted on wearing a Parachute Regiment tie. I know quite a few heavily muscled (and of necessity aggressive) chaps who served in the Paras, and to pretend you were one of them when you weren't really isn't a good idea – honestly.

Something of the kind happened in the case of Ernest Straney aged 34, Edward Wiggins aged 26 and 25-year-old George Wiggins, who were not gangsters but three night-duty printers. At 5 o'clock in the morning, they set out for what was later described in court as 'a breezy time' and were arrested for drunkenness and assaulting the police. But prior to their arrest, they boasted to Major Poole MC, the licensee of The Buck's Head Hotel, Croydon, 'We're the Sabini boys', and this claim not unnaturally found its way into the press. It was haughtily repudiated by Darby Sabini, who made a personal visit to the hotel to inform Major Poole that the three miscreants (none of whom had previous convictions) had never been associated with his gang; and the trio, who later appeared at Croydon Police Court, penitently paid fines and costs to a total of £47 15s 0d. Darby, quite out of character, was for once in his life telling the truth. However, he refused to let this deter him, and he soon carried on much as before, lying his head off and ensuring that witnesses were bribed so that he could continue to act pretty much as he pleased.

Of course, the use of the Sabini name in the case of Straney and Co was the result of silly, drunken boasting; but one year later, another case involved naming Sabini which had much more sinister and believable overtones.

Gaston Reynaud was a cook who had lodged at the house of a Frenchwoman, a Mme Roux, in Old Compton Street, Soho. There had been an altercation between Reynaud and a fellow lodger, Giovanni Periglione, and as a result, Reynaud was arrested, appeared in court and was bound over to keep the peace.

This led to Wilfred Jerome Cooper, a waiter, visiting Reynaud and telling him that Periglione intended to attack him with a razor and a broken glass but that in return for payment he could offer him the protection of the Sabini gang, of which he was a member. On a further occasion, Mme Roux, Reynaud's erstwhile landlady, hid under his bed at his new address at Stacey Street and overheard the demand, and on yet another occasion, £20 was demanded from Reynaud by both Periglione and a 33-year-old general merchant from Denmark Street named Georges Modebodze.

The demands continued, with Cooper now wanting £110 to ensure Reynaud's safety, and Reynaud finally (and wisely) decided that the police were the best people to ensure his safety. Detective Sergeant Lander, who spoke fluent French, took a leaf out of Mme Roux's book, hid under Reynaud's bed to coincide with Cooper's next visit and was able to hear a threat that if Reynaud failed to pay the money he would be glassed. Cooper then went on to say, 'I am the chief of the Sabini gang and since the police have interfered with the two gangs – the Sabinis and the Cortesis – we have declared an armistice.' He added that Periglione was a member of the Cortesi gang and had witnessed the murder of a man named Le Chevalier. Of course, there was not a word of truth in any of Cooper's assertions, but all the incriminating conversation in French was dutifully jotted down by Lander.

Arrested and charged with demanding a total of £130 with menaces, the trio appeared at Marlborough Street Police Court, where an interpreter was required for the depositions of that part of the proceedings which took place in French. When the Clerk of the Court referred to 'The Sabini Band', there was huge amusement in court when this was interpreted as '*L'orchestre de Sabini*'.

So as well as a useful tool for putting the frighteners on susceptible victims, the utterance of the name Sabini was also regarded as a 'get out of jail card' by artful offenders. It happened when James Moore, a 32-year-old native of Newcastle, appeared at Southampton Quarter Sessions in October 1929 charged with breaking into a Southampton house and stealing a watch. Not only did Moore admit the offence but, although evidence was given that no money had been stolen, he was also absolutely adamant that he had stolen £40. He added that there were two accomplices when the burglary had been committed. They had since threatened and blackmailed him, demanding £50, and he added that they were members of the Sabini gang. Despite his fulsome confession, he had refused to give police details of the men for fear that 'they would wait for him'.

It was a clever ruse to ensure that the saucy Mr Moore was bound over to keep the peace for twelve months.

⋆   ⋆   ⋆

Maurice Fireman was a fairly unlucky fellow; boxing as a light-weight under the ring-name of Jack Levene, he won only two of his eight professional bouts. Next, he was sentenced to four months' imprisonment for his part in the affray at Salisbury Railway Station in 1921; and then, when he put up a pitch at Epsom Downs on 4 June 1923, he was told by a man named Thomas, 'This is our pitch.' Additionally, the same day, he incurred the wrath of the Sabini brothers, Darby and Harry, and their 23-year-old accomplice, George Dido. Fireman's pugilistic skills appeared to have dissipated since his last fight, some five years previously, because the three men were able to hit him in the face and head with a knuckleduster, and Harry – now recovered from last November's bullet wound to the stomach – held a knife up to his eye, telling him, 'I've a good mind to knock your eye out.'

Arrested, Darby told Detective Inspector Shuman, 'All I did was to stop the boys fighting. It was a fight amongst the Jews.'

Harry's explanation was, 'I saw them fighting and let them get on with it.' Dido stated that he had had a stand-up fight with Fireman. It's difficult to say why Dido was in the Sabinis' company; he was an associate of Dodger Mullins, who was in direct confrontation with both the Italian Mob and the Yiddishers.

Naturally, they were all released on bail, and unsurprisingly, the case started to crumble almost immediately. A witness to the fight was produced who said that no knife or knuckleduster was seen, nor could either be found. Dr Beckitt of Aldgate said that Fireman's injuries might have been caused by a fist and a ring, but they did not appear serious enough to have been caused by a knuckleduster. This provided Dido with the excuse, when he gave evidence, to say that during his fight with Fireman he had been wearing a ring 'which might have been mistaken for a knuckleduster'. Then the trump card produced by the Sabinis was the testimony of Irish/Canadian Sergeant Major Michael O'Rourke VC, MM, who was recuperating as a patient at the Ministry of Pensions Hospital, Epsom and who corroborated the defendants' evidence, saying that Fireman (whose previous conviction was mentioned in court) was the aggressor. Who could possibly doubt the word of a war hero with two medals for gallantry? Certainly not the bench at Epsom Police Court, and on 18 June the charges were dismissed.

Nor was Fireman the only unlucky person in the case; whatever beneficence was bestowed upon O'Rourke by Darby, it was soon dissipated, and he was reduced to living on Skid Row, in Vancouver, British Columbia on a pension of $10 per month.

CHAPTER 10

Death at the Eden Social Club

Despite a number of brushes with the law, Alfie Solomon led a charmed life. On 14 February 1921, he was charged with eleven cases of welshing at Windsor Police Court which were dealt with under the Probation of Offenders Act; he was ordered to pay £10 damages and costs of £2 5s 0d. Then the same year, as we know, he was acquitted of shooting Billy Kimber after saying it was an accident; and two years later, he was again acquitted at the Old Bailey on a charge of conspiracy to cause grievous bodily harm to William Homer. Solomon's murderous instincts remained; his luck, however, was about to change.

On 22 September 1924, Solomon, together with fellow hard-men Edward Emanuel, Harry Mansfield and others, left the Alhambra Music Hall and entered the Eden Social Club, at 5 Eden Street, a cul-de-sac near the corner of Hampstead Road. The club was on two floors over a garage. About forty people were in the premises, and a game of faro was in progress. One of the customers was a bookmaker's runner, who was known as Buck Emden but whose real name was Barnett Blitz, and a very unpleasant character to boot. A professional boxer 'who was not particular at using his fists only in a scrap', his four-contest career had come to a halt in 1916, when at Bow Street Police Court he was bound over, having hit someone in the face with a bottle. In the same year, at Old Street Police Court, he was ordered to pay £20 to a police officer whom he had stabbed with a bayonet; incredibly, he had been spared imprisonment, and these were just two of his nine previous convictions for violence. He and Harry Moss, a commission agent's clerk and a boxing friend, had been to The Ring boxing booth that evening and they arrived at the club at around 11.30 pm. The two men had a drink, then Moss went to one end of the room to play cards. There was little love lost between Blitz and Emanuel; in 1923, Blitz had sold bookmakers' lists at the Epsom Spring Meeting, and Emanuel, of course, saw this as his monopoly. Perhaps as a result, Blitz had been arrested as being a suspected person, and although the bench at Epsom Police Court had sentenced him to three months' imprisonment, he had successfully appealed. But Blitz was in no doubt that it was

Emanuel who had set him up to the police and now, seeing him at the bar, he shouted, 'There's the copper!'[3]

At his reputation being thus impugned, Emanuel swore, then threw a glass of beer into Blitz's face; when Blitz retaliated, Emanuel ducked and the beer mug struck him on the head, cutting it severely, later requiring five stitches to be inserted. Emanuel clutched at Blitz's coat collar, shouting, 'What are you doing? Get off!', and the two men fell to the floor, struggling, until some of the faro players separated them.

The two men then went to the ground floor, and when Solomon saw his friend bleeding, he picked up a large carving knife from a table and plunged it violently into Blitz's neck, severing the left internal artery and the left internal jugular vein. The doorman, Mick Abelson, tried to separate Blitz and Solomon and take the knife off Solomon, who slashed Abelson severely in the leg; he was later taken to the London Temperance Hospital. Blitz should have died instantly, but he staggered out of the club, and a witness, Raymond Andibert, saw him run down Eden Street and collapse, blood gushing from his mouth. A number of men emerged from a nearby house; two picked him up and one of them said, 'He's done for.' Then, with a distinct lack of sympathy, he dropped Blitz into the gutter, where he stayed until the police arrived.

The majority of the club members had rushed off into the night leaving their hats and coats behind. A member of the club told a reporter from the *Daily Mirror*, 'Before you could count ten, there was a terrible cry from one of the tables. There was a rush to the injured man, a scramble and a rush to the door by some people.'

Later that morning, Detectives Duby and Nunn arrested Solomon, who they found sitting in a taxi in Covent Garden, and brought him into the CID office at Albany Street police station. There he was seen by Detective Inspector Steele, who had just returned from the mortuary at University College Hospital, where he had seen Blitz's body. He showed Solomon the knife that he had retrieved from the club and said, 'You were seen to strike Blitz and Mike Abelson with this at the Eden Street Club this morning. You will be charged with the murder of Blitz and the attempted murder of Abelson.'

To that, Solomon replied, 'That's what they say. What I have done, I have done in self-defence. I saw the doorman had a knife in his hand. I wrestled with him and got possession of

---

[3] This was an expression in common use at the time; he meant that Emanuel was a police informant.

the knife. All I know is that during the struggle someone pulled me off him.'

On 26 September, the inquest opened at St Pancras Coroner's Court, and among others, a barman at the club, Edward William George Trinder, described the attack on Blitz.

'Was there any reason why you did not get Blitz assistance?' asked Sir Walter Schroder, the coroner, to which Trinder replied, 'I wasn't feeling too grand after the blood and the fighting', and added, 'and what could I have done?'

It was suggested that Blitz had said to Solomon, 'I don't care for no one. If you want to, you can come downstairs and have it out. So can the rest of you.' But if indeed this was said, it was not heard by Trinder.

Harry Moss, who witnessed the struggle between Blitz and Emanuel, was asked, 'Had Blitz ever told you he thought anyone desired to do him an injury?'

'Yes,' replied Moss. 'He told me that Emanuel was making friends with Solomon with a view to hurting him.'

'They all seemed to be going mad', was the opinion of witness Harry Mansfield, who saw Solomon attacking the doorman with the knife and stopped him. Another commission agent, Isidore Hyams (the part-proprietor of the club), described how, when Blitz and Emanuel were starting to go downstairs, Solomon 'darted like lightning across the room' and stabbed Blitz in the neck.

Having seen Blitz, his head bleeding, rush down the club's stairs, Charles Samnel was asked why he did not fetch a doctor; he replied that owing to the character of the club, he did not wish to give it any publicity.

The coroner's jury had little hesitation in declaring that Solomon was guilty of wilful murder, and with a rope metaphorically caressing his neck, he was committed to stand his trial at the Old Bailey. Only a miracle could save him now, and one was found, in the form of Sir Edward Marshall Hall KC.

* * *

Hall was known as 'The Great Defender', and it's possible that the knighthood was conferred on him for services to drama. In his first case in 1894, he defended a 41-year-old prostitute named Marie Hermann, charged with murdering a client. With tears streaming down his face, Sir Edward cried to the jury, 'Look at her, gentlemen, look at her! God never gave her a chance – won't you?' It was sufficient for Ms Hermann to escape the hangman's noose and receive instead six years' penal servitude for manslaughter.

One astonishing acquittal followed another, but by the end of 1923 he stated, 'I am now declining all sensational criminal cases and hope to confine myself in future to the High Court.'

But as his 1929 biographer, Edward Marjoribanks MP noted, 'However, he was never allowed to avoid, nor indeed, could he resist the less lucrative but more sensational call of the Old Bailey.'

He certainly was unable to resist the lucrative fee of £1,000 in folding money to defend Solomon which was offered by Darby Sabini, when he arrived, together with a small retinue, at Sir Edward's Welbeck Street flat. As Sir Edward's biographer noted, 'Did they think that he would be more amenable to reason if they approached him direct, instead of through the medium of his lynx-eyed and vigilant clerk?'

Indeed he was, and together with Mr Roland Oliver and Mr G. L. Du Cann, he set about manufacturing a defence more watertight than a mermaid's brassière for the trial that commenced at the Old Bailey on 17 November 1924.

★   ★   ★

Edward Emanuel was called by the prosecution and said that Blitz hit him so hard with the bottle that 'I lost all reason.'

'Was Blitz a man with a strong feeling against you?' asked Sir Edward. 'A mug who, as you say, had wrongly accused you of putting him away?' to which Emanuel replied, 'Yes.'

'Had he told everybody you tried to bribe the police to get him locked up?' Emanuel was asked, and again he replied, 'Yes.'

Emanuel was able to untruthfully tell Solomon's barrister that Blitz and Solomon were friends. But more important than that bare-faced piece of perjury was the fact that the jury had had the opportunity of seeing the wound on Emanuel's forehead which had required five stitches. That, as will be seen, would be utterly essential to the defence.

Abelson hobbled into court on crutches and told the jury:

> During the struggle in the club, I saw Solomon swing up his arm. He had a knife in his hand. I saw him plunge the knife into Blitz's neck. I tried to get hold of Solomon but he started slashing out at me and when I tried to retreat, I tripped over a chair. Solomon was holding the knife, and was slashing at me but I kept him off by kicking out with my feet. A member of the club got hold of Solomon's arm and I made my escape.

After Hyams, who had employed Blitz to attend race meetings, described seeing Solomon plunging the knife into Blitz's neck, Sir Edward used a favourite barrister's trick of belittling a witness; he asked, 'What did you do?'

'I ran away', replied Hyams.

Affecting astonishment, Sir Edward gasped, 'You say you saw your friend stabbed in the neck, *and you ran away?*'

'I ran away because I was afraid of getting stabbed', replied Hyams. 'What would you have done in that case?'

'Don't ask me questions or you may get answers you don't like', responded Sir Edward tartly, although precisely what he meant by that is difficult to say. He also roundly condemned the Eden Club, saying that it was 'frequented mostly by the racing fraternity, members of the Jewish persuasion and the sooner that sort of place was shut, the better for everybody concerned.' But since it was stated that it was members of the Jewish community (as well as the Italian) who had raised the money to pay for Solomon's defence, Sir Edward told the jury, 'The prisoner could not be such a scoundrel as has been suggested.'

However, given the weight of evidence against his client, Sir Edward was far too shrewd to put him in the witness box. Instead, Solomon produced a written statement which was read by the Clerk of Assizes:

> I do not know what happened that night. It is no use to say I did. All I remember is seeing Emanuel bleeding like a pig from his head. I thought Blitz was going for him again.

And what that meant was that by not going into the witness box Solomon could not be cross-examined by the prosecution. Now Sir Edward could adduce evidence of Solomon's 'good character' – incredible, as we know, because of the violent attacks he had carried out in the past which had nevertheless ended in acquittals – and do his best to convince the jury that Solomon was guilty of manslaughter, not murder. He spoke of Solomon's service with the Royal Fusiliers and hinted that his medals were awarded for gallantry, although they were, of course, only the service medals to which every combatant during the war was entitled. Mr Percival Clarke for the prosecution did his best to prove otherwise, saying that there was no hint of drunkenness in Solomon's behaviour, that he had been sober enough to play faro and that there existed a feud between the racetrack gangs.

Divisional Detective Inspector Hambrook told the court he had known Solomon since boyhood and that he had a good character until he was discharged from the Army, when he fell in with the racecourse gangs.

But in the end, Sir Edward's rhetoric and histrionics won the day. He was drinking from a glass tumbler when suddenly he leaned forward, smashed the glass on the desk in front of him and held up the jagged shards for the gaping jury to see. They had heard of what happened to Emanuel, they had seen the scars, but now they had seen, first-hand, how an everyday item could be transformed into a deadly instrument capable of inflicting the most dreadful injuries, mutilating a person's face and even severing vital arteries. Suddenly it was forgotten that Blitz was the victim, and Solomon was acquitted of murder and found guilty of manslaughter. In sentencing him to three years' penal servitude, Mr Justice Salter observed, 'This stabbing is too common and must be checked.' Abelson's stabbing attracted no punishment at all; it was left on the file. It was as though it had never occurred. There were, of course, those who thought that Solomon had got away with murder. They also had long memories, which would lead to retribution being exacted some twelve years later.

CHAPTER 11

Widespread Gang Warfare

Fifteen months after his acquittal for attacking Maurice Fireman, Harry Sabini was at it again, this time at the Wye Races on 29 September 1924, when after the last race bookmakers Harry Fellows and Joseph Taylor were chased by a group of men who knocked them to the ground.

Fellows received the worst injuries; one of the gang held his head up, while another punched him in the face with full force – the wound on his forehead was said to be 'as big as the palm of one's hand' – and both men were kicked four or five times.

However, this time the assaults were witnessed by Detective Jenner, and as a result, Antonio Alfred 'Babe' Mancini was arrested at the scene, whilst the others fled. But warrants were soon issued for Thomas Mack, Pasqualino Papa and Harry Sabini, and the four men appeared at Ashford Police Court.

The Sabini acolytes were true to their code; Harry was absolved of all blame, his case was dismissed, and the others were each sentenced to one month's hard labour. As a footnote, Mancini – who also liked to use the name 'Stevens' – was a mixed bag of criminal talents. Violent, certainly, on this occasion, but also a sneak thief. In July 1935 he was sentenced to three months with hard labour for being a suspected person loitering to pick pockets, and then three years later, Woodbridge Justices packed him off to hard labour for twelve months for pinching a wallet and a coat. Mancini was a fervent Jew-hater and whilst he was serving this sentence he displayed his anti-Semitic disposition by spitting in Jewish prisoners' food. Unfortunately for him, one of those affected by his expectorations was Jack Comer, better known as gangland boss Jack Spot, who promptly smashed the living shit out of him. It was the beginning of a downward path for Mancini, as in due course we shall see.

Six months after that acquittal, Harry Sabini featured once more when William Thomas Presswell became involved in an argument in a café in Upper Street, Islington with the Phillips brothers, Johnny and Arthur. After a while, Arthur left but then returned with another man, plus Harry Sabini. Sensing danger, Presswell went to leave the café, at which point Arthur hit him on the head with an iron bar. The two men grappled, and the bar was dropped, but it was picked up by Johnny, who used it to strike Presswell on the back of the head. Sabini handed a knife to Johnny, who struck out at Presswell's face; the latter received defence wounds on the back of his hands in protecting himself.

And yet, it was only Johnny Phillips who appeared in the dock at Clerkenwell Police Court.

'Sabini cut me in the face at Brighton and I had twenty-six stitches put in', Johnny told his defence counsel, Mr Ricketts (practically doubling the number of stitches inserted on that occasion, for dramatic effect, as well as omitting the names of Messrs Langham and Ford and inserting Sabini instead).

'I suggest you were attacked by the Sabini gang?' said Mr Ricketts to Presswell, who replied, 'The Phillipses had had enough beer at the time but it would have been all right, but for Sabini.'

But Harry steered clear of the dock, and another case fizzled out.

Thus the attacks continued: in February 1925, five men were razor-slashed and kicked at Aldgate in front of a large crowd; two months later, another five men were attacked with razors and iron bars behind Euston Station, and in August two gangs, totalling twenty men, fought it out with razors in Shaftesbury Avenue. In the same month, racetrack gang members were travelling on top of an omnibus when a fight broke out in the Woodford Road. The conductor, Mr G. Allen, ascended the stairs in order to quell the trouble, was hit on the head with a bottle and knocked from the top of the bus into the roadway. Taken to Woodford Hospital for treatment, he reported for duty at Leyton garage the following day, but his condition worsened and he was placed sick again. Mr Allen was yet another innocent casualty of the racetrack gang wars.

★   ★   ★

Thomas Edward Bennyworth – he was known variously as 'Monkey' and 'The Trimmer' – could only be described as a pretty horrible character. Born in 1894 in South London, he was a very large and vicious bully. In 1917 he was flogged for attacking a warder, and according to Saffron Hill folklore, it was his jaw that was broken by Darby Sabini for insulting a lady. He was sentenced to three months' hard labour in 1921 and the following year, to eight months' hard labour. Hardly had he been released from a three-month sentence imposed in 1924 than he turned his attentions to Moses Levy in February 1925.

Levy had enjoyed the patronage of Alf Solomon (currently unavailable due to his enforced absence from the streets after killing Barnett Blitz) and the Sabini family, for whom – if it was true that Darby Sabini had knocked him out – Bennyworth had little affection. That night, as Levy strolled down Aldgate High Street, Bennyworth was in good company, which included Dodger Mullins, Ernest Watts, Stephen Martin and John Jackson. They attacked Levy like a pack of wild animals; his face was razor-slashed, he was knocked to the ground and mercilessly kicked.

From his bed at St Bartholomew's Hospital, Levy provided Detective Inspector Crocker with the details of his assailants; they were arrested without trouble and all proclaimed their innocence.

At the Guildhall Justice Room on 17 February 1925, police evidence only was given to Alderman Jenks, and the prosecution was lambasted by the prisoners' friend, Mr G. L. Hardy, for having the impudence to put his clients in the dock unsupported by any testimony; he suggested they be bailed immediately. In fact, they were bailed in the not insubstantial sum of £500 and on 25 February they appeared once more, to discover, unsurprisingly, that the charges had been dropped. It appeared to be business as usual.

Three months later, on 20 May, John Jackson hired a large blue car, a Landaulet taxi cab – he used the name Mr Dickinson – from Messrs Powell Ltd., at the Baker's Arms, Leytonstone. Together with a driver, Albert Henry Croke, who had been supplied by the firm, they first went the Rising Sun public house. After half an hour they left and visited a number of other pubs, finally arriving at The Rock, where six other men, including Tommy Bennyworth, George Watts, Leonard Winter and Dodger Mullins got into the car. Jackson directed the driver to take them to a dance hall in Windmill Street, then to the Bouverie Club, Bouverie Street, Paddington, which they entered and where a number of men were attacked and robbed – Alf White being one of them. The gang returned to the car, carrying a hat and two overcoats. They drove to Moody's Club in Tottenham Court Road, where two men got into the car for about five minutes. They then drove to 17 Maiden Lane, The Strand, where they kicked in the door, but nothing was stolen. The police were alerted, and the men drove off at high speed towards Trafalgar Square. Two shots were fired near the junction of Edgware Road and Harrow Road – these were heard by a constable on duty at about 2.00 am – and the driver was under the impression that the shots were fired to frighten anybody who was following them.

Albert Croke was directed to drive to Walworth, but then they stopped at the junction of Cambridge Street and Whitechapel Road. Croke was told to turn the car around while the men went to a coffee stall, but he seized the opportunity to drive off back to Leyton. Upon arrival there, he found that in a burst of mindless vandalism his passengers had cut the interior of the car to pieces.

Although Alf White was not willing to give evidence, he nevertheless provided police with the identities of his assailants. It soon became clear that apart from Alf White, the gang were looking to hand out punishment to the brothers of Alf Solomon, and although the matter was investigated by Divisional Detective Inspector Stevens, formerly of the Flying Squad and now stationed at Bow Street, it was his erstwhile colleagues from the Squad who were called in to assist.

Four days after the incident, Jackson and Mullins surrendered to police and Bennyworth and Watts were arrested; after being put up for identification, the latter two were picked out and charged with breaking and entering the dwelling house of Mr Lionel Barrett, 17 Maiden Lane, The Strand with intent to commit a felony and with assaulting and robbing several men at the Bouverie Club.

Bow Street Police Court was told by Inspector Stevens that the case had gained a certain amount of notoriety, that he wished to place the matter before the Director of Public Prosecutions and that he was 'anxious to arrest a number of other men'; the prisoners were remanded in custody.

The following day, Leonard Winter was arrested and said, 'I admit I went with them from the Rock public house, but I want the driver to pick me out.'

Mr Croke did just that, and Winter was charged and remanded with the rest.

The men appeared at court again on 2 June, when evidence for the prosecution was given, with G. L. Hardy once more bellowing for dismissal of the charges; and after overnight consideration by the magistrate, Sir Chartres Biron, Mr Wallace for the prosecution said he had no further evidence to offer. The Magistrate said he had no doubt that there was a great deal more behind this case than had come out. It was quite clear, he said, that the defendants were in search of one or more persons. They were, he added, a menace to the peace of London and evidently a dangerous gang who would not hesitate to employ violence – but not, of course, on this occasion.

He bound the prisoners over in the sum of £100 each and required another surety in the same amount to be of good behaviour for twelve months, or to go to prison for three months.

That case was quoted when six men appeared at Birmingham Police Court on 23 June 1925 after Thomas McDonough was attacked with an iron bar and razor-slashed from ear to lip. What were described as 'a loaded stick and two metal weapons' were found in the pub where the men were arrested. Matters were made rather difficult for police when McDonough told them, 'It's your place to find out who did it', and it was suggested that the Sabini gang were responsible for the attack. Not so. Not only was William Kimberley (also known as William Williams) a member of the Camden Town gang, he was also born in Birmingham. A year previously, he had been released from his twelve-month period of hard labour for attacking Steve Griffin with a broken glass. Perhaps it was a private quarrel, but it led to him, Moses, Isaac and Charles Kimberley plus William Weston and William Whitehouse appearing in the dock – although not for long. McDonough refused to give evidence, so the prosecuting solicitor suggested that the Stipendiary Magistrate take a leaf out of the book of his Bow Street counterpart, Sir Chartres Biron, and bind them over; and with the exception of Charles Kimberley, who was discharged, the others were bound over to keep the peace for six months. McDonough was charged with disturbing the peace and was offered a bind-over; he promised not to attempt any reprisals in Birmingham.

'You mean you will get your own back, somewhere else?' asked the clerk of the court, to which McDonough replied, 'I've made up my mind, I don't care who knows it, to get my own back.'

'You had better take care', said the magistrate, adding that McDonough would think better of matters presently. Since the deeply unpleasant McDonough had been previously birched and sent to hard labour for grievous bodily harm and assaulting the police, this may have been a forlorn hope.

Attacks were not restricted to any one area. At Walsall Police Court, George Edis was sentenced to three months' hard labour for attacking two members of a rival gang with an iron bar; this was part of a longstanding feud and coincided with the release from prison of members of a gang who had previously been sentenced to six months' imprisonment after attacking Edis with knives.

'Don't let Walsall be turned into another Sheffield' (where there had been a gang-related murder), urged the prosecuting solicitor in the case, and the Magistrate intimated that strong measures would be taken in the event of any further trouble.

That wasn't very likely, with many of those who were arrested ending up being bound over or otherwise walking free from court.

A classic case was that of Isaiah Elboz, a London bookmaker, who on 30 July 1925 had allegedly either attacked or insulted Sidney Payne, a Birmingham commission agent, in Brighton's Embassy Club. Payne returned to his hotel, where he was staying with Thomas Armstrong, who four years previously had escaped the death penalty (or indeed, any kind of penalty) for killing bookmaker Philip Jacobs. So Armstrong, together with Payne and fellow Birmingham Boy, 37-year-old William Glynn, returned to the club, and at 2.30 am as the dancers were leaving, an eye witness heard men arguing:

> Blows were exchanged and there was turmoil. Someone drew a razor and there were screams followed by a free fight. There was great alarm in the street and all the available police in the district were rushed to the scene.

Before the arrival of the police, Elboz half-walked and was half-carried to a car. He, together with two other men, Thomas Mayhew Welton and John Melville, both stewards at the club, had been brutally razor-slashed. Elboz had suffered the worst injuries. When the police did arrive, they found a bloodstained razor with a broken blade in the club, and the three men were arrested.

The matter was considered so serious that when the men appeared at Brighton Police Court charged with inflicting grievous bodily harm on Elboz, the county's Chief Constable personally stepped into the witness box to apply for a remand in custody, which was granted.

But upon their next appearance at court on 6 August, to answer charges of wounding Welton and Melville, matters changed dramatically. The prosecuting solicitor, Mr C. J. M. Whittaker, told the bench, 'You have to deal with a gang of very dangerous and violent men, who terrify people', adding, 'I have never heard of a more cold-blooded and ghastly attempt to maim and disfigure men from sheer spite.'

But Elboz, swathed in bandages, replied to almost every question, 'I cannot recollect', and was treated as a hostile witness; and although the three men in the dock were committed for trial, they also walked free on bail.

The gratuitous violence that was being dished out came to a head at 10.30 pm on 30 August 1925 at Victoria Station. A large group of drunken racegoers were returning from Gatwick races and began to argue amongst themselves and with other train passengers. Probably the worst behaved was 29-year-old William Rowlett, who had vomited on the station platform. William Gatford, a 54-year-old Southern Railway Police Constable, arrived and was spoken to by 21-year-old Harry Taylor (alias Joseph Newman), who said, 'Are you the first-aid man? We don't want you.'

Gatford took hold of Rowlett, who was holding a broken glass tumbler which he smashed into Gatford's forehead. Gatford struggled with his prisoner but was attacked by Rowlett's associates, who punched him, then threw him on to the railway line, where he lost consciousness. This was witnessed by a fellow railway constable, Harry Robbins, who was attacked by James Newman and others, punching and kicking him. Police Constable Leonard Collins of the Metropolitan Police rushed in to assist Robbins and when he was attacked by Rowlett, Collins drew his truncheon and 'sticked' Rowlett so severely that as well as flattening him on the spot, he also hospitalized him. Collins also arrested another man, but was set upon by more of the gang, who released him.

Charged with causing grievous bodily harm and assaults on the police, the three men, plus 17-year-old Charles Newman, appeared at Westminster Police Court the following day, made the mistake of refusing to give their fingerprints and were remanded in custody.

With the exception of Charles Newman, who was discharged, the other three were found guilty at the London Sessions of the assaults on 7 October. Rowlett and Joseph Newman both had convictions for assault and both were sent to hard labour, Rowlett for fifteen months and Joseph for twelve. The Deputy Chairman, Mr A. J. Lawrip KC, postponed sentence on James Newman, remanding him in custody until the next sessions, when he stated that James would be released under the Probation of Offenders Act on condition that he abstained from intoxicating liquor for the period of one year.

The prisoners were part of a bunch of tearaways known as the Battersea Boys, and although the trouble had started when they returned from the racetrack, they were just a bunch of drunken slags and should not be confused with the likes of the Italian Mob or the Birmingham Boys. But what had happened was all grist to the media's mill, and in 1925 the *Daily Mail* and the *Daily Express* both published lists of the gang-related outrages throughout the country which made impressive reading for the general public. Moreover, there's nothing like a bit of public disquiet to cause the Home Secretary's sphincter to twitch, which was what happened in this case.

CHAPTER 12

Questions in Parliament

Winston Churchill wrote, 'The worst that can be said about him is that he runs the risk of being most humorous when he wishes to be most serious'; he was referring to Sir William Joynson-Hicks – known popularly as 'Jix' – who was Home Secretary from 1924 to 1929. He was popular with the police but had done very little to stamp out the racecourse gangs during his tenure as Home Secretary. Still, the press coverage in the tabloids demanded firm (if flowery) rhetoric, which he duly delivered at full flow in the Commons:

> I intend to break up the race gangs. These fights show the existence of a state of affairs which cannot be tolerated in a civilised society. It may be difficult to break these gangs all at once, but give me time. The responsibility is mine; I mean to discharge it. It is monstrous that in a civilised country, this kind of rowdyism should take place. I shall take the necessary steps to put an end to this particular kind of atrocity.

He was backed up by Edward Shortt KC, who believed the race-track gangster was as dangerous as a mental patient and that a proper sentence should be to confine the perpetrator to an institution as a criminal lunatic during the King's pleasure. All very well, but Shortt really should have taken the matter by the scruff of its neck during his own tenure as Home Secretary between 1919 and 1922; he was referred to by a parliamentary colleague as being 'capable but obstinate'.

The Flying Squad were appointed to eradicate the race gangs, although they had been combating them for the past six years with limited success.

There was a flurry of letters between 'Jix' and Brigadier-General Sir William Horwood, the Commissioner of Police; Horwood was not a popular commissioner ('An unattractive man who mistook arrogance for leadership', recalled a clerk in his office), and when he consumed a poisoned chocolate sent through the post by a lunatic named Walter Tatam, the rank and file gleefully dubbed Sir William 'The Chocolate Soldier'.

The letters from Sir William were not a great deal of help; he underplayed the disturbances, pointed out the problems of policing race meetings and, using 'the overworked press term of "'race gangs'", pointed to the tendency of the press to label petty disturbances as 'race-gang related'; he did his best to assure the Home Secretary that many of the attacks reported by the *Daily Express* were exaggerated, with little evidence in many cases of any involvement by racing men. Indeed, he believed the reports of the razor fight in Shaftesbury Avenue to be 'pure invention'.

It was sufficient for the Home Secretary to tell the commissioner, 'Go on as you've been going.'

*   *   *

It appeared the courts were 'going on as they'd been going' as well. On 7 December 1925, a fight broke out after a number of bookmakers had left Tattersalls, England's main auctioneers of race horses, in Knightsbridge. In fact, a police constable stated that there was a crowd of 300–400, of whom at least twenty were fighting. Two of the combatants were arrested: George 'Brummie' Sage, who at fifty-one was confident enough to take on a 27-year-old costermonger named Robert William Penfold; it appeared there had been a betting dispute between Penfold's father and another man. In fact, the scene was so dramatic that after the two men were arrested, the fighting continued, and it was not until more police, one of them a mounted officer, arrived on the scene that the crowd was dispersed.

Whatever injuries Mr Penfold Sr. had sustained, it was not a matter that he wished to pursue, and at Westminster Police Court Penfold Jr. pleaded guilty to disorderly behaviour, his solicitor informing Mr Boyd, the Magistrate, that his client was 'a man of the highest character, and very much regretted that he should be charged with an offence even of that nature'. Sage, of course, could not be awarded such an accolade, simply said, 'I plead guilty to fighting, sir', and both were bound over in the sum of £10 to keep the peace for twelve months.

And then something rather odd happened. On the same day that Messrs Sage and Penfold were weighed off at Westminster Police Court, a couple of miles away to the east, at the Royal Courts of Justice, the Lord Chief Justice was hearing a libel case brought by Darby Sabini.

*   *   *

On 12 April 1924, the magazine *Topical Times*, published by D. C. Thompson & Co. Ltd, ran a piece to the effect that Darby had been referred to as being concerned in the operations of the Sabini gang, who were alleged to carry revolvers to terrorize bookmakers. In particular, the article stated:

> No story of the turf wars could be complete without reference to one or two men whose activities have made themselves notorious. The Sabini brothers, Harry and Charles Darby Sabini, have earned themselves enough publicity.

Since this was entirely accurate, Darby would have been well advised to swallow these impertinent words and say nothing, but instead, he sued the newspaper group for libel. Obviously, he believed that D. C. Thompson would cave in and be delighted to have the matter settled out of court at the earliest opportunity.

If that was so, Darby thought wrong; the newspaper defended the action, claiming the defence of truth and justification. But then, seeing the writing on the wall, Darby decided to discontinue proceedings, although – out of either obstinacy or tight-fistedness – he would not instruct counsel for leave to withdraw the action. So on 15 December 1925, not only did counsel fail to appear at the King's Bench Division, neither did Darby.

Consequently, Mr E. B. Charles, on behalf of the newspaper, asked the Lord Chief Justice for judgement upon the plea of justification. The Lord Chief Justice agreed and furthermore ordered that Darby should pay costs, directing that because the matter appeared so serious, it should be referred to the Director of Public Prosecutions.

Darby Sabini may have been as cunning as a fox, but when dealing with matters such as civil law, not only was he completely out of his depth, he was also profoundly stupid. On 11 June 1926, the creditors for D.C. Thompson arrived at the London Bankruptcy Court to claim £737, the cost of the defamation proceedings. Darby had already refused to pay the sum and he now further aggravated the situation by failing to appear; the Official Receiver stated that unless he put in an appearance, a warrant for his arrest would be issued. On 29 June, he did appear and gave details of his circumstances which were inaccurate, exaggerated and dramatized. He laughed as he denied both being the leader of the Sabini gang and making between £20–30,000 per year, and said instead that out of his weekly earnings of £8 he paid £1 5s 0d in travelling expenses plus 5s 0d a day for food and drink. If he was working five days a week, it's difficult to see how he could have provided for himself and his family on the 10s 0d that was left. He stated that he now lived in a furnished apartment in Russell Street, Brighton with his wife and three children. He added that he had no assets, had never had any money and could make no offer of payments for his debts; the examination was concluded with Darby being declared bankrupt.

Three years later, Darby was in trouble again. At Hove Greyhound Stadium he accused bookmaker David Isaacs of welshing; a fight ensued between the two men at a restaurant, followed by another, during which Darby knocked his opponent down. At Brighton Police Court on 28 October 1926, when Darby was accused of assault, Isaacs was asked why he had not brought any witnesses.

'How can I get witnesses against a man like this, when everyone goes in fear of their life of him?' he replied.

Darby, on the other hand, brought four witnesses to say that Isaacs was the aggressor, but for once his usual ploy failed to work. Perhaps the Chairman of the Bench had perused the recent law reports, because he found the case proved and fined Darby £5, with the alternative of twenty-eight days' hard labour. Despite the alleged absence of any assets, Darby paid up.

The Sabinis had diversified, running gambling clubs in London's West End and busying themselves on the greyhound racing scene, but Darby was beginning to slide. Alf White and his family were showing a greater interest in the money available from greyhound racing, and cracks were appearing in the coalition, especially with regard to the Jewish elements. Darby spent more and more time in Brighton and Hove and was becoming a spent force.

CHAPTER 13

Preventative Measures

It's time to leave the blood-letting for a bit. Since the outbreak of gang violence, on the occasions when gangsters were convicted it had become the norm for detectives to speak up in court for them, depending on which faction they supported. They would tell the open court of how this gangster or that had provided information to the detriment of other criminals, but this – in my opinion – was a foolish thing to do. In those halcyon days when police officers prosecuted at the lower court – prior to the introduction of the catastrophically inept Crown Prosecution Service – there were other ways of letting a court know of a defendant's helpfulness; or not, as the case might be. But openly stating a prisoner's cooperation not only suggested that the man in the dock was a grass (for which retribution could be and very often was taken), it also hinted that in speaking up for him, the police officer concerned was corrupt.

Darby Sabini was said to have paid out £5,000 per year in bribes to police, although that figure appears to have been wildly exaggerated. If Darby bunged a venal copper £50 each time – and make no mistake about it, during the 1920s, £50 was an enormous sum, representing eight times a detective inspector's weekly wage – it meant Darby was disbursing that amount one hundred times a year. Were he and his cohorts in danger of being nicked one hundred times during the space of one year? Not very likely. It's a boast that gangsters have used for years (and probably still do), so that their acolytes believe they have crooked coppers by the dozen in their pockets, thereby enhancing the boss's status. Easy to say, impossible to refute.

* * *

It seemed that former Detective Chief Inspector Tom Divall who, following his retirement, policed the racetracks, ran with the hare and hunted with the hounds. Admittedly, his was a difficult job since he had no actual police powers, and although in his time he had been a very tough cop indeed, he showed allegiance to both the Italian Mob and the Birmingham Boys. He described James

Ford, the bald-headed former boxer with a shocking record who had recently been released from a six-month sentence for wrecking the New Avenue club, as being 'a decent, quiet fellow', a reformed character who now had a freehold house and was earning 'a lucrative living'. Precisely what that living was, Divall neglected to say. He was a little premature in his effusiveness; as will be seen, following a savage attack in 1928, Ford collected another two-month sentence.

Following the racing at Hawthorn Hill, when Divall was surrounded by some toughs who appeared intent on killing him, he praised Darby for knocking one of his adversaries to the ground, which defused the situation. At Doncaster, an ugly situation arose between some miners and bookmakers' clerks; on that occasion, it was Billy Kimber who poured oil on the troubled waters, telling Divall afterwards that his actions 'saved you from any trouble and worry'. It was Kimber and George Sage, too, whom Divall appeared to side with, especially after Sage had helped him quiet some rowdy behaviour, and he later praised both men, who on separate occasions had been attacked by the Italian Mob, saying:

> Just to show what generous fellows Sage and Kimber were, they would not give any evidence or information against their antagonists and stated that they would sooner die than send those men to prison.

Nevertheless, Scotland Yard and the Home Secretary received a number of anonymous letters highlighting gangsters' activities and also castigating police officers.

In September and October 1922, the then Home Secretary, Edward Shortt, received letters signed 'Tommy Atkins';[1] this pseudonym was one of those along the lines of 'A lover of justice', 'A British Ratepayer' and 'An Englishman', all of which had a jingoistic flavour, castigating Jews and those of Italian extraction.

The first letter, in all its illiteracy, read as follows:

> The Financier and Brains of this gang of Cuthroat(s) on the Race Courses of England are Foriengers [sic] named Edward Emanual and Gurchen Harris, these two men finance all the large clubs and Gambling Houses in the West End of London, and they pay large sums of money to other foriengers [sic],

---

[1] A reference to British private soldiers' nickname during the First World War.

'The Sabini Gang' also the 'Flying Squad' of Scotland Yard to
safeguard their interests.

Chief Inspector Brown inserted an advertisement in the personal
column of the *Daily Express* urging 'Tommy Atkins' to arrange an
interview to discuss his grievances, and three days later, although
it looks as though Mr Atkins failed to make a personal appearance,
he sent a further letter in which he suggested ways to 'reconstruct
your evidence against this Wild, Foreign, Murderous Band of
Italian Jews'.

Eight months later, another letter, this one completely anonymous, was received, again targeting Emanuel and referring to the
number of police officers who kept him company, particularly in
the Titchbourne Club in Edgware Road.

A further letter, similarly anonymous, arrived after the incident
at Mornington Crescent, when the Italian faction shot at George
Sage and Fred Gilbert. It is rather confused and contradictory,
because Alf White, George West and Joseph Sabini were among
the aggressors, and the writer seems to suggest that one of the
English faction – probably White – should not have been arrested,
saying:

> And what is more the police are against him for why, because
> he happen(s) to be an Englishman, if he, had been Italian, there
> would have been know [*sic*] notice taken off [*sic*] the charge . . .

Of course, the writer may have been referring to Sage and Gilbert,
remanded in custody on the blackmailing charge – but then the
victim was Jewish, not Italian. As it appeared, all rather confusing
and, if one discounts the writer's illiteracy, perhaps it was meant
to be.

One month later, another letter arrived, this one signed
'Timewell Force', a reference to a Royal Commission in 1906.
A committee known as the Police and Public Vigilance Society had
been set up to investigate police malpractice under the auspices
of one James Timewell, who instructed Earl Russell to act on their
behalf. The peer described Timewell as 'a fanatic . . . prepared
always to believe anything he was told against the police and to
resent, with some indignation, the demand for proof which a
lawyer always makes'.

Timewell had been assisted by Arthur Harding, a vicious,
vindictive and thoroughly unscrupulous criminal, who had acquired
a thin veneer of education, read some law books and, by own
account, managed to get himself acquitted on twenty-seven

occasions. Harding was a contradiction in terms: he had a loathing for police in general and the Flying Squad in particular, since the Squad was the brainchild of Fred Wensley, who was his bitterest enemy; however, he was also a self-confessed snout for the post-Second World War Ghost Squad. Because the letter was reasonably literate, it is possible that Harding was its author, and it mentioned the shooting in Gray's Inn Road and the association between Detective Rutherford and the Sabinis. In part, it read:

> I first of all refer to the shooting case in the Italian Colony, when Rutherford was supposed to have been shot at. He was drinking with these men in a certain Public House, and words which were passed by the famous detective and these loafers in the betting world, the shots were among themselves and not in any direction for this drunken detective and one of the Flying Squad.

A twelve-page report was commissioned for the Home Office in which these allegations were dismissed one by one.

If Harding was the author of the letter he got his comeuppance a few years later, when he was followed from St Pancras to Leytonstone High Road by Detective Sergeant Dan Gooch of the Flying Squad who arrested him for being a suspected person; and with a considerable amount of evidence against him, Harding pleaded guilty at Stratford Police Court on 12 April 1928 and was sentenced to three months' hard labour.

John Rutherford came in for another hammering when, on 27 November 1928, a tailor named Montague Lester was savagely attacked at the Horseshoe Hotel in Tottenham Court Road by James Ford, his brother Harry and James Paul. This was as the result of a race gang feud which had originated in Manchester. It was said that Rutherford and other officers were present but did nothing to stop the attack – although it was quite possible that due to the numbers of people present, it was not possible to do so. The trio escaped, and the brothers Ford then went on to attack a commission agent, Charles Ricketts, in a first-class compartment of a race train at Paddington. This latter charge was dismissed by the Magistrate at Bow Street Police Court on 23 February 1929, but the prosecution on the first charge came in for fierce criticism from Mr Laurence Vine, for the defence.

He stated that the case had been 'much exaggerated' and complained that the matter had been taken out of the hands of the local police and entrusted to a Flying Squad officer, Detective Sergeant (later Detective Chief Inspector) Frederick 'Nutty' Sharpe.

This, said Mr Lawrence, was because Sharpe held a grudge against the Fords due to one of them having complained about him to his superiors. Sharpe replied that he had no knowledge of such a complaint.

Of course, there could have been a modicum of truth in those assertions, since Sharpe was not one to forgive or forget a slight. Early in his career as a Squad officer, Sharpe had arrested a pickpocket at Earl's Court Tube Station and got his struggling prisoner into the lift. Five of the pickpocket's associates crowded in behind him, attacked Sharpe with so much force he was knocked unconscious and made good their escape, together with the prisoner. Sharpe made it his business to identify and trace them – and within a year he had arrested all six men.

However, it was not pure vindictiveness that prompted Sharpe's involvement in the matter; racetrack gang feuding was the Flying Squad's prerogative, and James Ford, who had served two months for the shooting at Albany Street eight years earlier, now received another two-month sentence, while James Paul got one month (both with hard labour) and Ford's 21-year-old brother received a £25 fine.

Sharpe, an ex-miner who once had himself nailed up in a packing case, complete with eye-holes, and delivered to a warehouse that was experiencing thefts, was not only as hard as nails, he was also a dedicated race-goer who combined business with pleasure. As head of the Flying Squad, he received information that a wanted criminal would be attending Newmarket races. Resplendent in top hat and cutaway and with binoculars slung round his neck, Sharpe stepped into his 4½ litre Flying Squad Bentley but told his driver (and namesake) Police Constable George Sharp to drive first to King's Cross Railway Station, where a 'Race Special' train was due to leave at 9 o'clock. He walked slowly down the platform, looking in every carriage, and as soon as he spotted known cardsharps he opened the carriage door and told them to 'clear off'. None demurred. Returning to the Bentley, which then purred away in the direction of Newmarket, Sharpe spent a successful and lucrative day at the races, pausing on his way back to the Yard only to deposit his prisoner in the cells at Cannon Row police station.

Ted Greeno was another tough Flying Squad officer who, like Sharpe, possessed an encyclopaedic knowledge of the gangs who frequented racetracks. He was hugely disinclined to accept any kind of abuse, be it verbal or physical, from anybody. 'I've given some villains some awful hidings', he once said, without any hint of contrition.

Two of his clients were Jack 'Dodger' Mullins and Timmy Hayes. Both were pieces of dreg from London's East End who were simply mindless thugs. By the time he was twenty-three, Hayes had been convicted on ten occasions, three of them for wounding and one of them for kicking, biting and punching police officers. At that time, in November 1914, Hayes, together with William Driscoll, was sentenced to three months' hard labour for pickpocketing.

At one stage, Mullins – a small man with a razor-scarred face – had been at daggers drawn with Alf White, but he and Hayes were opportunist thugs, sometimes working with gangs, sometimes alone, and on one particular occasion, together, when they were each sentenced to three years' imprisonment for warehouse breaking.

Mullins has been mentioned several times in this narrative; now, it's time to take a closer look at him. Dodger became fed up with a woman that he was living with and pushed her out of a window. His supporters argued that the window was not very far from the ground. Indeed it wasn't, but it was a car window that the unfortunate woman was ejected from, and at the time the vehicle was travelling at a considerable speed. According to East End legends (among them Reggie Kray, a fervent Dodger-worshipper), Dodger was caught at Epsom Downs, where his arrest was effected by a copper who punched him in the face with a knuckleduster. Whether or not this account was true, some readers will be relieved to hear that that mode of arrest has now been discontinued by the Metropolitan Police.

In trying, unsuccessfully, to extort money from a billiard hall owner, Mullins and Hayes smashed the place up, and Greeno single-handedly arrested them both for blackmail. At the Old Bailey on 2 July 1926, Mullins said that the case had been got up by the Sabinis and the Yiddisher Mob to get them off the streets, but the jury disagreed and both were sentenced to four years' penal servitude, with Hayes receiving a further five years' preventative detention for being a habitual criminal.

But Dodger was unstoppable. No sooner was he released than he, brothers George and Charles Steadman, motor driver and news vendor respectively, 31-year-old Henry Richard Barton, also a motor driver, and Jack Sangers, a 26-year-old clerk, together with five others, burst into the Argus Club, Soho on 25 January 1930, demanding drinks. Although they were told by the club secretary, John Lewis, that it was too late, they adopted a threatening attitude and were duly served. Mullins then demanded to know if there were any 'Raddies'[2] in the club. Lewis was seized and dragged into the clubroom, where they spotted one Angelo Costognetti – and in the absence of any other 'Raddies', they decided that he would do.

This band of heroes tore into the unprotected young man, punching, kicking and hitting him with coshes and chair legs. As Costognetti lay on the floor, Mullins got hold of him by his waistcoat and with his other hand ruthlessly wielded a cosh. The mob was shouting, 'Kill him! Burn him!', and witnesses said that all of them were hitting him with something; his clothes were literally torn from his body, glasses were smashed and one of the gang was flourishing a revolver.

I said that Costognetti was unprotected, but one person did try to come to his assistance; this was Edith Milburn and she clung to the feet of the men kicking the Italian, screaming to the club secretary, 'Stop them, Jack, stop them!' She was manhandled and badly assaulted, and Lewis seized the opportunity to leave the club to telephone for an ambulance and the police. When he returned, he was confronted by Mullins, Barton and another man.

'Where have you been, Jack?' asked Mullins.

Lewis replied, 'I've just phoned for the ambulance.'

'Have you been to the police?' asked Mullins, and Lewis replied, 'No.'

'Are you sure?' asked Mullins, then added chillingly, 'I hope you've not spouted against me. God help you if you have. You know I'm a thick 'un and you know what it means for me. I shall do you, if you have.'

It was unfortunate that the gang were released on bail; it afforded Mullins and Barton the opportunity to see Costognetti in a pub at King's Cross; Lewis, too, was threatened.

When the courageous quartet next appeared at Marlborough Street Police Court on 18 February 1930, Costognetti gave evidence; he had identified Mullins as one of the gang; but when Mullins stood up in the dock, Costognetti could not swear that he was one of the attackers. Furthermore, he had never seen the men before the night in question, he did not know of any grudge they might have against him and, what was more, the men who had attacked him were not those in the dock.

---

[2] A slang term which originally referred to those Italians who were considered 'radicals', although the expression was later used to refer to Italians of any political persuasion.

Lewis gave his evidence and asked for police protection, saying
he was afraid of the men; at the conclusion of the day's proceedings,
Mr Dummett, the magistrate, refused to consider bail, telling Lewis:

> You have given your evidence courageously. They will not
> molest you, as they are in custody. If any of their charming
> friends approach you in any way, let the police know at once
> and they will do their utmost to protect you.

One week later, the case resumed, with the defence doing their
best to discredit Lewis. Although he had used the name 'Lewis'
for fifteen years, he admitted his baptismal name was Morris
Gorsch. He denied being the promoter or one of the proprietors
of the club, saying that a man named Robinson was the owner.
He denied that he had ever been under observation as a mental
case, or that he had concocted this 'highly coloured story'. When
the matter of bail was raised, Divisional Detective Inspector John
Horwell stated that in the interests of justice bail should not be
allowed, and it wasn't; but with little effect. On 5 May 1930, all
of the prisoners were found not guilty at the Old Bailey and were
discharged.

Still, there was a little light on the horizon. Twenty years later,
Jack Sangers was cut to pieces by Billy Hill (more of him later),
and later in 1930, Mullins tried to tap his old comrade Arthur
Harding for £2 and verbally abused Harding's wife when it was
refused. Whenever 'the code of the East End' is mentioned,
Harding can properly be omitted. As well as being a grass for the
Ghost Squad, he propped Mullins up to the police for demanding
money with menaces and saw him sentenced to six years' penal
servitude. In an effort at credibility in his outrageously untruthful
and inaccurate memoirs, he whined, 'His people straightened
me up – they gave my wife £50 or £60 so I was lenient in my
evidence.'

By the time Dodger passed on in 1967, having escaped punishment for the 1932 Dartmoor Mutiny, he had notched up several
hundred court appearances and fifty-one convictions, the last in
1956 for the improbable offence of pickpocketing at the age of
sixty-four.

★   ★   ★

Even though 'Jix' had appointed the Flying Squad to get rid
of the racecourse gangs, they had an enormous area to cover and
naturally, not every racecourse could be policed; nor could they

necessarily contend with the trouble that broke out. Often the gangs would be tailed by Flying Squad vehicles out of London, and once they had determined the route the gang was likely to take to a particular racecourse, that information would be relayed to the Yard, who in turn would telephone the constabulary concerned in order that their local officers could be sent to the racecourse. Sometimes it worked and sometimes it didn't, so preventative measures were taken; at a racecourse where trouble was expected, one of the Squad's well-known Crossley Tenders would be ostentatiously parked at the entrance as a warning to the gangsters. At other times, it would be the duty of a lone detective to forestall any trouble. One such was my friend, the late Detective Superintendent Bob Higgins who, as a detective sergeant with the Flying Squad in the 1930s, was on duty at Goodwood when he received information that the Nile Mob were on their way to the racecourse by coach. He intercepted the coach as it drew up and told the driver to 'return to London – or else'. The Nile Mob's spokesman told him, 'We didn't mean any offence, Guv', and they went.

These were the men who, like Henry 'Chesty' Corbett of the Squad, spent their mornings attending the police courts to see who was appearing before the Beak and, just as important, who was accompanying them – as well as memorizing their faces. Corbett, who, at $\frac{1}{8}$th of an inch over the (then) minimum height limit of five feet eight, was almost as broad as he was tall and would maintain a lone patrol on foot at night and arrest pickpockets, four-, five- and sometimes six-handed. He was aided by his enormous physical strength, reinforced by working out with a chest expander and a 56lb weight on a daily basis, and he told a colleague, 'They can't get away from me once I lay my hands on them!'

So those were some of the Flying Squad officers, who knew their adversaries and cracked down hard on them; but their successes brought allegations of malpractice, as we have seen – and in 1930 a particularly craven letter from one of the most vicious gang members.

CHAPTER 14

Alf Solomon Needs Help

On the morning of 18 February 1930, the Director of Public Prosecutions wrote to Sir Trevor Bigham CB, the Assistant Commissioner (Crime), enclosing a letter which he had just received and asking Sir Trevor to take whatever action as he might think right, 'for reasons which will readily occur to you'. The letter read:

Sir,

In November 1924 I was charged at the Old Bailey with murder, and was convicted of manslaughter and sentenced to 3 years penal servitude. Another charge of grievous bodily harm was put on the file. I served my sentence and was released.

Since being released I have got a respectable livelihood on the racecourses betting and never been in trouble since and do not want to get into any.

I am earnestly asking for your advise [*sic*] and protection under these strange circumstances.

A month ago, I happened to go to Clapton dog races for the first time. After racing I went into the Bar with a man named Bernie Dorrie, who owns and runs dogs there. A conversation was overheard while having a drink. A man named Luper took the biggest part in this, and he is a confidential friend of Superintendent Brown, who are always to be seen together. On leaving the Clapton Stadium, this particular night I was followed by a gang of men with Luper the leader under the protection of Inspector Pride. I was followed through a number of turnings, my life was threatened by a gang who is now remand [*sic*] at Marlborough Street, who [*sic*] Dodger Mullins is the head. I can't say that Inspector Pride was there then, but he was in the Stadium drinking with them until 11 o'clock at night. The words I heard used that night was 'Let's do him', and 'We've got the Big Five behind us now.'

The appeal I am making to you is, as this man Luper is working under the protection of Superintendent Brown, what protection have I got. If necessary to hold an inquiry into this affair I am quite willing to come and give evidence in front of you, as I have got further news to tell you, that will surprise you, and I can bring witnesses.

Hoping you will give me your protection as I don't know
which way to turn.

Yours faithfully,
Alfred Solomon

The matter referred to regarding Mullins was this: three weeks
before the letter was written, he and four others had been arrested
following an incident at the Argus Club in Soho's Greek Street,
where Angelo Castagnetti had been very badly injured indeed –
but the usual amount of intimidation ensued and, as has been
recounted, on 5 May 1930, Mullins and Co walked free from
the Old Bailey.

So that was the position; Solomon, a violent, murderous,
out-of-control thug transforming himself into a victim, with the
half-promise of becoming an informant.

The best person to deal with this matter was the Superintendent
William Brown mentioned in the letter, and a very different picture
soon emerged. Early in February 1930, an anonymous telephone
call revealed that police could anticipate trouble at several dog-
racing tracks in London – including Clapton – between two
racetrack gangs, one led by Alf Solomon, the other by Dodger
Mullins, and the divisional detective inspectors of the Metropolitan
Police divisions concerned were accordingly alerted.

On the evening of 7 February, Alf Solomon, Jack Burman and
others had gone to the dog track at Clapton, where they tried to
extort money from bookmakers. Solomon was seen in the club
room, was requested to leave by the club manager, Mr Luper,
and eventually ejected. On the evening of 18 February – the day
after Solomon's letter was sent – Mr Luper and his wife visited
Wembley Stadium dog-racing track, whereupon the gang attacked
him and Burman hit him with an iron bar; this led to Burman
being sentenced to two months' imprisonment and being bound
over to keep the peace for six months in the sum of £100.

There is no doubt that Luper was Brown's (as well as other
officers') informant, and being both a licensed victualler and
manager of the dog track, he was well placed to act as such.

So it became clear that Solomon wanted two main adversaries
out of the way, diverting the attention of the police from him
(on the thinly-veiled promise of supplying information) and making
them concentrate on keeping Dodger Mullins and the Bethnal
Green Boys under observation, while making damaging allegations
against Brown. There was certainly no love lost between Solomon
and Brown, since Brown had been the officer in the case when
Solomon stood trial for murder, and Solomon had displayed

considerable antipathy towards him. As Brown mentioned in his report, 'It was generally considered at the time that he was exceedingly fortunate not to have been convicted of the capital charge.' Brown was in no doubt that the letter was written out of spite, adding in his report that several days before the letter was sent, Solomon had boasted to his contemporaries that he intended to send it.

In forwarding his report to the AC(C), Brown attached a list of Solomon's court appearances, adding, 'He is a dangerous rascal and his enemies are far more in need of protection than he is', and there the matter ended.

★   ★   ★

Although Darby Sabini appeared to have retired to Brighton and Hove, the Sabini flag was still being waved.

In January 1935, five or six men – one was Harry Sabini and another was James Sabatini – entered the Majestic Social Club, Wardour Street, looking for two men, one of whom was referred to as 'Baby'. This was quite possibly Antonio Mancini. However, if it was him, there must have been a falling-out, because eleven years previously, Mancini had been one of those who had taken the blame for a racetrack bashing, in order to let Harry Sabini off the hook. Then again, alliances between racetrack gangsters could be and often were broken.

Sabatini told the proprietor, Jack Aaron Isow, the details of men they were looking for, whom they 'wanted to belt', and Harry added, 'It's my intention that you get rid of these two, and unless you do, if it costs £200, we'll come and do a down on you.'

Isow knew this was no idle threat, because the same gang had previously smashed up a club with which he had been associated; in fact, he had been obliged to close it because the members were frightened away. On 29 April 1935, just before midnight, a group of men which included Sabatini, Thomas Mack, Sidney Buonocore and Michael Tiano aggressively barged into the club and, because they were not members, Isow told them to leave.

Buonocore shouted, 'You fucking well ruined Harryboy (Harry Sabini) and we're going to ruin you!'

'We warned you a few months ago', said Mack. 'As you haven't carried out our warning, we've come to enforce it', and then added, rather illogically, 'You'd better go and bring the police.'

Isow looked for the key in order to lock the men in the premises but found it missing. However, he telephoned the police and when he returned he discovered that seven windows, some crockery, a lampshade and a table in the card room had been smashed.

This evidence – plus quite a bit more – was given by the witnesses at Bow Street Police Court on 1 May before Sir Rollo Graham-Campbell. The case was remanded; unfortunately, all of the accused were admitted to bail.

When the case resumed on 20 May, the situation became farcical. During the initial, previous appearance, the doorman, David Godfrey, said that when the men had entered the club, he was pushed against a table. He had told the court, 'The members were rushing about and didn't know what to do. The noise was terrible. These men were like a lot of animals. I have never seen human beings behave like that. The members flew for their lives; when I got an opportunity, I flew myself.'

Nineteen days later, Godfrey retracted his evidence and declared that the accused men were 'absolutely innocent'. Asked who had broken the windows, Godfrey replied, 'Mr Isow might have broken them himself; I don't know.' He added that Isow had promised him a better job and a new suit if he would give evidence against the defendants, but he had gone to the defence solicitors and made a statement to them because 'I wanted to get it off my conscience.'

Not unnaturally, he was treated as a hostile witness, but when his statement to the police was read out in court, he said that he had been bullied into making it. 'No one ran out of the club panic-stricken', he said. 'One or two walked out. There was no fighting.'

Asked, 'Did you run out panic-stricken?' Godfrey artlessly relied, 'Me? No. I took a walk.'

The craven (and highly mendacious) Mr Godfrey was not alone. John Rosenberg, an assistant at the club who originally said that Mack had struck him and Tiano and Sabatini had tried to, now said that he didn't know who had hit him. Asked to explain the bruises that a doctor had found on his arms, he lamely replied, 'Perhaps I might have knocked myself.'

Morris Copple, a tailor, also changed his evidence and he, too, was treated as a hostile witness. He now said a cup was thrown through the window of the card room, other windows were broken and two men jumped on to the table where he was playing cards. Someone punched him, but he could not say who, since he was under the table at the time. In cross-examination, Copple insisted he was not terrified of anyone, but this was contradicted by Detective Sergeant Wakeling, who told the court that Copple had told him he was afraid of having his throat cut.

Antonio Amadio said that some of the statements which he had sworn in support of an application for an arrest warrant were inaccurate, and while the prosecution had wanted to call another witness, they had been unsuccessful in their attempt to find and serve a subpoena on him to secure his attendance.

The defence stated that the whole case had been manufactured by Isow, that there was not a scrap of evidence against the four men and that if the case should go to trial, eight witnesses would be called to say the defendants had left the club prior to the trouble starting.

It would have been laughable but for the seriousness of the matter.

In the event, each defendant was bound over in the sum of £200 with a surety in the same amount, to come up for judgement if called upon to do so within twelve months, to pay costs of £38 (this included the damage to the amount of £13) and not to visit the club premises ever again. So there.

It appeared quite clear that when witnesses could be bribed and/or intimidated, those racetrack gangs, on or off the track, could do pretty well as they pleased. Alf White and his sons certainly thought so.

CHAPTER 15

A Cowardly Attack

Adance was held in the Wharncliffe Rooms at the Great Central Hotel, London on 17 April 1935 to raise funds for the Paddington General Hospital. Among the 900 people at the dance were John McCarthy Differary, the manager of the Yorkshire Stingo public house in the Marylebone Road, and his wife, Queenie; so were Alf White, his son, also named Alf, and a second son, William.

Differary took a £1 note from his wallet – it contained £12 – to pay for a round of drinks, when suddenly he was struck a terrific blow in the left eye by William White, and as he staggered from the assault, White's father, brother and others joined in the attack. Alf Sr. picked up a glass-topped table and smashed it over Differary's head, he was then punched and when he recovered consciousness he discovered that his wallet was missing. So was his left eye.

When William White was arrested he told Detective Sergeant Cory, 'A man took a liberty with my girl, struck at me and I hit him back.'

Alf Sr. and Alf Jr. denied any knowledge of the affair. Differary denied interfering with anyone and said that the Whites were complete strangers to him.

At the Old Bailey, Colin Symons, Master of Ceremonies at the dance, gave evidence:

> Just after midnight, I saw a man go up to another and give him a terrific punch. The man struck fell to the ground. I started to remonstrate with his assailant. Things simmered down for a time and then there was more trouble of which some women, in my opinion, were the cause. The fellow who had struck the blow pushed a woman in red, and before you could say 'Jack Robinson' forty or fifty people started fighting and women started screaming and crying.
>
> It was not one of the accused who struck the first blow. I should think he had been a boxer; he knew how to punch.

So that was the beginning of a clever defence – Differary had certainly been attacked but not by any of the accused – and there was more to come.

Next, a certain Gertrude Evans was called for the defence; Differary stated that he had never seen her before in his life. This was confirmed by Miss Evans, who stated she had never seen Differary before. Miss Evans described herself as William White's fiancée and said it was somebody else who had insulted her. That was backed up by William White as well: he had never seen Differary before – it was another man whom he had punched. And that was the opinion of a dozen witnesses who had originally picked out the genus White on identification parades but subsequently changed their minds.

With only Mr and Mrs Differary out of 900 people stating that it was William White who had delivered the attack, it was rather amazing that the three members of the White family were convicted of anything. The charge of inflicting grievous body harm was rejected by the jury, but the Whites were convicted of the lesser offence of causing actual bodily harm. By the way, actual bodily harm means bruising or perhaps a little blood-letting; obviously the jury believed that this included the loss of an eye.

The jury were not made aware of the written threats made against the prosecuting barrister, Mr Horace Fenton, that should any of the family be found guilty, he would get 'the hiding of his life'. He was afforded police protection, but perhaps the presence of forty members of the scowling Sabini gang in and around the court may have swayed the jury to conclude that with company like that the White family were not quite whiter-than-white.

Alfred White Jr. had no previous convictions, William White, just one for taking and driving away a car for which he had been fined £1, whereas Alf Sr. possessed five previous convictions. In 1913 he had been sentenced to three months' hard labour for stealing a purse, and five years later, he was bound over for assault. In 1922 he was fined for assaulting the police; the following year, he got eighteen months' hard labour for conspiracy to incite a breach of the Prison Act; and in 1927 he received three months' hard labour for unlawfully wounding a police officer. Even disregarding all the offences that he'd got away with, this was a pretty damning indictment of violent law-breaking, but the Recorder of London, Sir Holman Gregory, stated that he would take no notice of those previous convictions. A former Liberal Member of Parliament, 71-year-old Sir Holman had succeeded Sir Ernest Wild as Recorder the previous year.

Detective Inspector Griffey told the court that the records showed Alf Sr. 'as a member of a gang of racecourse ruffians who begged from and subsequently blackmailed bookmakers', only to be coldly told by the Recorder, 'That does not affect me.'

And when Inspector Griffey added that he had interviewed 12–15 bookmakers and publicans who attended the dance, from whom he had been informed that he would obtain useful evidence, and told the Recorder, 'In each case they declined to give information and I felt sure that they were in physical fear of Alfred White Sr.', it made not one jot of difference.

It's rather surprising that with that show of irrelevance, on 3 July 1935, the Recorder sentenced the White family to twelve months' imprisonment each.

The other gang members who took part in that disgraceful, cowardly attack possibly included Thomas Mack, James Sabatini, Michael Tiano and Sidney Buonocore who, twelve days after the assault and perhaps on a high, turned their attention to the Majestic Social Club – but who can say?

CHAPTER 16

Dirty Work at Croydon

Time to clear up the misconceptions of several writers who have claimed that there was a robbery at Croydon Aerodrome on 6 March 1936. Bad phraseology and bad research. First, the incident in which three boxes containing three gold bars, 5,000 US gold coins and 5,800 sovereigns, with a total value of £21,000 – probably £1,200,000 in today's values – were stolen was not a robbery at all; robbery means that violence (or the threat of it) is involved, and it wasn't. The boxes were stolen, unseen, from a warehouse on which duplicate keys were used. And second, the theft occurred one year earlier, on 6 March 1935.

At face value you might think there would seem to be little correlation between an audacious theft and racetrack gang warfare – and you might be right. But let's take a look at what happened.

At one o'clock in the morning of 6 March, taxi driver George Manson was woken by repeated knocking on his front door. He answered it, to discover that a man whom he knew only as 'Little Harry' wanted him to pick him and three other men up at King's Cross railway station in three hours' time. He duly did so, and drove them to Croydon Aerodrome, where the boxes, the property of Imperial Airways, were loaded into the cab and taken to an address in Harringay. The theft was discovered at 7.00 am, but unfortunately for those involved, at 5.25 that morning, the taxi, followed by a small green car, had been spotted near the aerodrome by Alfred George King, who was cycling to work; he thought this rather strange and jotted down the taxi's registration number. What was more, a widow, Mrs Laura Scholz, who rented the ground floor rooms of her house at 3 Pemberton Road, Harringay to a Mr and Mrs Cecil Swanland, looked out of her window at 6.30 am to see her lodger with another man at the gate. He took something from a car and rushed inside the house, then she heard banging, as though something was being forced, and later heard a downstairs window being opened out of which smoke billowed, possibly because the chimney had caught fire.

Twelve hours later, she saw Swanland carrying an attaché case which looked very heavy and which he placed in a waiting car.

When Swanland received a visit from Chief Inspector Alec Duncan (soon to become head of the Flying Squad) the following afternoon, he laughed and denied any suggestion that he was involved in the theft, saying, 'If you think there's any gold here, you're quite at liberty to search.'

'That', replied Duncan grimly, 'is just what we intend to do.'

Duncan didn't find any gold; what he did find was a copy of the *Daily Express* open at the page which reported the theft, with pencil markings at the pertinent parts, an Imperial Airways timetable and a long wire key in Swanland's jacket which fitted the lock of the inner door of the Croydon strong room. There were pieces of paper on which were written the number of ounces to the kilo and some prices per kilogram for the freightage of gold as charged by Imperial Airways; also, although Swanland had no children, there was a large lump of plasticine. There were nineteen nail heads, a metal band, two more nails and a piece of a seal, five more burnt seals, twelve burnt nails, a quantity of charred wood and a piece of string. All these items were identified as having been used in the packaging of the stolen gold, and Swanland was well and truly nicked.

Detective Inspector Alf Dance of the Flying Squad saw Silvio 'Shonk' Mazzarda in a Soho café, beckoned him outside and arrested him; and 74-year-old John O'Brien was also brought in.

The three men were picked out on identification parades by the taxi driver, Manson, who very definitely identified 'Shonk', saying he had known him for over twenty years; and given the size of Mazzarda's proboscis, he would have been difficult to miss. But of the gold – and of 'Little Harry' – there was no sign.

Matters started to crumble almost immediately. Following Mrs Scholz's initial appearance at Croydon Police Court, she was approached in the street by an unknown person and told to 'shut her mouth' and not give any further evidence. However, Mrs Scholz was made of sterner stuff, and she did. George Manson was not, and he didn't. He entirely repudiated his identifications and statements, saying that he was unsure if he had driven to Pemberton Road, could not recall his statement being read to him (the contents of which he disputed) and had only identified 'Shonk' (whom he had never seen before) because the police had shown him the suspect's photograph.

Unsurprisingly, the prosecution asked permission from the Chairman of the Bench to treat Manson as a hostile witness, to which Mr J. Davis, representing Mazzarda and O'Brien, stated,

'If he is going to treat him as a hostile witness, let him do so. He has either got to adopt him or throw him over', adding, rather dismissively, 'I don't mind which he does.'

Nevertheless, the three men were committed to stand their trial at Croydon Quarter Sessions, but thanks to Manson's testimony, there was so much doubt as to Mazzarda's and O'Brien's culpability that they were acquitted. The evidence was somewhat stronger against Swanland, and the jury retired for only seventeen minutes before finding him guilty. He had seven previous convictions, which included having served three, four, five and six years' penal servitude, and on 29 April 1935 he received another helping – seven years.

Prior to the trial, Swanland, twenty-six years older than his 21-year-old wife, had purchased gold cufflinks, clothing worth £59 and a £50 brooch for her. Following his arrest, Mrs Scholz lost no time in evicting Mrs Margaret Swanland who, with a very healthy bank account, went to live with her mother at Dean Street, Soho; it was believed that the gold had been transported there. Thoughtfully, she also made an application at Wandsworth Prison to lodge £30 for her husband.

A couple of years after his acquittal, Mazzarda stated to the police that they had obtained copies of the strong room keys allegedly from Burtwell Peters, the chief unloader at the aerodrome, for which he was said to have been handsomely recompensed. There was no problem with that disclosure; in those days, once someone had been acquitted they could not be tried again.

The police believed that at least five men were directly involved in the theft. O'Brien was an old sparring partner of the repellent Arthur Harding, and Mazzarda was an associate of Darby Sabini.

So who was 'Little Harry'? It could well have been Harry Sabini, because it was believed that he was the brains behind the plot – he and Bert Marsh, aka Pasqualino Papa.

It's time to take another look at him.

CHAPTER 17

Death between Friends

It was a strange killing; the two men had been friends since boyhood. They played together, attended St Peter's School and went to Mass at St Peter's Church. When they grew older and their careers diverged, they were still friends; Pasqualino Papa boxed as a professional under the ring name of Bert Marsh, and Massimino Francesco Antonio Monte-Colombo cheered him on. Not that he wanted to join his chum in the ring; Massimino had dashing good looks which he didn't want spoilt, since they were guaranteed to bring the maids of Saffron Hill rushing down the cobbles towards him, arms outstretched and skirts flying. He had small, uncredited bit-parts in films, including *Educated Evans*, a film about horseracing and crooks; the popular actor Gordon Harker attended his trial at the Old Bailey.

Massimino and his brothers worked as asphalters – they were skilled at their trade – but after Marsh started work at Wandsworth Park Royal dog-racing track he offered Massimino and his brother Camillo jobs there, which they accepted. Massimino later asked Marsh if he could find a position at the track for another of his brothers, and this Marsh promised to do.

In the summer of 1936 the two men were still friends, but then came a falling-out. It appeared that there was jealousy regarding Marsh's position at the track; Massimino wanted Marsh's job; he felt that Marsh was not paying him enough; and when the third brother, Nestor, failed to secure employment there, that was the catalyst for the situation to erupt into violence. At least, that was Marsh's interpretation of the situation.

On the evening of 1 September 1935 at 7.50 pm, Myer Rosenberg saw Marsh walking towards the pitch of a man named Hart. 'Just as he got to Hart's pitch . . .', he said, 'Camillo came behind him and punched Marsh on the jaw. Marsh went down on the floor. On rising, Massimino attacked him over the head with a cosh. He caught him on the head and Marsh fell down again. Then he got up, again.' Rosenberg added that Camillo then picked up a stool and aimed it at Marsh's head. 'Marsh put out his hand to avoid it, but doing that, Camillo kicked him.'

Rosenberg's account was more or less backed up by Albert Cutler, a bookmaker's clerk. He was in the half-crown ring that evening and, referring to Camillo as 'Miller', he said he saw Marsh and, 'I was going towards him when I saw Miller strike him in the back. Marsh half turned and Miller struck him again and Marsh fell to the ground. Massimino came on the scene and he had a weapon in his right hand.' He was referring to a cosh and he continued, 'He was swinging this weapon by his wrist and hit Marsh while he was on the floor. Then Wilkins came on the scene.'

Cutler was referring to 23-year-old Herbert Wilkins, who joined in the struggle, in which Camillo received severe gashes to his face and body. But it was Massimino who received the deadly wounds: Dr William MacCormac would later tell an inquest that Massimino had a deep slashing wound, eight inches long, running down his neck from the level of the upper part of his ear. He also had three puncture wounds, the first on the right side of his upper body, puncturing the chest and lungs, the second on the side of his left lower chest, injuring a rib, and the third on the inner side of the left arm, penetrating to the bone. All in all, a frenzied attack. He was conveyed as quickly as possible to St James' Hospital, Balham, where a fourth brother, Leonelli, provided blood for a transfusion in a desperate attempt to save him, but it was too late. The detectives who had been waiting at the foot of the bed hoping for a statement left to pursue their enquiries elsewhere. They had heard of problems arising from race-gangs which did not coincide with the accounts given by the pro-Marsh witnesses.

Following the incident, having had a drink, both Marsh and Wilkins left the stadium. Marsh was suffering severe injuries to his head, cheek and abdomen, and Wilkins, suffering from shock, had bruises to his left eye. That night, they consulted a doctor saying they had been attacked. Their account might have had more veracity had Marsh not told the doctor that his name was John Anderson, and Wilkins, that his was Murray.

Two days after the killing, Marsh and Wilkins, accompanied by their solicitor, the pro-Sabini Mr John A. Davis, surrendered themselves at Wandsworth police station.

They were arrested, whereupon Marsh said, 'I am not the guilty person. I nearly got murdered myself.'

Wilkins said, 'Am I being charged with murder? I'm not guilty.'

When they were formally charged with the murder and attempted murder of the Monte-Colombo brothers, Marsh repeated his original denial, while Wilkins replied, 'I'm not guilty. All I did was to go to try to help Marsh.'

Pointing to the cosh, Marsh said to Divisional Detective Inspector John Henry, 'Do me a favour and have the fingerprints taken off that; it's not mine.'

At their first appearance at South-Western Police Court, Wilkins asked for bail on the grounds that he had been badly injured, and DDI John Henry told the court that Marsh 'had certainly been knocked about a bit' but was fit to be detained, and both men were remanded in custody.

It now emerged that neither the two prisoners nor the two Monte-Colombo brothers had been employed by the stadium but by a certain Mr Jim Wicks who, a little later on in his career, would manage the heavyweight boxer, Henry Cooper.

It was not until 9 October that Camillo was well enough to attend the Police Court to give evidence. 'I saw a scuffle between Marsh and my brother', he told the court. 'I rushed towards them and got Marsh by his back because I knew he carried an implement. I saw Wilkins rushing over. I heard him say, "I'm with you, Bert". I felt a sharp blow from Marsh in my chest. They were both facing me and I saw them both with shiny objects in their hands . . . I felt a shock in my back and I went down.' He then burst into tears as he described how he found his brother with his head bending forward, his tongue between his teeth and the two prisoners 'pushing things' at him.

John Eggeman, a confectioner, said that three men appeared to be trying to get to grips with two others and trying to force them back. The two men were defending themselves but also trying to attack, and one of the two men had a stool in his hand.

One week later, both men were committed for trial at the Old Bailey.

There had been a remarkable funeral cortège for Massimino – he was known variously as Massimino the gallant cavalier, Massimino the generous, Massimino the brave – the like of which had seldom been seen in 'Little Italy'. It wound its way from Clerkenwell's Italian Church, bedecked with flowers and wreaths that cost £500, to his grave at Kensal Green, the route thronged with crowds. Camillo was still in hospital and could not attend; his younger brother, Anesio, was so ill with grief and shock in his bedroom at the family's top floor flat in Margaret Street that the doctor refused to allow him to leave his bed.

'He was kind and he was nice', said Louisa Cimini, one of the many mourners. 'They all liked him. That is why all the Italian girls of the Hill gave their coppers, sixpences or shillings – just what they could afford – for his wreath. They all gave because he was so grand.'

The sister of the brothers, Ada Monte-Colombo, said, 'We want to thank them all for their wonderful flowers and their sympathy for their love for Massimino.'

The opulence of the funeral was matched by the abundance of barristers, eleven of them, including three KCs, who filed into the legendary No. 1 courtroom at the Old Bailey. They were accompanied by a procession of bookmakers, their clerks and hard-faced men from Clerkenwell, there presumably to 'keep an eye on things'.

When Norman Birkett KC for Marsh suggested to Camillo that 'without the slightest provocation and without a word of warning' he had struck Marsh such a blow from behind that 'he went down, like a felled ox', this was strongly denied.

Camillo told the jury that his brother called out, 'Get away – they've got razors!' He felt a blow from Marsh's elbow against his chest, so he struck him twice on the jaw with his fist. 'I saw the glint of instruments in their hands', he said, 'and as Wilkins passed me, I felt a blow in my side. My legs collapsed and Marsh took a kick at me and missed. I picked up a stool and swung it at Marsh several times. They left me and I saw them attacking my brother under the stand. When I got there, they disappeared. I had no weapon.'

Birkett produced a leather life preserver with a weight inside, alleged to have been in Massimino's possession, for the judge and jury to examine, and Camillo told the court, 'In the racing world and the underworld, they call it a cosh. If my brother had had that in his hand, he would have been alive today. He could have kept them at bay.'

When Birkett suggested that Marsh had never used any implement, Camillo's dark eyes blazed as he retorted, 'Who caused my brother's stabs, then – the invisible man? All sorts of people are afraid to come up. You can't get proper witnesses here, because of the gang.'

With a barrister's typical pomposity, Birkett told him to 'behave himself', but Camillo scored another goal when he told John Flowers KC for Wilkins, 'Witnesses are being employed by one man who has been blackmailing everybody on behalf of the defence.' He went on to say, 'In this racing game, if you have been hurt and rush to the police, there is a black mark against you and you're not wanted. I thought if my brother lived, I would not inform the police; my brother died and I then made a statement to the police.'

Both prisoners gave evidence. Marsh said he suddenly received three or four blows to the jaw from behind. 'I went to the floor and

as I went to rise, I saw Massimino with a cosh in his hand', he said.
'He struck me on the head and as I was falling, I was kicked by
Camillo in the stomach two or three times.'

His counsel, Birkett, asked, 'Had you made any attack on
Massimino before you received these blows?'

'No. I never laid a finger on him.'

'Had you made any attack on Camillo?'

'No.'

'Had you said any words, provocative or angry, to either of
them?'

'No.'

A bookmaker's stool was produced which Marsh said he had
seen in Camillo's hand and he was asked, 'After you were struck
by the stool by Camillo, what happened next?'

Marsh replied, 'I don't remember any more.'

In re-examination, Mr L. A. Byrne for the Crown asked, 'You
can throw no light on how Massimino came to receive his fatal
injuries?' and unsurprisingly, Marsh replied, 'No.'

To hammer the point home, Birkett asked, 'Had you have any
part or not in causing these wounds on Massimino or Camillo?'
and Marsh replied, 'None whatsoever.'

Next it was Wilkins' turn; he told the court that he had been
employed at the stadium for about three years and on the evening
of 1 September he had seen Camillo approach Marsh from
behind and punch him on the jaw. Marsh fell to the floor, then
Massimino had begun to hit him on the head with the cosh; as
he tried to get up, Camillo kicked him in the face and the groin.
Camillo picked up a stool and started hitting Marsh with that.
'I thought they were going to kill him and I ran towards them',
said Wilkins. 'At that time, I had no weapon at all.'

But not for long. 'I put up my arm to protect myself; as I did so,
I saw a stiletto on the ground. This was while they were attacking
me', said Wilkins. 'I picked it up and struck out with it. I didn't
mean to injure anybody.'

'The attackers of Marsh evidently preferred to use a stool and
a life preserver, rather than a stiletto?' asked Byrne and Wilkins
replied, 'That would be so.'

'Do you recall whether you stabbed him with this stiletto or that
it went into this man's chest?' asked Byrne and Wilkins replied,
'I could not say.'

It appeared that, bearing in mind he was prosecuting a capital
offence, Byrne's cross-examination was pretty feeble, although
when he addressed the jury he did say that Wilkins' evidence might
have surprised them, because he had said the stiletto was actually

in his hand. Could they accept his evidence? Bearing in mind that one of the stab wounds in Massimino's chest was an inch-and-a-half deep, did they think that the stiletto could have been plunged into his chest without Wilkins being aware of it?

In his closing speech to the jury Birkett submitted that to convict Marsh on the evidence would be a grave miscarriage of justice: 'I beseech you not to pay any attention to anything said by the witness Camillo. These two men would not be on trial for their lives if Camillo had not started the trouble.'

Birkett had submitted that there was no case to answer on either charge of murder or manslaughter, saying that no evidence had been presented by the prosecution as to who had struck the fatal blow and that there was no evidence of common design. John Flowers KC for Wilkins agreed, adding that when the affray started, his client was not present.

In response to these submissions, the judge thought it undesirable at that stage of the trial that he should say any more other than that there was evidence fit to be considered by the jury.

However, when the case had been committed for trial, the magistrate at South-Western Police Court, Mr Claud Mullins, had said:

> I have taken a great deal of trouble in reading the evidence of Camillo Monte-Colombo and I feel I should be usurping the authority I have if I said that this evidence did not amount to evidence of murder. I do not propose to give in detail the reasons for my decision as they might embarrass the judge and jury.

The judge certainly adopted the Magistrate's words because in his summing up he told the jury:

> You might not think it right, on the evidence, to return a verdict of murder. It seems to me the only case against the prisoners which you have to consider is the alternative charge of manslaughter.

The jury, which included three women, were out for twenty minutes, before returning to find both men not guilty of murder but guilty of manslaughter. However, Marsh still had a trump card up his sleeve.

★ ★ ★

On 28 October, while Marsh and Wilkins were on remand at Brixton prison, they were among some thirty prisoners in the exercise yard. Suddenly, a powerfully built man leapt at Prison Officer Payne, knocked him to the ground and seized him by the neck. Marsh and Wilkins went to the rescue; Marsh seized the prisoner by the shoulders, Wilkins by the legs, and they tried to drag him away from the warder. Although the prisoner kicked out, sending Wilkins 'spinning across the yard', he was overpowered by Marsh and, having appeared to have had a brainstorm, was inserted into a straitjacket.

Well, that was helpful for Prison Officer Payne, wasn't it? Pretty helpful for the two prisoners as well, not to mention the alleged lunatic in the straitjacket who must have handsomely benefited financially from this staged assault. These were the sort of amateur dramatics which, over the years, have been staged time and time again by cunning criminals with a few bob to chuck about to do themselves a bit of good. The same sort of criminals who, if they saw a copper getting a kicking in the street would be only too glad to join in with the perpetrators.

In court, DDI Henry gave details of the prisoners' previous convictions but stressed that while Marsh was 'quick-tempered, excitable and easily provoked, there had been no complaints against him and he had caused no trouble since he had become associated with the Wandsworth Park Royal and Catford tracks.'

Passing sentence, Mr Justice McNaughton told the prisoners:

> The jury after a most patient hearing, and after all the forensic skill on your behalf, have found you guilty of the manslaughter of Massimino Monte-Colombo.
>
> They have rejected the evidence which you gave in the witness box; they have rejected it as untrue. I agree with their verdict. I have no doubt this man met his death because on that night, each of you used knives. It is a very grave offence – the use of a lethal weapon resulting in the loss of a human life. I can take into consideration, Marsh, that for some years you have shown amendment of your ways, and I can take into consideration for you, Wilkins, that you are a young man, and for both of you I intend to take well into consideration that fact that when you were in prison on remand, you came forward to save a warder from what might have been his death. That was a service for which you will gain reduction of the sentence I am about to pass. It is impossible for me to overlook the facts, however.

Marsh was sentenced to twelve months' imprisonment, Wilkins to nine months, and racecourse frequenters in the courtroom began to tic-tac their congratulations to the smiling prisoners in the dock.

Leaving court, Camillo declared that he was finished forever with the racing game. 'No more dog tracks for me', he said. 'I'm going back to work as an asphalter. I was never afraid of anyone, but after you've been cut up once, it isn't nice to think of being cut up again. I could never use a knife, I haven't the blood to do it.'

He added that he would seek police protection. So did Marsh, feeling that saving the prison warder 'from certain death' had put him beyond the pale. He had been given permission to exercise alone at Wandsworth Prison and intended to ask the visiting magistrates for 'special protection'.

It was said that the defence, which consisted of eight barristers for the two men, cost £2,000, and that 'pretty young Mrs Marsh with a daughter of eight' had pawned her jewels and withdrawn her life savings to pay for it. There is a school of thought which suggests that Bert Marsh's cut from the theft at Croydon Aerodrome paid for the defence, but there was a far stronger inference that contributions had come fairly willingly from the Italian Mob and, far less willingly, from the honest shopkeepers in and around Clerkenwell.

CHAPTER 18

The Battle of Lewes Racetrack

Apart from terms of imprisonment (albeit short ones) for two deserving thugs, something good arose from that court case, because almost four months previously, Wilkins' brother Harry (who had served three years' Borstal Training for receiving stolen goods) had been sent down for two years' hard labour; so hopefully the brothers were reunited in the penal system.

The reason for Harry's incarceration (and that of fifteen others) was what became known as 'The Battle of Lewes Racetrack', and this is what happened.

Various explanations have been given of what prompted that cowardly attack at the racetrack on 8 June 1936, but there had been confrontations at various times since 1934 between the King's Cross Boys, the Hoxton Mob and members of the Yiddisher Gang, first at Walthamstow, then at Liverpool Street Station. The main protagonists were, on behalf of the Hoxton Mob, Dick Hutton – noticeable by a livid scar down one side of his face and described as 'a really tough guy' – and on the opposing faction by a character known as 'Conky'. It appears that Dodger Mullins of the Bethnal Green Boys and fresh out of prison was also involved, but the fact was, he and others from the Hoxton contingent got the worst of the confrontation and, forming a coalition with the Elephant Boys, decided upon a suitable revenge against 'Conky' who, they knew, was great friends with Alf Solomon. There was an added inducement: one of the Hoxton Mob was the brother of Barnett Blitz, who had been killed by Solomon twelve years previously. Albert Blitz, aged twenty-four, who had convictions for larceny, receiving and possessing housebreaking implements by night, thus had a very strong incentive to be part of that motley crew.

Therefore the scene was set for an all-out confrontation at Lewes Racecourse on Monday, 8 June, when it was known that Alf Solomon would be in attendance, as well as – hopefully – 'Conky' plus other members of the Yiddisher Gang. In addition, if any members of the Italian Mob were present, that would be a bonus.

But before dealing with the events that would take place forty-five minutes prior to the first race being called, it's also time to deal with a commonly held misconception regarding the policing of the racetrack.

'It's going to be off at Lewes on Monday' was the anonymous telephone call allegedly received by the Flying Squad and, as a result, Brighton Borough Police were informed and, according to the memoirs of Ted Greeno and Fred Sharpe, the Flying Squad turned up in force at the racetrack. Additionally, the Flying Squad driver, PC George 'Jack' Frost, mentioned in his memoirs being one of the drivers of two Flying Squad cars containing a total of ten officers, including Greeno, Sharpe and Dan Gooch, and taking them to the racecourse. Regarding the sickening nature of the attack that followed, Frost informed his readers, 'I will not attempt to give details.' It was probably just as well. Had the Squad been there, they could have intercepted the two carloads of gangsters who escaped. They could also have assisted in the arrests of the attackers and given evidence in court; but if indeed they were there, they must just have stood back and watched events, because they took no part in the arrests at all.

Frost's account is open to serious criticism. Fred Sharpe was not then a member of the Flying Squad, being engaged on other duties in C1 Department at the Yard and with another six months to go before he took over as head of the Flying Squad. Frost also mentioned Dan Gooch being present, but he had resigned as head of the Flying Squad on 22 December 1935. It could, I suppose, be said that he was taken along for a day out, had it not been for the fact that Gooch was killed in a car accident on the Guildford bypass over four months earlier, on 25 April 1936.

It's such a pity that in order to embellish their memoirs – which in fairness did not need bolstering at all – some officers felt the need to resort to publishing utter bollocks such as that.

It has been suggested that the police were tipped off by the Sabini family that there was going to be trouble at the racetrack, so that the police would be in attendance to deal with any disturbance when the Hoxton Mob arrived armed to the teeth; then the Sabinis could quietly disappear and arrests could be carried out. It wasn't true. Nobody in the world of law and order had any idea of the affray that was going to take place.

So – no. In this particular instance, we can forget about the Flying Squad – worthy opponents of the racetrack gangs though they most definitely were – and concentrate on the real heroes of the day, who were two detectives, both members of the Brighton Borough Police Force.

*   *   *

Stanley George Janes had joined the Force in 1925 and after making a series of good arrests was appointed to the CID. Heavily built and standing at 5 ft 11 inches, on 8 June 1936 he was partnered by Detective Sergeant Walter Collyer, who was as tough as his subordinate and who referred to Janes as 'a stout companion in any kind of trouble'.

It was clear that neither officer – nor any other police officer – was expecting anything particularly untoward to happen on that oppressively hot June day; there was a smattering of uniformed police officers drawn from over the local county, but not in excessive numbers. That was the norm at a race meeting where trouble was not expected; in fact, the officers' biggest concern was that the heat would be very tiring. Arriving at the racecourse at 12.45 pm, they walked towards the bookmakers' stands; having years of experience, they wanted to identify any bookmaker who they thought was crooked.

Standing close to the 3s 0d ring, they suddenly saw a group of men, some forty in number, walking from the car parks in the general direction of the bookmakers' stands.

'Here comes a fine gang of cutthroats', commented Collyer, to which Janes replied, 'Yes. They look good for anything up to murder.'

Collyer later recounted:

> I decided that it was absolutely necessary to follow them . . . we walked along only a pace behind the rear members of the gang. How they didn't see us there, I do not know, except that it became obvious that they were searching for someone in particular and became blind to anything or anyone else.

Dick Hutton was in the lead of the gang and he remarked, 'It's no good here, boys – too many "Top Hats" around.'

This was a reference to uniformed officers – but not to Janes or Collyer, since the gang was unaware of their presence. The gang retraced their steps and then stopped, as they spotted their prey. Neither 'Conky' nor members of the Italian Mob were present, but Alf Solomon and his clerk, Mark Frater, were.

The leader of the gang was James Spinks, aged twenty-nine; weighing in at twenty stone, he had both a formidable presence and a past. As well as having convictions for a miscellany of offences, including two cases of inflicting grievous bodily harm and several for assaulting the police, he had, according to Hoxton folklore, killed his girlfriend in a drunken rage by taking a heavy mirror off the wall and smashing her over the head with it. Splattered with her blood, Spinks ran out into the street and attempted to board a bus, but the conductor, seeing this disturbing looking thug covered in blood, refused to let him board. And yet the conductor and several of the passengers who witnessed this spectacle were unable to identify him thereafter. Indeed, several of Spinks' friends came forward to say that at the material time he was in their company, miles away. With the possible exception of members of her family, the memory of Spinks' unfortunate girlfriend faded away. Undoubtedly there were some who thought she deserved her fate. It left Jimmy Spinks, bare-knuckle boxer who of course never, *ever*, terrorized the shopkeepers in the Hoxton area (where women walked the streets in perfect safety), to become even more of a hero. Now his reputation would be further enhanced.

'Here they are, boys – get your tools ready!' he shouted and drew out a hatchet; the rest of the gang also produced a variety of murderous implements.

Solomon received several heavy blows to the head but managed to escape; Frater was not so lucky. While Blitz pinioned his arms, Spinks hit Frater on the head with the hatchet, shouting to the others, 'Let him have it!' Frater was wearing a bowler hat and the force of the blow smashed it in, as well as causing an inch-and-a-half-long cut to the left side of his head. Other gang members crowded round, kicking Frater.

'Here they are, boys – blow!' shouted a gang member as uni-formed officers arrived, one of whom was Inspector Harry Stripp, a Littlehampton officer, who saw Frater lying on the ground bleeding heavily from his wound; he also saw a piece of rubber, an improvised baton and a large hammer. They had been discarded by the fleeing gang, as had a truncheon wielded by 36-year-old Charles Spring, who had a record just as bad as Spinks' – wounding with intent and assault – as well as having served a term of imprisonment and three years' Borstal Training.

Frater was taken to Lewes Victoria Hospital, where he was detained; Solomon's less serious injuries were treated initially by the St John's Ambulance Brigade at the course, then later at the hospital.

Meanwhile, Collyer chased after Spinks and caught him after he had discarded the hatchet yards away from the attack, noticing as he did so that Dick Hutton, as well as a number of others, was fleeing for the car park – he was never arrested. Collyer then arrested Joseph John Kilby, a 26-year-old labourer who had served a term of imprisonment for assaulting the police. Handing his prisoners over to uniformed officers, Collyer saw a Standard sports saloon car; in the driver's seat was Harry Bond, a 25-year-old florist whose past revealed convictions for shopbreaking. Next to him was 30-year-old George Gardiner, and in the back was Michael Illingworth who, like the front seat passenger, had no previous convictions. Not so his other back seat companions, the brothers Bennis: 33-year-old Stephen Patrick had served Borstal Training for wounding, plus being a suspected person, and after being released in 1931 from serving six months' imprisonment had gone into Dorchester and bought a packet of tobacco, which he helpfully threw over a prison wall to his chums inside, receiving one month's imprisonment for his trouble. His younger brother, Timothy, had also had a chequered career, with convictions for larceny, being a suspected person and having housebreaking implements.

Collyer was joined by Inspector Shipp who, like the detective, was able to say that all five men had been involved in the affray. 'I've only just got here and I've taken the wrong turning', protested Bond, but Shipp told them, 'You're members of that gang, and I shall hold you here.'

'Not us, we've only just got here', came a shout from one of the back seat passengers, but their protestations appeared rather flawed when an iron bar and a knuckleduster were found underneath their seat.

Standing on the car's running-board, Collyer told Bond to start it up and drive to the station's lock-up, but Bond took the opportunity to set off in the opposite direction on the road back to Lewes, until Collyer and Shipp both shouted 'Stop!' and Collyer wrenched the steering wheel round.

'All right, Guv'nor', said a penitent Bond, 'I'm sorry.'

Spring was spotted crouching behind a parked car; he was arrested by the inspector. Tommy Mack (whose exploits have already been recounted in these pages) was being chased by Detective Constable Janes. Mack, a small man, tried to facilitate his escape by ducking under a roped-off fence. Janes took the more direct route and leapt over the barrier, landing on top of Mack and squashing him. Told why he was being arrested, Mack's reply was, 'Not me, Guv'nor' and he tried once more, unsuccessfully, to get away.

Police Constable James Lynch, a Chichester-based officer, had seen the attack on Frater; he chased and arrested Blitz. He would later deny that on the way to the lock-up, Blitz asked him why he was being arrested; and he would similarly refute the suggestion that he answered, 'You'll see.'

Police Constable William Groves from Durrington saw two cars come out of the car park and the men in one of the cars jump out and run. He chased after them and saw George Churchill, a 29-year-old bookmaker's clerk, disappear into some bushes, where he found him lying on the ground. 'It's all right, matey, I'm just resting', explained Churchill, who also liked to be known as George Jones and had served imprisonment for larceny.

'Come along and rest with me', suggested PC Groves. This exchange later caused a great deal of amusement in court.

At the lock-up, a piece of steel tubing was found under the seat where Mack and Leslie Edward Hain, a 26-year-old labourer, had been sitting; both denied any knowledge of it.

That tubing was one of the twenty-one offensive weapons collected by police that day, including a splintered billiard cue, a short iron bar with a two-inch nail driven through the top, an axe, several lengths of solid rubber, hammers, truncheons and a piece of wood with a razor blade tied to it.

It's interesting to note also that when the sixteen men were searched, their total wealth amounted to £20 8s 9d. Four of them collectively possessed £19, which left the other twelve with just about 2s 4d to share between them; this effectively nullified any hope that they might have had to claim that they'd come along for the racing.

★   ★   ★

The prisoners, who had been charged with loitering with intent to commit a felony and who made no reply or said, 'Yes' or 'I understand' – with the exception of Spinks, who imprudently said, 'I expected assault' – appeared at Lewes Police Court the following day.

Superintendent Waghorn outlined the facts of the case to the Bench saying, 'This is a very bad case', and adding, 'No doubt they came down from London with the intent to cause injuries to certain persons.'

When the court was told that Blitz was holding Frater whilst he was struck, Blitz took the opportunity to shout, 'It's a lie, Sir, I was nowhere near Frater!'

A spirited attempt was made for bail, which was opposed by the superintendent, and the Chairman of the Bench, Mr J. I. Blencowe, remanded the men in custody.

At a further hearing more evidence was produced, and Dr Herbert Vallance, the Medical Superintendent at the hospital, described Frater's wounds, saying he thought they had been caused by 'a blunt-edged instrument with an irregular edge'. Upon being shown the bloodstained hatchet, Dr Vallance's expert opinion was, 'That is the very thing which could have done it', and when

Mr Cassels for the defence suggested that the wound could have been caused by the victim falling on to a stone or a piece of glass, the doctor replied, decisively, 'It's extremely unlikely.'

But by now, since 16 June the men had all been granted bail in the sum of £50, with a surety in a similar amount. They were committed to stand their trial at the Sussex Assizes, a request to have the case tried at the Old Bailey having being refused. But most worrying of all was that after being discharged from hospital the day after his admission, Frater had disappeared. The police had made the most exhaustive enquiries, but nobody knew his whereabouts.

The trial of the sixteen men, charged with malicious wounding and riotous assembly, commenced on 28 July 1936 before Mr Justice Hilbery. And who should walk into court but Mark Frater, appearing not as the prosecution's star witness but as the principal witness for the defence?

★ ★ ★

Frater agreed that he had been at Lewes Racetrack on 8 June 1936 as a bookmaker's clerk to Alf Solomon when he saw a lot of men coming up the hill towards them; that was the end of his truthful evidence.

'I don't know what did happen', Frater told the court. 'I got it, and that's all I know.'

'Can you help the court by telling us who it was who struck you?' asked John Flowers KC for the prosecution.

'I could not see. I have no idea who struck me', replied Frater.

'Can you identify any of the men you saw? Any of the men who came towards you?'

'No. Not one.'

He was then cross-examined by Mr J. D. Cassels KC. It was said that £1,000 had been raised for the defence, not much when one considers the £2,000 acquired for the defence of Bert Marsh and Wilkins, but then those two were represented by eight barristers. Cassels was one of just three barristers who appeared for all of the defendants. His manner was said to be brusque and he had been labelled 'the second rudest man at the bar'; not on this occasion, though. His tone was positively avuncular; after all, Frater was his star witness.

'Looking at these men here now', he said, indicating the sixteen defendants, four of whom were in the dock, the rest on a bench in front of it, 'have you any dispute that you know anything about, with any of them?'

'I have no dispute.'

'It is said that a man called Spinks struck you on the head with a hatchet', said Cassels. 'Let Spinks stand up.'

The twenty-stone monster lumbered to his feet, and Cassels asked Frater, 'Tell me, do you know that man? Did that man strike you on that date?'

'I have known him for two or three years, now', replied Frater, adding that Spinks had never made any threat against him.

'Can you say that that man did strike you on that date?' asked Cassels, to which Frater replied, 'No. I couldn't say that he did.'

'Let Blitz stand up', said Cassels, and as he did so, Cassels asked Frater, 'Do you know that man?' and Frater replied, 'No.'

'As far as you can say, did you see him upon that date?'

'No.'

'What name do you know Spinks by?' asked Cassels, and Frater replied, '"Spinkey", something like that, a nickname.'

Now Cassels asked his all important question: 'You have seen him, have you, since this charge was made?'

To this Frater replied, 'No', which was not what Cassels wanted to hear because (a) he knew full well that he had and (b) this was an essential ingredient of his carefully cooked-up defence.

'Didn't you meet him on 16 June?' persisted Cassels, to which Frater again replied, 'No.'

At that moment, the judge intervened.

'I have observed you looking towards the men in the dock', he said. 'It would be much better and you would feel more comfortable, perhaps, if you looked towards counsel who is asking the questions or even towards the jury. You know, Mr Cassels is asking if you met Spinks or Spinks met you on 16 June – that is since the hearing of the police court. Is that true? Has Spinks been meeting you?'

Once more, Frater replied, 'No.'

Cassels, seeing the carefully constructed defence slipping away, asked very urgently, 'Let me put it very definitely. You and Spinks *have* met since 16 June and you actually had a drink together?'

'I was thinking you meant the sixteenth of this month', said Frater lamely, adding illogically, 'I was thinking it was June.'

Mr Justice Hilbery, who had been appointed to the High Court only the previous year, was now becoming rather irascible. 'You were just giving evidence, you know, about being at Lewes races on 8 June', he snapped. 'Did you realize you have been giving evidence about 8 June, and that was not this month?'

'Yes', replied Frater. 'I realize that.'

'Then counsel was asking you about 16 June?'

'I thought he meant 16 July.'

'Do you remember having a drink with Spinks after 16 June?' asked Cassels once more, and Frater now realized what was demanded of him, because he replied, 'Yes. I did meet him one night.'

'What did he say to you?'

'I asked him, was he the man who was in the trouble, and he said, "Yes". I told him I was the man who got hit and he said he didn't know it was me.'

'And have you remained friendly with Spinks ever since?'

'I have got no animosity against him.'

'Has any threat of any kind been made against you in regards to this case?'

'No.'

'Had you any fear at all in coming into that witness box to give your evidence?'

'No.'

In re-examination, Frater told John Flowers that after coming out of hospital he had been away without leaving an address.

'Nobody could find you', said Flowers. 'Where were you?'

'I didn't know I was wanted', replied Frater. 'As soon as I knew I was wanted, I came straight back. That was as soon as I saw it in the papers.'

'Can you tell us where you met Spinks?' asked Flowers, to which Frater replied, 'Outside a public house in Harringay', adding, 'You might meet anybody in a place like that.'

Indeed one might, although that pub could hardly be referred to as 'the local' of either of the men, since Spinks was living five miles away in Maidstone Street, Hackney at that time, while Frater was residing in Biddulph Mansions, Maida Vale, seven miles away. It was, of course, pure coincidence that the men had met on the same day that Spinks had been admitted to bail.

The police officers gave their evidence, and very strong, unshakable evidence it was too. Janes was asked by prosecuting counsel if he had noticed anything remarkable about the prisoners when they were charged; he replied that practically all of them had holes in their trouser pockets which acted as repositories for the weapons. It has since been suggested that Wal McDonald distributed £5 notes to dull police memories, but if this was so, it was a wasted exercise. As one of the Elephant Boys who was supposed to have been present but escaped before he could be arrested, why should McDonald have distributed this beneficence? None of his gang appear to have been arrested, since the addresses of all sixteen defendants were north of the River Thames. It was far more likely that this was a gang leader's vainglorious boast about his non-existent power over the police.

There was also evidence from a lorry driver, Douglas Clayton (admittedly brought to court on a subpoena), who saw one man kick another on the side of his head and then hit him with an iron bar wrapped in paper; he had drawn a constable's attention to this. He also identified Spring as being a member of the gang because he struck Clayton as being 'rather out of the ordinary'.

Cassels now opened the defence, which was simple: all of the men in the dock had been wrongfully arrested, having had nothing to do with the affray.

Gilder gave evidence that he was not a member of a race gang, did not know Solomon or Frater and, in fact, had never been to the races before. He did, however, possess convictions for larceny, being a suspected person and assaulting the police and had served terms of imprisonment and Borstal Training.

Blitz stated that he was employed as a tic-tac man by a book-maker and said that he was nowhere near the scene of the attack. Asked in cross-examination by Flowers, 'Do you know Solomon was convicted of the manslaughter of a man called Barnett Blitz in 1924?' Blitz replied, 'No.'

'It is simply a coincidence that one of the men attacked was a man called Barnett Blitz?' asked Flowers, to which Blitz replied, 'Yes.'

Since Barnett Blitz was the brother of the defendant, his answer left untruthfulness far behind and vanished into the realms of absurdity.

Arthur Bonniface, a 28-year-old fruiterer with convictions for conspiracy to rob, assault and inflicting grievous bodily harm, denied taking part in the assault, as did Illingworth, Churchill and Tyler, the last having convictions for larceny, shopbreaking and assaulting the police. Gardiner, who had told the arresting officer he was resting when he was discovered in some bushes, told the court, 'I fell, the officer got hold of me by the arm and I thought for the moment that he was assisting me to my feet.'

'You have been identified as being in the attacking mob', Flowers told Mack in cross-examination, to which Mack replied, 'I'm getting to believe that, myself!'

Amidst laughter in court and when told this was not a laughing matter, Mack replied, 'I'm not laughing at it; I'm nearly crying.'

Spinks – despite his claim that he never intimidated Hoxton shopkeepers, he was said to have taken umbrage with a fish and chip shop proprietor who requested payment and as a mark of his displeasure to have thrown the shop's cat into the fryer – now gave evidence.

He told the court that he had gone with Churchill to Lewes to sell fruit. He denied he had taken any part in the assault and said that there was no truth in the assertion that he was a member of a race gang which was concerned in a dispute with either Solomon or Frater. Frater, he said, he knew well but he had never quarrelled with him.

'It is said you struck Frater across the head with the hatchet', suggested Cassels, and Spinks replied, 'I had never seen it before until it was put up at Lewes Police Court.'

'It is said Blitz held Frater while you struck him', said Cassels, to which Spinks replied, 'I don't know Blitz.'

Spinks told the jury that he was having a drink at a pub in Harringay when Frater walked up to him: 'He said, "Were you the man who was charged with using a hatchet? It was me." I said, "I didn't know that; did you see me there?" and Frater replied, "No".'

Spinks added that he had challenged the police to find his fingerprints on the hatchet but they were unable to produce them.

The jury had been told by John Flowers:

> You might think the circumstances of this case reveal a some-
> what remarkable state of affairs to have happened in this
> country. So far as acts of violence of this kind are concerned,
> we may hope that this country is fairly free.

After a period of three hours – including the luncheon adjournment – the jury returned a verdict of guilty on both charges – inflicting grievous bodily harm on Frater and riotous assembly – on all sixteen defendants.

However, Sergeant Collyer, who had been approached with the offer of a £200 bribe 'to make a muck of his evidence', had been informed that he was not likely to live two days longer should the men in the dock be found guilty; also that heavy sentences would not only result in a united demonstration in the dock but that a real attempt would be made by the gang's hangers-on, who had spent the trial inside and outside the courtroom. This information was passed on to the Crown counsel and the judge, and stringent precautions were taken in and around the court. When the verdicts of guilty were announced, the doors of the court were locked, and the defendants' records were recounted by Superintendent Waghorn.

Addressing the prisoners, Mr Justice Hilbery said:

> Crimes of gang violence in this country will meet with no
> mercy, let that be understood by each one of you, and let it be
> understood by your many friends who have congregated at this
> Assize to hear your trial and to be about the precincts of this
> court – that you sixteen men stand convicted of acting together
> as a gang to inflict grievous bodily harm on Mark Frater. Your
> common purpose was effected and you did inflict grievous
> bodily harm on Frater. By the mercy of providence, Frater was
> not killed. I said the mercy of providence but perhaps, too,
> through the alertness of the police and the prompt execution by
> the police of their duty. It certainly was not through any mercy
> any one of you was disposed to show to your victim. You did
> arm yourselves with weapons which lie on the table, there, and
> which have been aptly described as villainous instruments to
> attack or use upon a fellow human being. You showed no mercy
> to your victim, you intended to show no mercy and claims of
> gang violence in this country will meet with no mercy. Gang
> violence is not only a brutal breach of our law, but it exercises
> terror on the victims. The consequence is that you men who
> employ gang violence in this way, hope to escape. I have not the
> least doubt that in this case you thought that because Frater
> would not dare, for fear of identifying one of you, you might
> escape. There is no cause here for leniency. You will receive
> sentences which I hope will teach you once and for all that
> crimes of this sort cannot pay in this country and it will teach
> those who are listening here, or may read about what happens
> in this case afterwards.

Sentences of penal servitude were imposed, five years each for
Spinks and Spring, four years for Blitz and three years each
for Gilder, Tyler, Mack, Boniface, and Stephen Bennis. Hard
labour next: two years each for Churchill, Bond, Wilkins, Kilby
and Timothy Bennis, followed by eighteen-month sentences for
Gardiner, Illingworth and Hain. It added up to a swingeing total
of 43½ years' imprisonment and it stunned the racetrack gangs;
it was all a far cry from the one month's imprisonment, fine or
bind-over which hitherto had been the norm. Furthermore, for
whatever reason, there were no police officers present to tell the
court what useful contacts the defendants had been in providing
information about rival gangs, since the prisoners had all stated
that they had no involvement with the racetrack gangs. Telling the
judge that the cat's immersion in the chip shop fryer had occurred
because its tail had slipped out of Spinks' grasp would not really
have been seen as mitigation.

The doors of the court were opened, and the news of the sentences spread like wildfire. Collyer was informed that a mob was waiting outside with the express intention of causing him harm. Together with Janes, Collyer confronted a dozen of them and asked if they wished to speak to him.

'You can do it', he told them, 'but bear in mind, you'll go the same way as those who've just gone down.'

It was absolutely the right course of action to take; their nerve broke, one muttered, 'That's all right, Guv'nor', and they shambled away. Dick Hutton, who had orchestrated the violence but had got clean away, was a believer of running with the hare and hunting with the hounds. Although he had a marked antipathy towards Alf Solomon and others of his race, ten years later he was employed as a strong-arm man by a Jewish bookmaker. However, when he hit a Jewish lad with his binoculars at a race meeting, Jack Spot came looking for him. Hutton kept a low profile for months, but at the same time armed himself with a revolver – just in case nemesis, in the form of Spot, caught up with him.

Both Janes and Collyer received a Watch Committee's commendation on 14 October 1936 for displaying outstanding initiative during the incident.

The novelist Graham Greene capitalized on the case in 1938, in his novel *Brighton Rock*, later made into a 1948 film directed by John Boulting in which a scar-faced Richard Attenborough played the gang leader 'Pinkie' Brown, although he looked about as menacing as Liberace. It was said that 'Pinkie' was a wordplay on Spinks' nickname, 'Spinkey', and a rival gang leader named 'Colleoni' (played by Charles Goldner) was thought to have been based on Darby Sabini.

The case effectively broke the power of the racetrack gangs. There were, naturally, other examples of violence but none on the scale of the Battle of Lewes Racetrack. The proof of the pudding came in the disparity between two race meetings: in 1923 110 arrests had been carried out at Epsom racecourse, for blackmail, welshing and pickpocketing. On Derby Day, the year after the imprisoning of the gang at Lewes, the arrests numbered just eight.

CHAPTER 19

Downfall of the Sabinis

It appeared that with the heavy sentences imposed at Sussex Assizes the power of the gangs had dissipated. There were, naturally, sporadic outbursts of violence, but after the Sabinis and Alf White had split up, White turned his attentions from the horses to greyhound racing. However, he was a spent force; being beaten up by a group of tearaways from Stoke Newington at Harringay Greyhound Stadium rather knocked the stuffing out of him. It was thought there would be reprisals from Alf's sons; but none came.

With the arrival of the Second World War, many race courses were closed, and Regulation 18B of the Defence Regulations, 1939 was one of many new pieces of legislation rushed in to crowd the statute books. It provided for detention without trial of those persons considered because of their origins, background or political associations to be a danger to the country. This included Italian citizens, after Italy joined in the war on the Axis side on 10 June 1940.

British hostility to Italians was high, and there were some unpleasant incidents in and around the Soho area of hostility to Italian shopkeepers and café owners, among whom few, if any, could be accused of being a danger to British citizens, and who put up signs proclaiming, 'We are Swiss' and 'This is a British Firm'. Nevertheless, on 17 June 1940, a newspaper report stated:

> Gangsterdom is by no means confined to the younger Italians, but the removal of a few Italian undesirables may well leave the small and offensive British element without opponents, so that old quarrels may die of inertia. For many years, the best known gang has gone under the name of 'The Sabini Boys' and its personnel included Italians as well as other riff-raff of Soho's dim back streets.

Apart from its jingoistic content, the message could not have been clearer. A total of 1,847 people had been detained under the regulations; included in their number were Darby and Harry Sabini.

Given that the Sabini brothers were only half-Italian, had an English mother, did not speak Italian and had never been to Italy, it is difficult to see what danger they represented, since it also appeared that they were not members of any subversive political party. Was their arrest and detention unlawful? It certainly seemed to be, but as will be seen, it was in fact completely lawful because the legislation did cover the brothers' circumstances. In any case, Darby and Harry had been a thorn in the side of the British authorities for far too long, and this was a perfect way to get them out of circulation. It was rough justice; but the brothers had got away with so much for so long, that this was a case of the biter bit.

Darby, who had been living at Old Shoreham Road, Hove, using the name of Fred Handley, had been arrested – perhaps slightly prematurely – on 6 June 1940 at the Hove greyhound stadium. For the previous three years he had been working as a bookmaker under the name of Dan Cope. The local chief constable stated that he knew Darby as Fred, that he was a bookmaker at Hove dog meetings, collected money from racecourse book-makers for protection and for racecards, and that he and his brother Harry were at one time regarded as feared by bookmakers on horse and dog racing tracks.

Former Detective Superintendent F. Taylor was asked for his views regarding Sabini and, stating that he had known Darby for twenty years – in what capacity, it is unclear – said, 'His livelihood has always been among the racing world. To me, Sabini appeared straightforward and one who would go a long way to prevent trouble.'

To a cynic it might appear that the former detective felt the need for his pension to be inflated, but in any event, Detective Inspector Ted Greeno redressed the balance when he added his own unequivocal comments:

> He is a drunkard and a man of most violent temperament with a heavy following and strong command of bullies of Italian origin and other undesirables. A dangerous gangster and a racketeer of the worst type.

Darby appealed against his detention, and the matter was examined in December 1940 after he had written, saying:

> My real name is Octavious Sabini, not Frederick Sabini or Frederick Handley. I used the name of Fred Handley has [sic] my boxing name. Darby is my nickname. My friends call me

Fred but I am not the same has [*sic*] Frederick Sabini, my brother.

> Signed: Octavious Sabini.

Having used so many aliases and so many misspellings of his name, it was probably difficult for Darby to decide who he actually was, but during his examination he told the committee, 'It is like going to church today, on a racecourse. All that rough business is finished.'

Two months later, the Home Office advisory committee recommended his release, and the following month, a report was sent to the Home Secretary from Brighton police:

> There is little doubt that Sabini was the head of a race gang, and considerable trouble was experienced by police with this gang and others, running in opposition on various racecourses. These gangs were finally broken up and it is safe to say that that gang warfare during the past few years has been practically negligible owing to police action whilst the Sabini gang can rightly be said to be non-existent.

The appeal was successful and Darby was released; for the time being, that is.

★   ★   ★

Harry was detained eight days after brother Darby's arrest. A police report described him as being dangerous and violent, and although he appeared to be a fairly wealthy man, he did not appear to be engaged in any honest employment.

In a further report Ted Greeno conceded that Harry had no known interest in politics but repeated the description of Darby when he wrote that Harry was:

> One of the leading lights of a gang of bullies known as the Sabini gang who under the cover of various rackets have, by their blackmailing methods, levied toll on bookmakers. He is a dangerous man of the most violent temperament and has a heavy following and strong command of a gang of bullies of Italian origin in London . . . He is a dangerous gangster and racketeer of the worst type and appears to be a most likely person who would be chosen by enemy agents to create and be a leader of violent internal actions against the country.

Harry appealed, and on 20 December 1940 a writ of habeas corpus was granted at a Divisional Court by Mr Justice Humphreys.

The application was made by Harry's barrister, Mr G. O. Slade, who said that his client had been detained since 14 June on an order issued by the Home Secretary, Sir John Anderson, stating that he had reasonable cause to believe that Sabini was a person of hostile origin and that it was necessary to exercise control over him for that reason.

In fact, said Mr Slade, his client was British-born; his father had been Italian but had died when Sabini was eighteen months old, his mother was English, he could not speak Italian, had never been to Italy and was entirely loyal to Britain's cause in the war. Everything he owned, a substantial amount of house property, was in England.

Furthermore, on 27 November 1940, stated Mr Slade, his client had received a document headed 'Reasons for order made under Regulation 18B against Harry Sabini, alias Harry Handley'. He had never been known by that name and could only assume that he had been confused with another person bearing the name Sabini. Apart from a single summary conviction many years ago for a trivial offence, his client had never been convicted, and he most emphatically denied Greeno's assertion that he was liable to lead internal insurrections in this country.

The court was told that on 3 December 1940 Sabini had appeared before the Advisory Committee of the Home Office, at which time no evidence was offered against him, and therefore, Mr Slade submitted, Sir John Anderson could not have had reasonable cause to believe that he was a person of hostile origin or that it was necessary to exercise control over him.

It was an impressive plea and it certainly convinced Mr Justice Humphreys, who stated:

> The main point in the application appeared to be that it might well be that the applicant had been confused with someone bearing a similar name, in which case there could be no grounds at all for holding him.

The application was granted and the matter was adjourned while a writ of habeas corpus was served on the Home Secretary as well as the commandant at the Ascot internment camp where Sabini was under detention.

Greeno was down, but being the tenacious detective that he was, he was by no means out.

On 20 January 1941, the writ was refused by the Lord Chief Justice at the King's Bench Division. The Solicitor General told the court that under Italian law Sabini was also an Italian subject, having been born to an Italian father. Italy was now an enemy of Great Britain and therefore Sabini's origin was hostile; the situation under consideration was not at the date of Sabini's birth but at the present time. Furthermore, added the Solicitor General, he had seldom seen 'such shocking perjury' as was shown in Sabini's affidavit; this was only emphasised when Greeno (now a detective chief inspector) informed the court that he had known Sabini as Harry Handley and produced certified copies of two convictions against him in that name, one of them for pointing a pistol at a man in 1922. Harry had offered his house at 44 Highbury Park, Highbury New Barn, described as 'palatially furnished' and worth £15,000, as surety for his release on bail, and when police went to that address and asked his wife the whereabouts of Harry Handley, they were told, 'Upstairs'. Evidence then came from former Detective Chief Inspector Godley, who stated in an affidavit that Mr Harry Sabini was known on racecourses as Harry Handley.

The court decided that Sir John Anderson's order was perfectly proper and, with Mr Justice Humphreys remarking that Harry had 'committed deliberate perjury and deceived this court' (and what was worse, had deceived the judge himself), the application was refused and Sabini was ordered to pay costs.

On 18 March 1941, Harry Sabini was released on the order of Herbert Morrison, by now Home Secretary; however, he was promptly arrested for perjury.

On 16 April, Harry was committed for trial from Bow Street Police Court after Mr Slade unsuccessfully argued that the false statement alleged was not material to the proceedings before the Divisional Court and that there was no case to go before a jury.

After a two-day trial at the Old Bailey, Harry was found guilty of perjury; Greeno was by now deeply involved in a series of murder investigations, so it fell to Scotland Yard's Detective Inspector Griffey to put the poison in:

> The Sabini gang has levied toll on bookmakers for many years, under cover of various rackets. He has two convictions – the last in 1922. The gang's activities have been cut down by the police and recently Sabini has supplemented his income by professional backing of horses and greyhounds. He is regarded by the police as a man of violent temperament and has a heavy following of bullies of Italian origin in London.

The Recorder of London acknowledged that Harry had kept out of trouble for nineteen years (that was, as far as he knew) and that he had taken that into account in fixing the sentence, 'but I cannot shut my eyes to the fact that perjury is a grave offence'; and on 8 July 1941, he sentenced him to nine months' imprisonment.

★   ★   ★

The property known as Buckham Hill House, Isfield, Sussex belonging to Mr John Mathison Fraser JP had been requisitioned during the war and occupied by American troops. Mr Fraser had stored items of glass, silver and wine in the cellar and, for added security, had the door bricked up on the outside, so that there was no entrance. On 10 May 1943, he had visited the house and discovered that the ventilator cover had been removed, giving access to a disused flue, and that a hole had been knocked in the internal wall, giving access to the cellar.

He discovered that 144 bottles of wine were missing as well as a silver table service, a half table service, forty-seven miscellaneous pieces of silver, 213 plates, two vegetable dishes and lids, eighty-three wine glasses, nine ornaments, two silver ladles, a christening set, an electric cleaner and a japanned tray; the total value of the missing property was £383 10s 6d.

Five US servicemen were quickly arrested, and some, just as quickly, had a lot to say; they admitted the burglary, which had occurred sometime prior to 6 May.

On 15 May, Mr Fraser was taken to an address where he identified 73 bottles of wine and quite a lot more of the stolen property. The address was in Old Shoreham Road, Hove, the home of Darby Sabini, now calling himself Fred Sabini. He and two others were charged with receiving the property from one of the servicemen; more items were then recovered to a total of £364 10s 6d, and Darby and others appeared at Uckfield Police Court on 4 June 1943, from where they were committed to stand their trial at the East Sussex Quarter Sessions.

On 17 June, the soldiers were all convicted and imprisoned; one of the three men charged with receiving was acquitted, but the other two were convicted, one of them being Darby Sabini. He had unsuccessfully tried to convince the jury that he had innocently purchased the items believing them to have come from a hotel that was being sold. Told by Recorder Gilbert Paul, 'It is men like you who lay temptation before soldiers. If there were none like you, there would be no temptation to steal', Darby was sentenced to two years' hard labour – the law had caught up with him at last. At fifty-five years of age, Darby's one and only prison sentence which incorporated hard labour must have been a heavy blow indeed.

If that was not enough, within months of his imprisonment, Darby received the news that his son, Flight Sergeant Harry Sabini, a member of the RAF Volunteer Reserve, had been shot down and killed on 14 August 1943 while on active service. He was buried at the Fayid War Cemetery, Egypt.

It was the end of the road for Darby. He died aged sixty-two on 4 October 1950 at his home in Hove; it was described as both a small terraced house and a semi-detached villa, situated opposite Brighton Grammar School, Dyke Road (now the Brighton, Hove and Sussex Grammar School). The cause of death was splenic anaemia: enlargement of the spleen, with a tendency to haemorrhage from the stomach which is associated with cirrhosis of the liver. His widow spoke warmly of his contributions to hospitals, adding:

> He always took a collecting box to the racecourse. He gave hospitals a lot of his own money. My husband did more good than bad. When he was younger, he sometimes got into fights. But all this nonsense about razors and protection money from bookmakers is untrue.

Darby was buried in Hove Old Cemetery, Old Shoreham Road, as was his wife when she died twenty-eight years later in 1978, the same year that brother Harry died. Billy Kimber, Darby's arch-enemy, had preceded him, dying in Torquay in 1945. Darby's estate was valued at £3,665, although his clerk was said to have been found in possession of £36,000 which belonged to Sabini and seems to be a much more realistic estimate of Darby's wealth.

Hero or villain? Hardly a hero, while some might have treated him as one, those who got hand-outs to pay the rent, although only the really reckless would have failed to repay him. Giving money to the hospitals was fine; if it had been his money that he donated. At the time of Darby's death, Ron and Reg Kray were doing much the same thing; the local newspapers would proclaim, 'Boxing twins donate a television set at a raffle.' So they had, but it was a set which they had frightened out of a retailer.

It was part of the Sabini legend that his daughters attended Roedean School and that he lived in a penthouse suite at Brighton's Grand Hotel. They did not, and he did not. The closest the Grand came to an encounter with gangsters was during the 1930s when a group of racecourse thugs entered the hotel, ordered drinks and, as time went by, became cantankerous and belligerent. When a rival gang arrived, matters became fraught and knives were produced. The manager, Sidney Thomas Smith, attempted to intervene but was pushed aside; the police were called and the gangs were arrested. At the risk of bad publicity, Mr Smith was obliged to give evidence in court.

But there was never any danger of the hotel receiving adverse publicity by permitting a gangster like Sabini to be one of their guests, because he never stayed there; a search revealed that he was not registered there under his name or any of his aliases. Following the evacuation of Dunkirk, the guests left the Grand in 1940 and it was requisitioned by the army; it did not reopen until 10 October 1946, by which time, Darby was ensconced at his home in Old Shoreham Road.

Ken Wood was Darby's great-nephew by marriage; his grandmother Rosie was the sister of Darby's wife, Annie, and in an anecdote sixty years ago he was told by her about how Rosie's husband Albert – by all accounts an obnoxious racist, sexist, homophobic type – got into a fight just after the First World War in the company of his father-in-law, Bill Potter, with a local Clerkenwell family named Tucker. Albert got the worst of the encounter, and Bill Potter escaped but returned just in time to pull his son-in-law clear of the tram tracks, where he had been dumped by the Tucker family, unconscious, to await the arrival of the next tram. Bill and Albert complained to Darby and retribution was administered to the Tuckers, with the addition of a grovelling apology.

Another Potter family anecdote related how Darby would come home from the races with his pockets full of 'the old white fivers', plus other folding money, and put the notes on the shelf over the fire; the children were then poised to catch any of the money caught by the fire's updraught and prevent the notes being consumed by the flames.

'Mad Frankie' Fraser gave fulsome accounts of Darby's generosity, of being a 10-year-old 'bucket boy' at the racetracks and Darby giving him half-a-crown 'to take home to your mum'. If that was the case, Frank had a long way to travel, because when Frank was ten years of age, Darby had forsworn London for Brighton and was conducting his shady deals on the Sussex coast. Nevertheless, for someone who was a member of the Richardson Torture Gang and derived immense pleasure from pulling out his victims' teeth with pliers and impaling their feet to the floor with knives, as well as generating electric shocks to their genitals, Darby must have been a role model, whether Frank knew him or not.

CHAPTER 20

Demise of the 'Tecs

Before dealing with 'what happened after that', I want to refer to the detectives who have so far featured in this tale, simply because they don't appear any longer.

First must come David Goodwillie, who joined the Met in 1902 and who, at the time of the fight at King's Cross Railway Station, was aged forty. He emerged from the fracas with great credit and one month after the court appearance was promoted to detective inspector (second class). He was an intrepid officer who, disguised as a dustman, had caught a number of counterfeiters and had been highly commended in 1911 for tackling a gunman who had shot a fellow officer. Goodwillie had taken a decisive role in the arrest of two countrywide burglars, as well as assisting in the arrest (whilst disguised, as usual) of the gang responsible for the sensational 'Great Pearl Robbery' of 1913. He might have gone on to greater heights but sadly, within five years and with the rank of divisional detective inspector, he was discharged as being medically unfit and retired to Fife.

As well as forming the Flying Squad, Fred Wensley went on to become Chief Constable of the CID. He completely reorganized the CID, was worshipped by his men and when he retired in 1929, had served in the Met for over forty years and took with him, as well as his medals, over 300 commendations.

Divisional Detective Inspector Bill Smith was a stern supervisor on the East End's 'H' Division; described as being 'one of the shrewdest brains in the Criminal Investigation Department', he was one of the officers seconded to investigate the 1923 Joseph Engelstein arson case, under Wensley's direction.

Detectives Selby and Dawkins were two of the original officers picked for the Flying Squad who, on the first night's patrol in the Crossley Tenders, were involved in a terrific punch-up with a gang of violent shopbreakers. Another of the originals was John Rutherford, who like the others was commended by the commissioner for his part in those arrests and additionally received a monetary award of £1 5s 0d. Rutherford had joined the Met in 1913 and it appeared that he had a glittering career in front of him; instead, he unexpectedly resigned with less than eighteen years' service in 1931. I was walking to work at a printers' company along Cleveland Street, W1 on the morning of 26 February 1965 and was unaware of Rutherford's existence at that time; therefore I had no idea that I'd walked past 30 Howard House, where he'd just died, aged seventy-two.

There were two detective inspectors on that initial, bruising Flying Squad patrol; one of them was Walter Hambrook, who used his heavy ash walking stick against the shopbreakers 'to great effect'. He had joined the Met in 1898 and, following a distinguished career of thief-catching, became the head of the Flying Squad in 1929. He rose to the rank of detective superintendent, was known as 'The Father of the Squad' and when he died, following a long retirement, at the age of ninety in 1966, his obituary in *The Times* noted that he was 'more likely to have been mistaken for a modest businessman than for the shrewd detective he was'.

The other detective inspector on that first patrol was Albert Grosse, who had joined the Met in 1899 and was posted to the very tough 'G' Division, where he thoroughly distinguished himself, winning commendations for 'Cleverness in arresting a man for burglary', 'Bravery in arresting a man who violently attacked him' and 'Zealous action in a case of housebreaking'. By 1919 he had been promoted to detective inspector and started his career with the Flying Squad and his battle with the racetrack gangs. After promotion to divisional detective inspector, he retired in 1925.

Divisional Detective Inspector James Berrett ('The Bearded Detective') took charge of the twenty-eight Birmingham Boys' fracas in 1921 and six years later also dealt with the brilliant and successful investigation into the case of Kennedy and Browne, who had cold-bloodedly murdered Essex officer, Police Constable Gutteridge.

As a chief inspector, Detective Superintendent Brown had led the investigation into the assassination of Field Marshal Sir Henry Wilson by the IRA in 1922, although later in his career he cherry-picked what he had to say about the racetrack gangs.

'Chesty' Corbett – he of the iron grip – rose to the rank of chief inspector. As well as service with the Flying Squad, he worked all over North and East London, where practically all of his prisoners were pickpockets. But despite his high standard of physical fitness, he was discharged in 1940 as being medically unfit due to coronary thrombosis and retired to Shrewsbury. However, his fitness must have counted for something. Despite suffering a heart attack, he managed to live for another twenty years, and that wasn't all. Although 5ft 8⅛ inches tall when he joined the Met, by the time he retired he had gained another ⅛ inch in height.

Walter Collyer and Stanley Janes both retired from Brighton CID, Janes at the age of forty-nine in 1953. He had been involved in several successful murder investigations and enjoyed what he described as 'a good and action-packed career'. In retirement, he was appointed as a security officer to a large business company.

Fred Sharpe retired as head of the Flying Squad in 1937. He received the last of his seventy-nine commissioner's commendations six weeks before retirement, being highly commended for his actions in a difficult case of murder. He had been a very skilful murder investigator although he would always be remembered for his actions against the racecourse pests – the gangs, the fraudsters and the pickpockets. Detective Superintendent Fred Narborough, then a junior member of the Flying Squad, recalled how Sharpe had led him and other Squad officers towards the silver ring at Epsom. As Sharpe's trademark bowler hat bobbed along through the crowd, the arms of the tic-tac men flailed wildly. It was not the prices they were signalling but the presence of Sharpe, and within seconds, gangs of pickpockets fell over themselves as they climbed the rails and dashed away to freedom.

Sharpe went into the bookmaker's business – hardly surprising for a man who once said, 'I do not think there is any place at which an enthusiastic detective can spend a more profitable day, than at a race meeting.' He first employed Isaac Bogard aka 'Darky the Coon' – 'They're a colourful, rascally lot, these wide 'uns', said Sharpe, and thereby hangs a tale.

Sharpe was pretty colourful, too, and had a very good press. Upon his promotion to chief inspector, the *Daily Express* hyperbolically reported that he was:

> A terror to old-time East End gangsters. Stocky, bird-like, close-cropped, slow of speech, brusque of manner; wears a stand-up stiff collar, (bowler) hat a size too small, a gourmet, hates publicity. Crooks call him, affectionately, 'Fred'.

But not too many crooks treated him affectionately, and their numbers were not restricted to the racetrack gangs. Sharpe upset a hornet's nest after his successful investigation into the murder of Max Kassel, a noted white slaver, and apart from the disruption which his enquiries had caused to prostitution in London, the thorough dislike the underworld had for him spread to Paris, where the trial was finally concluded at the Assizes de la Seine.

So in providing Isaac Bogard with employment, Sharpe would certainly have gained the displeasure of Arthur Harding who, with four others had attacked Bogard in the Bluecoat Boy public house in 1911; one of the gang cut his throat, the others smashed their tumblers and rammed them into Bogard's face and hands. Harding received the heaviest sentence: twenty-one months' hard labour plus three years' penal servitude.

So when the Yard received an anonymous hand-written note in block capitals on 6 July 1939, it is possible that Harding was either the author or perhaps the instigator. It read:

A FINE ADVERT FOR THE POLICE SHARPE A BOOKMAKER NOW – AS BAD STILL AS EVER HE WAS WORSE WHEN IN THE POLICE HE GOT AWAY WITH IT TO THE DISGRACE OF ALL OF YOU WHO SHOULD HAVE KNOWN THE GAME HE WAS HAVING FOR YEARS ONE OF THE WICKED SCOUNDRELS IN THE POLICE FOR YEARS.

(Signed) ON THE BEAT

On reflection, the letter's illiteracy seems to excuse Harding, who had a smattering of education, but the accusation was sufficient for the Yard to take the matter seriously and investigate it.

It transpired that Sharpe was associated with a commission agent named Tommy Williams, who had a shady reputation and was an associate of Phil Lee, the licensee of The Final public house, although no offences of any kind were disclosed. Questioned, Sharpe stated that he was in business with Williams' son and that Lee had ceased to be a partner one week after the anonymous note had been received. It appeared that the Yard believed that by associating with the son of an undesirable character he was somehow 'letting the side down'. Bearing in mind that all through his service Sharpe had been associating with 'undesirable characters' to get the job done, this really was a case of double standards.

The investigation droned on for over a year before it fizzled out, and Sharpe continued to draw his annual pension of £347 17s 2d for thirty-seven years before dying at the age of eighty-four.

CHAPTER 21

Death and Resurrection

What follows – although it describes a gangland murder – appears initially to have nothing to do with the racetrack gangs; but it has. It deals with one of those who figured in the racetrack wars, another who was on the periphery and, as he bowed out, introduced a newcomer to the racetrack gang scene who would dominate it for the next thirty years.

Whilst the Sabinis were interned, Alf White had formed an uneasy alliance with some of the Italian gangsters in Soho, but it was a shaky one, and many of the Italians and Jews ran the clubs. However, Alf had not recovered mentally or physically from the beating he had sustained in 1939 and he died in 1942, aged fifty-four.

There was a link with the racetrack gangs because one of the central characters in this account, Eddie Fletcher – his baptismal name was Eddie Fleisher – had been involved with Alf's son Harry ten years previously, when they had been both arrested for attacking Casimir Raczynski and William Fred Roche, a waiter at the Phoenix Club, Little Denmark Street.

Trouble had arisen on 14 January 1931 when, six nights after a police raid when the club was accused of selling alcoholic liquor without a licence, Ellen Coleman, Michael Tiano and Joseph Desmond had entered the club at closing time and noisily demanded drinks. When they were refused, they went behind the bar, helped themselves and then alleged that the manager, Nicholas Raczynski – he also liked to be known as 'Roberts' and was the brother of Casimir – had taken an iron bar, whacked Miss Coleman across the legs with it 'for no reason whatever' (as she indignantly stated) and bashed the two men over their heads with it.

Tiano had then punched Nicholas on the nose, said he would cut his throat and told him that his name was 'Sabini'.

The troublemakers were ejected on to the street, but when Casimir and Roche left to go home they were attacked by White and Fletcher, who were part of a gang; White slashed Raczynski across the throat with a razor and Fletcher hit Roche with a bottle and kicked him.

However, at Bow Street Police Court on 3 February 1931, the former secretary of the club, Thomas Jeacock, asked to be allowed to withdraw the statement he had made to the police, since Roche had assured him that Fletcher was not his attacker, he could not swear that the two men in the dock were involved in the attack and, indeed, he was almost positive that they were never even there. To nobody's surprise, the charges were dismissed; the club was struck off the register. Joseph Desmond and Michael Tiano failed to appear at court to pursue their allegation of assault; it's quite possible that they feared putting in an appearance in case they were identified as being members of the gang who attacked the two men. However, four years later (as has already been recounted), Tiano (naturally with some help) went on to industriously wreck the Majestic Social Club.

But on 22 April 1941, 'Fair-haired' Eddie Fletcher together with Joseph Franks had been involved in a fight with the doorman, Bert Connelly, at The Palm Beach Bottle Parties Club, situated in the basement of 37 Wardour Street, Soho. Fletcher had come off worse; in fact, two men had been charged with causing him grievous bodily harm, and the manager, Joe Leon, had banned Fletcher from the club.

Ten days later, on 1 May, Fletcher unwisely returned to the premises, and it was whilst he was playing pool in the Bridge and Billiards Club on the first floor that he was set upon by Joseph Collette, Harry Capocci and Albert George Dimes. It was Dimes – also known as Alberto Dimeo or 'Italian Albert' – at that time on the run from the RAF, who was the ringleader. The son of an Italian father and a Scottish mother, Dimes was twenty-five years of age, 6 feet 2 inches tall, strongly built and good looking, with an interesting background. He had served a period of Borstal Training and several prison sentences, one of four months for various offences, including breaking a police officer's jaw; but his reputation came from two violent interludes. The first was in March 1938, when Michael McCausland was attacked by five men who leapt out of a car and savagely attacked him. He later died, and although the Coroner's Court decided that he had died from natural causes, two men were charged with inflicting grievous bodily harm on him, one of whom was Eddie Raimo (more will be heard about him in the next chapter). The charges were later dismissed but it was thought that he and Albert Dimes were part of the gang of five who had attacked McCausland.

The second matter to enhance Dimes' reputation came from his having allegedly murdered an East End docker and hardman named Charles Edward 'Chick' Lawrence. His body had been

found on Sunday, 12 November 1939 at Spitalfields; he had
sustained severe and fatal head injuries. It was unusual for him to
visit this district from his home in Westgate Street, Hackney, and
an argument had been heard at three o'clock on the morning of
his murder. A car had drawn up and stayed for about a quarter
of an hour before leaving. Witnesses had heard things but seen
nothing. Police officers investigating the case pursued the theory
that Lawrence was the victim of a race gang attack. But whatever
they thought, there was no evidence to charge Dimes – or Eddie
Raimo, who was similarly suspected – with the murder, and
whether Dimes was connected with it or not, many believed that
he was, and so his persona grew.

There was certainly evidence of Dimes' violent disposition on
the night of 1 May at the Bridge and Billiards Club. The five billiard
tables were wrecked, the light shades above them were torn down
and smashed, billiard balls were thrown around the room, broken
glass was everywhere and Fletcher received a sustained beating by
the trio, who set about him using their fists, billiard cues and coshes.
Blood was seeping from a wound on the side of his head, and his
injuries might have escalated had it not been for the intervention of
his friend, 36-year-old Harry Distleman, a 'large lump' and a one-
time club owner, pickpocket and racecourse pest with six previous
convictions for assault. As a result, Fletcher's assailants fled, and
Distleman took his friend to have his wounds treated at Charing
Cross Hospital, as they had been ten days previously.

Fletcher was a chancer, no doubt about that; having been barred
from the club, he now decided to return on a second occasion that
night, saying later that it was merely to pick up his coat, although
it's far more likely he was simply asserting his authority – and his
ego.

But upon his arrival, his three attackers also reappeared and
the brawling began all over again. At the same time, the manager
of the Palm Beach Bottle Parties Club, having been alerted
by one Sammy Lederman,[1] arrived at Wardour Street; he was
39-year-old Antonio 'Babe' Mancini who, it will be recalled, had
had an extremely bruising run-in some two years previously with
Jack Spot, whilst the two of them were serving prison sentences.
In addition, who should turn up but Thomas Mack, fresh from
his release after three years' penal servitude for his part in 'The
Battle of Lewes Racetrack'. No one could be sure what part the

---

[1] Lederman claimed association with the likes of the Sabinis, Jack Spot,
Billy Hill and later on, the Kray twins; really, he was a hanger-on.

bald-headed former boxer played in the frenzied fighting; he vanished either before or at the time of the final denouement. The manager, Joe Leon, told Mancini to go to the door and let nobody in, whereupon Mancini ascended the stairs. Victor Dimes, Albert's older brother (and a professional wrestler), grabbed hold of his sibling and pinned him against one of the wrecked billiard tables, thereby preventing him from participating any further in the hostilities. This was just as well, because Mancini thrust a seven-inch-long dagger into Distleman's left armpit to a depth of five inches, sufficient to sever the axillary artery and the accompanying vein. Distleman – he was also known as 'Scarface' and 'Little Hubby' – staggered into the arms of three bystanders, saying to one of them, 'I am terribly hurt. He has stabbed me in the heart. Babe's done it', and to another, 'I am stabbed. I am stabbed. I am dying.'

Dumped on the pavement outside the club, the dying Distleman was found by two passing police officers.

Meanwhile, Mancini had gone completely out of control. Exhibiting a near-lunatic temper, he chased Fletcher around the billiard tables slashing at him with the dagger and severing the tendons in his arm; in fact, Mancini almost severed the arm itself, before dropping the dagger and going home. Fletcher made his way once more to the Charing Cross Hospital where, as a regular customer, they probably had a bed waiting for him. Meanwhile, six men were brought in for questioning, with a view to putting them up for identification the following day.

★ ★ ★

The officer deputed to investigate this matter was 40-year-old Divisional Detective Inspector Arthur Thorp from West End Central police station. A keen boxer, he used a number of unconventional practices. For example, if a punter complained of his wallet being stolen by a prostitute, Thorp would take him back to the premises where the encounter had taken place. To nobody's surprise, not only would the erring prostitute not be there, but the landlord would not admit to renting a room to a person who followed such a disreputable profession. Thorp would then suggest to the aggrieved party that 'he might like to work the room over a little' and avert his eyes whilst the room and all its contents were systematically wrecked. Just as eyebrow-raising was when Thorp attended the 1932 Derby; a colleague's wife had asked him to put 2s 6d each way on April the Fifth, which was not the favourite and therefore had a starting price of 100–6.

Thorp placed the bet with a bookmaker who was offering slightly longer odds and the horse, ridden by Fred Lane, romped home. But when Thorp went to collect his winnings, the bookmaker had vanished, leaving a number of angry punters at the empty space where his stall had been. However, before the day was out, Thorp spotted both the bookmaker and his clerk and arrested them both for welshing. Following their court appearance the following day, Thorp confronted the bookie, telling him, 'I think you owe me some money, don't you?' to which he replied, 'That's right, Guv. Let's see, now. How much was it?' and duly coughed up.

These forceful habits are now, I feel sure, outdated, and the very thought of them being currently practised would cause any present day senior officer to suffer severe respiratory difficulties.

However, Thorp was in more conventional mood when Mancini presented himself at the police station the following day and said, 'I admit stabbing Fletcher with a long dagger which I found on the floor of the club, but I don't admit doing Distleman. Why should I do him? They threatened me as I came up the stairs and I got panicky. In fact, I don't remember everything that happened.'

Thorp took a written statement from Mancini in which said, 'As I was going upstairs, I heard someone behind me say: "There's Babe" (meaning me), "Let's knife him!"'

Mancini believed that it was Fletcher who had uttered those words. When he got into the club, Fletcher and Distleman came in and a general fight started. The statement continued:

> Fletcher saw me and made for me with a raised chair. I saw the knife on the ground. It was a dagger, coming to a point. I picked it up to defend myself and struck him with it on the arm. I might have struck him again. I think I did. When the fight first started, I went to act as mediator and received a blow in the face and a push. I don't remember seeing Distleman from the time he entered the club. I was panicky the whole time I was in the club. I have known Fletcher and Distleman for about fifteen years.

When he was charged the following day, Mancini said, 'I'm sticking by the statement I've already made. I'll take my chance on it. The bit about finding the dagger on the floor is wrong. I had it with me, with a bit of rag wrapped round it.'

At Bow Street Police Court on 2 May, Mancini was remanded, and Joseph Collette took his turn in the dock charged with inflicting grievous bodily harm on Fletcher. Having been charged, he replied, 'I was there. I was in the fight. There was a general mix-up.

They were using broken cues. I got hit on the face. I know nothing about Distleman being stabbed. I would like to have a solicitor.'

Three days later, Harry Armando Capocci appeared at court facing the same charge as Collette. Detective Inspector Jeffrey told the court that the prisoner had told him, 'I read about it in the newspapers. I was there but I was not mixed up in any murder business. I don't see what a fight has got to do with causing grievous bodily harm.'

The inspector stated that since the arrest of the first two men, a number of people had been threatened by Capocci's friends; Capocci immediately told the court that he knew nothing about any attempts to interfere with witnesses, and in an effort to distance himself, his name and his ancestry from the anti-Italian feelings sweeping the country, he stated that he had been in England since he was three months old and that he was now industriously engaged in repairing bomb-damaged houses. He added, almost as an afterthought, 'I was definitely not there at the time of the murder', but he was nevertheless remanded in custody.

Mancini's counsel was keen to extract Thorp's confirmation that the man in the dock was not the same as 'Toni Mancini' who had been charged with (and acquitted of) the murder of prostitute Violette Kay in 1934; Thorp agreed that the two murderers were not one and the same, but although he would never know it, just before Mancini died in 1976, he admitted that he had been the murderer of the unfortunate Ms Kaye. That was that particular hurdle out of the way, but the complexities of the legal process were far from over.

There were several remands at Bow Street, during which Patrick Crowley, a doorman at the club, gave evidence that Mancini and Fletcher were involved in a struggle when Distleman intervened, whereupon Mancini pushed him away and continued his fight with Fletcher. It was not until 26 May that Eddie Fletcher, his left arm in a sling, was able to appear to give evidence in court. He described how a man named Albert rushed at him but was held back by his (Albert's) brother. Collette went to hit him with a billiard cue but, he told the court, he hit Collette first.

His testimony then continued:

> I ran round and Collette followed me. Mancini went towards the door, where Distleman was standing. Collette started hitting me with a cue and I saw Mancini running towards me. I left Collette and Mancini followed me and started slashing at me with what looked like a dagger or a stiletto. I kept running back until he got me one on the left wrist, which I put up to guard

myself. Blood started to spurt and I shouted, 'My hand's off!'
Mancini stopped and went out of the club.

In cross-examination, Fletcher denied that when he came into the club he said, 'There's Baby – let's knife him' or that he was the first to attack Mancini with a chair, telling the court, 'Mancini rushed at me like a bull.'

At the Old Bailey, Mancini was given the chance to plead guilty to manslaughter, and this was a plea that would certainly have been acceptable to the prosecution. Instead, in an act of almost unbelievable stupidity, he pleaded not guilty to Distleman's murder and manslaughter, as well as denying inflicting grievous bodily harm on Fletcher with intent to murder him or to cause him grievous bodily harm. It was crazy for three reasons: firstly, the considerable weight of the evidence against him; secondly, Italy had joined in the war on the Axis side thirteen months previously and anti-Italian feelings were running very high; and lastly, the jury was going to be made up of solid, middle-class English house-owners who would have a natural antipathy to beastly foreigners wielding daggers.

But Mancini – and his followers – believed that he would get away with it; as well as the few witnesses out of the forty who were in the club being threatened, the word was put about that a number of gang members were going to 'get' Thorp. It was stupid, empty boasting, but for a police officer with a reputation for toughness like Thorp to have ignored it would have been positively foolish. So he paid a solo visit to a club where the gang was in attendance and said, 'I believe you boys are looking for me. What can I do for you?'

Of course, nobody spoke, nobody moved. Thorp left, free to continue his depredations on landlords of shady establishments and recalcitrant bookmakers and to continue rising up the promotional ladder to retire, thirteen years later, with the rank of detective chief superintendent.

After the summing-up, and after a woman dressed in black shouted out something uncomplimentary from the back of the court and was immediately ejected, it took the jury fifty-four minutes on 4 July to find Mancini guilty of murder. Mr Justice McNaughton donned the black cap, the chaplain unctuously murmured something vaguely comforting and Mancini was sentenced to death.

Mancini appealed twice, and on both occasions the sentence was confirmed. But when a request was made for the Attorney-General's fiat to appeal to the House of Lords, the fiat was granted.

This was something that thoroughly pissed off William Barkley of the *Daily Express* who wrote on 3 October 1941:

> On May 1, five months ago, there was a row – or what Viscount Simon in the House of Lords yesterday called a 'scrimmage' – in a Soho club in which a man named Harry Distleman (Scarface Harry) was killed.
>
> A British citizen named Antonio Mancini was apprehended, tried by a jury and convicted of murder.
>
> But there was one point. Was Mancini provoked to the fatal blow?
>
> If you strike a fatal blow, said to be in retaliation, and you are convicted of murder, can you still cry in this country, although your name is Mancini, 'I am innocent of murder and I appeal'?
>
> Yes, you can.
>
> An appeal was heard against this conviction before three judges (Lord Chief Justice Lord Caldecote presiding), and adjourned by them to get two more judges for a court of five, on September 3.
>
> Meanwhile, 400,000 men bearing Italian names have been shot, hunted, harried or imprisoned without the slightest ceremony by our men, all through the wastes of Libya and Abyssinia.

Following this slightly biased piece, when the Law Lords finally rejected the appeal, Mr Barkley was relieved to inform the readers of the *Daily Express* on 17 October: 'Mancini: The law is "Content" after 5½ months. "3 times guilty",' and as he succinctly remarked, 'That's the end of that.'

It was probably the longest time in British history that a man had sat in a condemned cell, and the first time in twenty-three years that a gangster would be executed for murder.

He met his end on 31 October 1941 at Pentonville Prison at the hands of Albert Pierrepoint. It was the latter's first hanging as Chief Executioner – during his career, 434 more executions would follow – and he was rather unnerved, as he slipped the black hood over his client's head, to hear Mancini's slightly muffled voice say, 'Cheerio!'

Dimes, Capocci and Collette appeared at the Old Bailey before Sir Gerald Dodson, the Recorder of London, to deny a charge of wounding Fletcher. The eyewitnesses were not of the highest calibre, having somewhat defective memories, and on two occasions the Recorder plaintively asked prosecuting counsel, 'Is it worthwhile going on with this case?'

The prosecution obviously thought it was, although in his summing-up to the jury Sir Gerald commented, 'There is no evidence to show that they did anything more than engage in a rough-and-tumble', adding that what had occurred was 'a disreputable brawl in an abominable haunt'. In the event, Capocci was acquitted, and on 21 July 1941 Sir Gerald told the other two, 'You were probably expecting prison and no doubt you deserve it, but I am going to bind you over.'

Dimes and Collette were duly bound over in the sum of £5 to be of good behaviour for a period of three years, before Dimes received six months in the glasshouse for his absence from the RAF.

Upon his release, he – and his long-term friend, Bert Marsh – began to make inroads into the fiefdom which the Sabinis had vacated, and in September 1942 they formed an alliance with Billy Hill.

However, before dealing with the ascendancy of Albert Dimes, it's necessary to take a look at two other gang leaders, Jack Spot and Billy Hill, both of whom – Spot especially – professed an interest in horseracing activities, especially of the illegal variety.

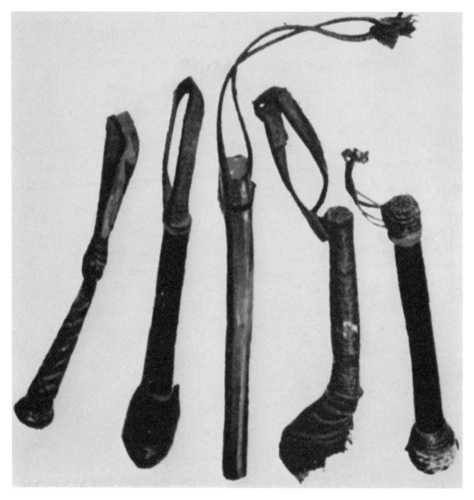

Above: Weapons used by the racetrack gangs.

Right: The chopper used on Mark Frater.

Chief Constable (CID) Fred
Wensley OBE, KPM.

Left: A Crossley Tender, as used by
the Flying Squad.

Below: Detective Superintendent
Walter Hambrook.

Above left: Detective Chief Inspector Fred 'Nutty' Sharpe.

Above right: Ex-Detective Chief Inspector Tom Divall.

Below left: Detective Chief Inspector James Berrett.

Below right: Detective Chief Superintendent Arthur Thorp.

Left: Detective Chief Superintendent Ted Greeno MBE.

Below: Deputy Commander Reg Spooner.

Above: Francasal (right) found in stables at Reading.

Below: One year after the horse switch, Santo Amaro and Francasal sold at auction.

Above left: Billy Hill.

Above right: Jack Spot.

Below left: Ron and Reg Kray.

Below right: Albert Dimes at Brighton racetrack.

Above: (L-R) Detective Inspector Bill Baldock BEM, Detective Sergeant Terry O'Connell, Sir Gordon Richards.

Below left: A bolus.

Below right: A discrepancy in height demands that the 6ft 1½ inch Terry O'Connell has to bend double to catch what Sir Gordon Richards is saying.

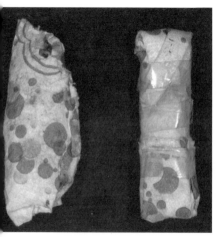

Above left: The Old Bailey, where . . .

Above right: 'Babe' Mancini met his fate . . .

Left: and Albert Dimes (plus many others) didn't.

CHAPTER 22

Jack Spot and Billy Hill

Jack Spot and Billy Hill were two feared gang leaders with a propensity for violence. Hill was a skilled thief, a thinker, a planner and had spent a considerable amount of time behind bars. He was canny, too, and when he served prison sentences he kept quiet, never misbehaved and got full remission; additionally, he made the acquaintance of a number of senior police officers; he knew how to horse-trade and strike deals with them. Hill could engage in single combat, although he preferred a cut-throat razor or a knife to do his fighting – or 'striping' – for him.

Spot, on the other hand, was simply a violent thug and although he used weapons as well, he was a feared fighter in an unarmed one-to-one confrontation. Although he had minor convictions for minor dishonesty Spot was not a thief; he was what was known (as the Kray twins would become branded) as 'a thieves' ponce' – someone who took a percentage of a thief's illicit payroll. He also scared money out of shopkeepers and bookmakers on the grounds that he was offering them protection. Both Spot and Hill were beautifully and expensively attired; not only were they gang leaders, but unlike the shabby Darby Sabini, they looked the part.

* * *

Billy Hill was born William Charles Hill in 1911 in St Pancras, London. He was one of a family of twenty-one mainly villainous children; his father was a fighting drunk, his mother was a receiver of stolen goods and his older sister, Maggie, was a member of the notorious 'Forty Thieves' gang of shoplifters. She possessed a saucy streak as well as a violent one; convicted of sticking a hatpin into a police officer's eye, the judge sentenced her to four years' imprisonment, adding dismissively, 'Take her down', before Maggie screamed defiantly, 'You didn't say that when you was fucking me last night!'

Hill's first conviction was at the age of fourteen when he broke into a tobacconist's kiosk, and over the next thirty years, for burglaries, smash and grabs and a robbery with violence, he was birched and sent to Borstal, as well as receiving several periods of imprisonment which included penal servitude; but by the end of the Second World War he had formed an alliance with Jack Spot.

*   *   *

Jack Spot was born Jacob Comacho in 1913 at Myrdle Road, Whitechapel. He was the youngest of four children born to Jewish parents who originally hailed from Poland. He was also known as John or Jack Comer although he soon became referred to as Jack Spot, either because of the large mole on his cheek or because, as he liked to say, whenever there was any trouble, 'I was always on the spot.'

In an area of such grinding poverty you either stayed where you were, to be usually trampled underfoot, or else you clawed your way up – and young Spot definitely opted for the latter course. By the age of sixteen he was running protection rackets from the stallholders and shopkeepers in the area of Petticoat Lane and earning a sizable pension. He was also six feet tall, a good boxer and a fearless fighter.

He had a couple of minor brushes with the law, the first when he was twenty, for which he was placed on probation; and two years later, he was bound over to keep the peace. Although he was greatly feared, many of the Jews who paid him a 'pension' also genuinely liked him; whenever they were threatened by gangs of tearaway gentiles, Spot really did appear 'on the spot' and dished out appropriate punishment to the mischief-makers.

Without doubt, the finest moment for his reputation came on 4 October 1936 at what became known as 'The Battle of Cable Street'. This was a pitched battle between Sir Oswald Mosley's anti-semitic, fascist Blackshirts, Communists, Jews and the police. Some 6,000 police officers were on duty, and in the civil disorder that followed, 175 people were injured, including women, children and 73 police officers.

Jack Spot was in the middle of it. Charging the black-shirted fascists who menaced the Jewish community he had sworn to protect, Spot swung a chair leg lined with lead, sending fascists flying left and right, including Mosley's bodyguard, 'Rough House' King Curtis, the heavyweight all-in wrestler. Spot's charge was halted when he was knocked unconscious by a mounted police officer's long baton, and he woke up to find himself in hospital, a casualty of one of the 175 arrests which had been carried out. This was followed by a prison sentence of six months, and when he was released he was lauded and feted as the Jews' hero of Whitechapel.

Unfortunately, this was all bollocks.

Jack Spot wasn't at Cable Street. It's extremely likely that the mountainous 'Rough House' wasn't there either. It follows, therefore, that there was no chair leg, and no squashed fascists. There definitely wasn't a prison sentence. But it was certainly a convincing story, promulgated by Spot, and many people believed it; Sammy Lederman, an East End thief and hanger-on, said he'd seen him, like some modern-day Samson smashing the living shit out of 1,000 Philistines at Ramath-lehi. But whereas afterwards, Samson 'went unto the hills', Jack Spot went unto the stallholders of Petticoat Lane where, without the encumbrance of 'half a stretch' – (to the uninformed, six months' imprisonment) – he had become a legend in his own lifetime.

But he did serve his one and only sentence of six months' imprisonment in 1939; he and others had been involved in a fight at the Somerset Social Club in Whitechapel and he was charged with inflicting grievous bodily harm and sent down at the Mansion House Justice Rooms. It was whilst he was serving his sentence that he had an encounter with 'Babe' Mancini, which was witnessed by Arthur Edward Skurry, 'The King of the Upton Park Gipsies', who was hugely impressed by Spot's pugilistic abilities. This would lead to an alliance between the two, but before that happened, Spot joined the Army in 1940 and served with the Royal Artillery. He did not see active service abroad, his service was marred by instances of indiscipline and fighting in the barracks and he was medically discharged in 1943. After that, he moved north to Leeds, Manchester and Birmingham, where he ran protection rackets, before returning to London.

It was then that Jack Spot formed an alliance with Skurry, together with Teddy Machin, Arthur 'Porky' Bennett and Jackie Reynolds. Skurry – whose ear had been bitten off during a brawl – and his gang had profited during the war by 'protecting' shopkeepers as well as distributing stolen foodstuffs to them, in an area from Upton Park out to Romford, Essex. Now this strong partnership ousted Jimmy Wooder (who was related to the White family) and the Islington Mob from their control of Ascot – Spot cut Wooder's throat from ear to ear – and Spot then decided it was time to eject the White family. Eddie Raimo was a strong arm man for the Whites who had served several prison sentences for violence and had been flogged; in 1938 he had been acquitted at the Old Bailey for grievous bodily harm after no evidence was offered. Additionally, during a confrontation with the recently released Billy Hill in the Yorkshire Grey pub in Clerkenwell he had smashed a glass and shoved it into Hill's face, cutting him above the eye. But matters changed dramatically in October 1946 after an elderly Jewish bookmaker, Moses Levy, was warned off his pitch at Yarmouth racecourse by the Whites.

Moses Levy had a chequered and a disfiguring past. He had been arrested with his brother David at Epsom in 1921 for possessing a revolver (as well as loitering with intent to commit a felony) and, like his brother, had been sentenced to three months' imprisonment with the addition of a £10 fine. But prior to that, in March 1921, he had entered into recognisances to be of good behaviour after being convicted of obstruction and assault; and following his release, he appeared at Old Street Police Court on 17 August to show why those recognisances should not be estreated.

Levy was wise enough to employ a barrister, Mr Purchas, who informed the Magistrate, Mr Clarke Hall, that the reason his client had taken the revolver with him to the Derby was because his life had been threatened and he had heard of dangerous gangs in the neighbourhood. Had the Magistrates sitting at Epsom Police Court been aware of the existence of those gangs, said Mr Purchas, 'They would have arrived at a different decision.'

'Having heard the explanation', said Mr Clarke Hall, 'I shall simply order that the recognisance will be enlarged for six months.'

It was a good result, but Levy's troubles did not end there.

As has already been mentioned, Levy suffered a severe razor-slashing in 1925 at the hands of 'Dodger' Mullins, 'Monkey' Bennyworth and Co (all of whom walked away scot-free), and one year later, he was the victim of another attack in which his throat was cut by Arthur Harding (who also walked free) and Charley Horrickey. The latter was described by Harding in his usual idiot-speak as being a 'half-breed' – meaning half-Irish and half-Jewish – and 'as ignorant as hell, although 'e was never dangerous'. The Judge, who obviously took a different view to Harding's character assessment of Horrickey, sentenced him to three years' imprisonment.

Levy did find his resolve again the following year when he gave evidence against Thomas 'Wassle' Newman and Alfred Hayes, who had demanded £3 with menaces from him. Newman was regarded as a terror in the East End; a fearsome fighter, he threw housebricks into the air and punched them on their downward journey to toughen his hands. (Like 'Dodger' Mullins, he was hysterically worshipped by Reg Kray.) At the Old Bailey on 19 September 1927, Newman was sentenced to three years' penal servitude after the Judge, Sir Ernest Wild KC, was told by Detective Sergeant Farquhar that Newman 'belonged to a well-known gang which infested the East End and made a practice of blackmailing bookmakers.' 'Hayes', he added sympathetically, 'was not a member of the gang and had probably got into trouble through associating with bad characters.'

It sounded as though Sergeant Farquhar was endeavouring to recruit Hayes as a snout, and the judge postponed sentence until the next sessions, although, snout recruitment or not, it ended in tears. Two years later, Hayes was one of a gang who attacked a Flying Squad officer with an iron bar after he leapt on to the running board of a stolen car; he was sentenced to four years' penal servitude.

But that apart, Moses Levy was not getting any younger and he needed some help. He got it.

Spot and his team – which included George Wood and Teddy Machin – paid a visit to the Whites, and after Eddie Raimo was badly hurt (as was Harry White), they backed down, with Raimo deciding to take early retirement.

More confrontations followed, and in January 1947 there was a pitched battle at Al Burnett's Stork Club in Sackville Street during which 'Big Bill' Goller, one of the White gang's hardmen, had had his throat cut so severely that it was thought he would die, and Spot went into hiding. Fortunately, Goller recovered, and a soothing poultice of £300 was applied to the incision, where upon Spot miraculously reappeared.

It was decided that there would be an all-out bloody confrontation between Hill and Spot on one side and the White family and their followers on the other, at Harringay Arena on 17 April 1947; this coincided with the Baksi v Woodcock heavyweight boxing match. The only injuries sustained that night were by Bruce Woodcock, who suffered a broken jaw and a detached retina after the referee stopped the fight in the seventh round, because Detective Chief Superintendent Peter Beveridge MBE, the head of the Metropolitan Police's No. 2 Area had heard about the planned confrontation. He had the heads of both gangs into his office – separately, of course – and warned them of the inevitable consequences with the police if they went ahead with their plans. Beveridge, who had headed the Flying Squad during the war years, was tough and well-respected. The gang leaders realized the wisdom of his words and called off the feud. Hill and Spot retained the horseracing rackets, the Whites kept control of the dog racing circuits.

Hill and Spot had opened a club in Southend (it proved to be a useful bolt-hole for Spot following the Goller throat-cutting incident) and left Jackie Reynolds and Eddie Machin to run it; alas, the two men fell out and were involved in a ferocious battle which an onlooker described as being 'like two mad fucking dogs fighting'.

'Porkie' Bennett left the alliance in 1948, having received a six-month sentence for driving over his wife's legs; after a resumption of gang-related hostilities, he absented himself a little longer in 1951 after he was sentenced to eight years' preventative detention after being convicted of slashing a customer in a Chinese restaurant. Arthur Skurry – who, it was said, had a penchant for smashing his adversaries in the face with a chain – also left the gang for good when he expired aged forty-three in January 1949.

The Hill/Spot amalgamation suffered a setback when Hill was arrested for a warehousebreaking, which he swore he had never committed. Given bail, he took the opportunity to flee to South Africa, but when he returned he gave himself up and was sentenced to three years' imprisonment.

Whilst he was serving his sentence, a daring raid was carried out at the newly opened Heathrow Airport on 29 July 1948 which was said to have been orchestrated by Jack Spot.

The raid should have netted the gang goods valued at £237,900 but unfortunately, Flying Squad officers were lying in wait for them and there was a terrific punch-up, the gang using iron bars, giant wire-cutters and a broken bottle, the Squad officers relying on their truncheons; fearsome injuries were inflicted on both sides, but eventually eight of the gang lay unconscious on the warehouse floor. Not all were captured; four escaped, including Teddy Machin and Franny Daniels, a well-respected thief who had worked with Spot and Hill.

The rest of the gang later appeared at the Old Bailey, where they were sentenced to a total of 71 years' penal servitude.

Spot was, of course, questioned by police but remarked that he had lent his car to 'a couple of pals' for a night out, denied any knowledge of the planned robbery and the matter could not be pursued against him any further.

But other matters could. The police paid so much attention to his gambling club at St Botolph's Row that it eventually closed. Another matter was far more serious. When members of his gang were caught and imprisoned, Billy Hill looked after their families financially; but Spot, a notorious tightwad, did not. It was also said that his meanness extended to failing to provide support for his son from a previous marriage. It was the first crack in the Spot/ Hill/Skurry amalgamation.

However, for the time being, they continued their activities, sometimes working together, sometimes not, Hill with his clubs and assorted criminality, Spot on the racecourses, sorting out any problems and working as a debt collector, charging a fee of 50 per cent of the monies recovered.

But matters started to go downhill for Spot. His clubs were raided, he was – at least, according to Spot himself – fitted up for carrying a knife and he was also fined for attacking newspaper reporter Duncan Webb, Billy Hill's trusted biographer.

At this point, it's time to turn to some different stories of racetrack crimes which were carried out without the assistance of any of the well-known racing gangs who have been already mentioned but with the connivance of just one of their members: Albert Dimes.

CHAPTER 23

The Francasal Affair

There was always plenty of press coverage of the slashings, clubbings and shootings of the racetrack gangs, but when a racing scandal occurred in Bath during the 1950s, it caused a furore. There was no violence, although bribes were offered to influential people and there was an attempt at jury-nobbling; but these peccadilloes were par for the course.

The publicity generated was not confined to England; the news flashed around the world. India's national newspaper, *The Hindu*, dated 26 July 1953, excitedly exclaimed that 'Police in England were cutting through a tangle of false trails, bogus clubs and wrong identities' and this was no mere press hyperbole – it was a clever conspiracy, two senior Scotland Yard officers were involved in the investigation (one more so than the other) and the matter was known as 'The Francasal Affair'.

* * *

A racehorse running as Francasal, owned by a Maurice Williams, won the two o'clock Spa Selling Plate at Bath Races on 16 July 1953. It had been unplaced in five of its previous races and had finished third in a sixth; hence its odds of 10–1. Thirty minutes before the commencement of the race, enormous amounts of cash began to pour in on Francasal with bookmakers all over England, Scotland and Wales. In turn, the bookmakers attempted to hedge their bets with the bookies at Bath, which would have resulted in the starting price on Francasal being reduced. In order to do so, they would have used 'the blower', the telephone service through which the off-course bets get back to the racecourse so that starting prices reflect the money invested. The bookmakers would have been successful had the London and Provincial Sporting News Agency, which operated the blower service, not reported that all telephone communications to the racecourse had stopped at 1.30 pm. Some of the bookmakers tried to induce others to hedge their bets for them, but when those bookmakers discovered that the blower was not functioning, they tried to find yet more bookmakers with whom they could lay off some of the bets to reduce their liability.

The telephone line of the blower had been severed; it had not, as originally stated, been struck by lightning, which was the initial deduction of the telephone engineers called to repair the inch-thick cable that connected the eleven telephone circuits to Bath racecourse. In fact, that was a reasonable assumption, because there had been a thunderstorm in the area at the time and the site where the cable had been cut was underneath trees. However, a later laboratory examination revealed that the cable had been severed not by lightning but by an oxy-acetylene cutter.

So Francasal had romped home by two lengths to win the Spa Selling Plate, the winner of which was directly offered at public auction immediately after the race. But strangely, Francasal was nowhere to be seen – neither was his owner.

The National Sporting League advised the bookmakers to withhold the £250,000 which represented the punters' winnings, the Chief Constable of Bath declared that there appeared to be 'a huge racing conspiracy' and the Yard was called in.

Detective Superintendent Reginald Spooner of C1 Department was recalled from his holidays at Eastbourne to investigate the matter; Spooner had been attached to MI5 during the war and later had received sensational press publicity over his arrest of the sadistic murderer, Neville Heath. He was a skilled investigator – indeed, the press had dubbed him 'The Great Detective' – but sadly, he knew nothing about the world of horseracing. He was going into the enquiry with both hands tied behind his back, because he had never even placed a bet in his life.

Detective Chief Superintendent Ted Greeno, on the other hand, knew everything about the track, so when, on 28 January 1953, Greeno first heard that people were trying to open bookmakers' accounts all over England, he knew that a big betting fraud was afoot and told the head of the Yard's Fraud Squad of his suspicions. When and where, he did not know – but because of his expertise at the track, he did know the names of those who were likely to be involved.

Of course, Greeno would have been the ideal man to have led the investigation when the matter was reported, but for the fact that as a superintendent, Spooner was 'in the frame' to deal with difficult, complicated investigations at the behest of the Director of Public Prosecutions, and Greeno, one rank higher, was one of what were colloquially known as 'The Big Five', since he was in charge of the Metropolitan Police's No. 4 District.

Fortuitously, amongst Spooner's assistants (unusually, at the same rank) was Detective Superintendent Fred Hodge. With Spooner badly floundering, Hodge knew what to do. He had been Greeno's sergeant on the Murder Squad during the war years – together they had successfully solved seven out of seven murders – and he was naturally aware of Greeno's encyclopaedic knowledge of the world of horseracing.

So when Hodge contacted Greeno for assistance, he received first-class information; but knowing someone has carried out a crime and proving it are two entirely different matters – and Spooner and his team deserve full credit for carrying out a meticulous and enormously complex two-month investigation. During that time, 1,000 people were interviewed and 80–90 would be called as witnesses at the trial that followed. However, it was due to Greeno's significant input into the investigation that the case was cleared up far quicker than Spooner could have hoped.

It was established that during the month prior to the race, Francasal was purchased from the owner's trainer, John Swaine, in Maisons-Lafitte, near Paris, for £500. The purchaser had been introduced to Swaine as William Maurice Williams by Lieutenant Colonel Victor Dill, a bloodstock dealer; not that this had been their first transaction. Two months previously, the same men had purchased a horse – one far superior to Francasal – named Santo Amaro from the same source for £2,000.

Dill gave his address as 38 England's Lane, Hampstead; it was also an address used by Williams and it turned out to be a first-floor, one-room premises run as a bookmaking business and styled 'J. Davidson'. The business had been started by James Davidson, a greengrocer, who occupied the ground floor of the premises but had sold it on 7 March to the man he was introduced to as Williams for £200. In fact, it was a bookmaker named Harry Kateley who was masquerading as Williams; he had been accompanied by Dill, who was using his middle name, Colquhoun. It was established that £3,500 had been bet on Francasal by Dill from that office, on Williams' instructions – the name of the bookmakers remained unchanged – and still, Williams was nowhere to be found.

But Francasal and Santo Amaro were found, at the premises of a horse carrier – and the two horses were virtually identical. Identity was established after the veterinary surgeon who had examined both upon their arrival in England found that they both had contrary tufts, known as 'epis', which went against the general direction of their hair. Francasal's epis were level with his eyes; Santo Amaro had one epi on his forehead, the left epi being above the level of his left eye. These marking were congenital and continued throughout a horse's life; it was impossible for them to be altered or faked. Because Francasal was, as Swaine put it, 'a very poor performer' the horses had been switched – Santo Amaro, running as Francasal, was a 'ringer'.

Williams now appeared at the Yard with his solicitor; Spooner established that he was the owner of both horses and released him; he wanted to find out who had supplied Williams with the money for the business and the horses, and who had provided the references necessary to set up a bookmaker's business. By now, Spooner knew that, apart from having two previous convictions and serving a two-month sentence in 1944 for stealing a parcel from a railway platform, Williams had also been suspected of switching greyhounds.

Spooner discovered that some of the references had come from Williams himself, and the co-tenant at Williams' offices was Harry Kateley. Therefore, this was the chain of the conspiracy: Kateley (who had been sentenced to nine months' imprisonment in 1932 at the London Sessions for receiving a stolen car) masquerading as Williams had accompanied Dill to France to purchase the horses, thus linking him to Williams – as was another bookmaker, Gomer Charles, who had also supplied references for Williams; but there was more.

Matters were now moving very quickly; on 5 August, Leonard Phillips, a Welsh rag dealer, was arrested for cutting the blower line and was remanded. He had been traced after a passer-by had seen two men in a vehicle parked by the site of the cable-cutting and had seen a man up a ladder cutting the cable with an oxy-acetylene torch; a check on the vehicle's registration plate had resulted in Phillips' arrest. On 17 August, the rather greasy Mr Charles – he had previously been warned off all racecourses in May 1951 after his involvement in a horse-switching conspiracy had been revealed by the Jockey Club – approached a fellow bookmaker, Lord Eliot, and asked him to see the chief constable of Bath and tell him that he (Eliot) was an unofficial member of the Jockey Club. Charles further asked Eliot to request that the chief constable prosecute Phillips on the minor charge of malicious damage so that the racing scandal could be hushed up. For this, the eldest son of the 8th Earl of St Germans would receive £500; the chief constable's wife, said Charles, would receive a fur coat!

Since Eton-educated Eliot had served as a Captain in the Duke of Cornwall's Light Infantry, was a Justice of the Peace and a Deputy Lieutenant, had owned several racehorses and was due to succeed his father to become the 9th Earl of St Germans and inherit the family's estates, the belief that he would accept the offer of a 'monkey' was rather insulting. Charles had certainly backed the wrong horse there, because Eliot refused to cooperate; within ten minutes of Charles leaving, he informed Spooner, who interviewed Charles the following day.

Charles hotly denied Eliot's allegations; in fact, he told Spooner, his only involvement had been to wager £50 on Francasal. This was a lie – he had bet at least £2,500 at odds of 10–1 and had advanced Williams most of the money to purchase the book-maker's property and the horses. Furthermore, Dill had told Williams that Santo Amaro would be unbeatable in a Selling Plate race but that he wanted to make sure. It was a mistake. Williams arranged for the horse to run secretly in a trial race at 6 o'clock one morning; he was identified by the racecourse hands as having been present.

Nor was Eliot the only person to whom a bung was offered; for the dropping of certain charges against certain persons, Spooner was informed he could become £20,000 the richer. It didn't work; on 19 September, the day after Leonard Phillips was sentenced to three months' imprisonment for cutting the blower line, Williams, Charles, Kateley and Dill all appeared at Bow Street Magistrates' Court charged with two cases of conspiracy to cheat and defraud.

During the committal proceedings, the prosecution brought to the attention of the magistrate that a witness whom he proposed to call had received an anonymous letter indicating to him the evidence that he should give.

The first trial, which commenced at the Old Bailey on 12 January 1954, was abandoned after hearing sixteen days of evidence when the jury failed to agree; there had been allegations of jury-nobbling, and the twelve male members of the jury were followed from dawn to midnight by detectives. The Trial Judge, Mr Justice Sellers, was impelled to inform the jury – and not for the first time:

> I repeat to you the necessity of being most careful. If anybody speaks to you, telephones you or writes to you about anything at all connected with this case, do not fail to let me know. Keep your own counsel and do not let anybody interfere with you.

The second trial lasted twenty-three days, during which time some very dodgy evidence was produced for the defence and more attempts were made to nobble the jury; but on 17 March, after deliberating for four hours and seventeen minutes, the jury returned a verdict of guilty.

Telling Kateley, 'To my mind, you were obviously the head and front of this conspiracy', Mr Justice Byrne sentenced him to three years' imprisonment. Charles was told, 'You kept yourself well in the background, but I have not the slightest doubt that you were in this conspiracy from early days, and I have not the smallest doubt that you provided the money to buy the second horse', and he and Williams each received two years' imprisonment and were jointly ordered to pay prosecution costs of £4,500. Dill, who had been mentioned in dispatches in 1917 and awarded a Military Cross during the First World War for extinguishing a fire in an ammunition dump, was a broken man and was dealt with accordingly – nine months' imprisonment – with Mr Justice Byrne telling him, 'I am distressed to see a man such as you convicted of this offence. You were down and out and were brought into this by Kateley and Williams to give an atmosphere of respectability to it.' A fifth defendant was acquitted. The cost of the two trials was estimated at £30,000.

A month after the trial had finished, in April 1954 the Jockey Club sustained the objection to Francasal and declared the real winner to be the runner-up, Pomonaway. Furthermore, both Francasal and Santa Amaro were disqualified from racing for life, as were the four defendants. On 26 July the two horses were sold by auction at Epsom on the orders of the High Sheriff of Surrey: in less than fifteen minutes, Francasal sold for 160 guineas and San Amaro for 400 guineas.

One of the reasons why the men had been caught was their greed; if they had wagered lesser amounts they might well have got away with the scam.

It was greed that brought the downfall of Gomer Charles, although not his own; he answered the doorbell to his home at 22 Park Place, Cardiff at 9 o'clock on the evening of 11 December 1966 and was shot dead by three robbers. Two of them had previously broken into another house, where they had stolen the murder instrument, a 12-bore shotgun – they were subsequently caught and sentenced to life imprisonment. For some reason, when he opened the door, they had panicked and after shooting Charles dead, ran off, unaware that they had left behind them £25,000 in his safe.

Leonard Phillips died, as did Dill, in 1986 at the age of eighty-nine, and Kateley died aged eighty-eight in 1999.

The press heralded it as Spooner's finest case, and perhaps it was. The Magistrate, Sir Lawrence Dunne at Bow Street Magistrates' Court stated:

> I particularly wish to draw the attention of the commissioner to the work of the officers concerned in the investigation and conduct of this case. I consider it a model of what police work should be and it reflects the greatest credit on the Force and on the officers concerned.

Spooner and Hodge's names were mentioned, although not, of course, Greeno's.

It was one of those strange quirks of fate that the year following the trial, Spooner was promoted to detective chief superintendent and became head of the Flying Squad; a department that he had never served in previously. He later went on to become deputy commander.

So it's odd that Greeno retained the rank of detective chief superintendent for fourteen years (and retired with it). He had served on the Flying Squad for seventeen years in all ranks up to and including divisional detective inspector but never headed the Squad – he would have been as supremely capable as head of the Flying Squad as he would have been in charge of the Francasal affair. Instead, Greeno became a highly respected murder investigator before becoming one of 'The Big Five'.

'Mad Frankie' Fraser, fresh out of prison, was at Brighton racetrack when he was confronted by Ted Greeno and his deputy, the equally tough Detective Superintendent Bert 'Iron Man' Sparks. Greeno had received information that Fraser was going to shoot a gangland member and told him he was going to be searched. Fraser demurred, saying that Greeno would 'put something on him'.

According to Fraser, Greeno replied that it would be 'a straight search', but following an abortive examination he added, 'Next time, we may make out we've found something.' However, Greeno's account of the incident varied considerably from Fraser's.

But if one cares to accept Fraser's version of events, it was typical behaviour of the man who cleared the racecourses of the gangs by telling the leaders to 'clear off' (and punching those who didn't), and who retired in 1959, having been appointed MBE and taking with him eighty-six commissioner's commendations. Greeno had hoped to devote his retirement to his first love, the turf. When Pearl Diver won the Derby in 1947, Greeno had cleared

£5,000 – but as ever, much of it was dispersed in payments of
£25 or £50 to informants (this at a time when the going rate for
information from the Informants' Fund was 2s 6d) who brought
him the finest information. Now it was too late; cancer claimed
him and he died in 1966.

Chapter 24

The Dopers

Working on the dictum that 'there's nothing new under the sun', doping racehorses may have started as long as 2,500 years ago, when in ancient Greece, Euripides startled his fellow Athenians by informing them that some horses had been fed human flesh to make them run faster. Of course, that may have been a snippet of fake news to enhance his reputation as a tragedian. But a couple of centuries later – perhaps because any spare human flesh was used to feed the lions in the Roman amphitheatres – someone came up with the bright idea of supplying horses participating in the chariot races with hydromel, a liquor made with fermented honey and water, similar to mead. This was a risky business because anyone who was caught supplying this beverage to the animals was likely to be crucified.

In England, records show that in 1553 a stimulant (it was probably arsenic-related) was being administered to horses, and in 1812 a stable-boy was hanged on Newmarket Heath for doing just that. A specific law which prohibited horse-doping was introduced to the statute books in 1903, and in 1912 saliva tests were carried out to detect stimulants such as caffeine in a horse's system.

Doping was an offence which gained momentum in the 1960s, either to make horses run faster or to slow them down. It was considered extremely serious for three reasons: first, there was a great deal of illicit money to be made from the practice; second, the unfortunate horse in question was inevitably physically ruined; but even if it was not – and third – it was never permitted to run again, thereby losing the owner thousands of pounds. This was because, under the draconian Jockey Club rules, if after a race a horse's saliva or urine was found to contain a stimulant, its trainer's licence was automatically and immediately withdrawn, even if it could be proved beyond doubt that he was not responsible. Furthermore, the owner and the trainer were arraigned before the stewards. They were told the results of the test but that was all; no legal representation was permitted and none of the rules of evidence were observed. This practice thus spelled black ruin for both trainer and owner, as well as the horse. This disgraceful behaviour by the Jockey Club was far, far easier than taking decisive action to identify and prosecute the dopers.

When the former jockey and then trainer, Sir Gordon Richards, returned from holiday in Switzerland in April 1960 he was horrified to discover rumours, which had spread like wildfire, that members of his staff had fed stimulants to his horses. He was between a rock and a hard place; do nothing and his horses could be ruined, as well as the likelihood of any doping becoming known to the Jockey Club. Alternatively, if he made it known officially, the Jockey Club might still ban him. Sir Gordon simply could not allow himself to stand idly by; in spite of the implied risks he contacted the Jockey Club. Amazingly, they advised him to sack all his staff who had been named as being in the pay of a doping ring, and that, presumably, would be that; but Sir Gordon could not bring himself to take such arbitrary action and instead, he contacted Scotland Yard.

Fortunately, this was not done through official channels; had it been, it would have been referred to C1 Department and the next detective superintendent who was 'in the frame' would have been sent; and that officer might well have been as uninformed as Spooner had been when he was sent to investigate the Francasal case.

Therefore, the 'old boy network'[1] was utilized, corners were cut, contacts were consulted and, as a result, Detective Inspector Bill Baldock and Detective Sergeant Terry O'Connell of the Flying Squad were sent; they could not have been a better choice. As a wartime police constable, Baldock had been awarded a BEM for meritorious service during the Blitz, prior to volunteering for four years' wartime service with the Army's Special Investigation Branch. Before his thirty years' police service came to an end with the rank of detective superintendent, he was commended time and again for arresting gangs of armed robbers as well as criminals described as 'dangerous, cunning, persistent, violent and troublesome'.

This was the first of three postings to the Flying Squad totalling ten years for O'Connell (later Commander O'Connell QPM), who had cut his teeth on racetrack gangs and dips, working the courses at Liverpool, Ascot, Cheltenham and Goodwood.

Discreet investigations were carried out at race meetings and stables all over the country, and the name which kept cropping up

---

[1] Of which the author was a fully paid-up member.

was the same one that Sir Gordon had passed on to the officers; that of Bertie 'Bandy' Rogers.

Enquiries revealed that 66-year-old Rogers, a former trainer, had had an interesting career. In 1950 he had been strongly suspected of horse-doping and horse-ringing and had been investigated by the police, but there had been insufficient evidence to prosecute him. The same happened in 1953; he had been responsible for switching the two horses prior to the race at Bath, keeping hold of Francasal while its alter ego, Santo Amaro, went off to the racetrack to win. Then in 1954, together with a chemist's assistant, he had been investigated by West Riding Police regarding allegations of horse-doping in the Wetherby area. It was believed that the two men were associated with two crooked bookmakers and a professional big-time punter. But within a few days of that interview, the chemist was found dead; it was believed to be suicide, and although the matter was referred to the Director of Public Prosecutions, the investigation was dropped. In 1959, Rogers found another chemist from whom he hoped to obtain drugs to dope horses; then he, too, died. But more than that, Rogers was a garrulous and, in drink, boastful character, telling people at the local pub how 'his powders' provided him with winners. He might have been regarded as an eccentric had it not been for the fact that in his wallet, which he ostentatiously flourished, was crammed about £1,000 in £5 and £10 notes.

Rogers – who had been seen clandestinely meeting a glamorous looking couple, the woman described as 'a beautiful French blonde' – had his spirits dampened about a month prior to his interview with the Yard detectives. Two men arrived at his cottage – one of them was named 'Joe' – and Rogers drove off with them in their car. When he returned, hours later, he was covered in blood and bruises.

'He had a lump the size of an egg on his temple', commented his landlord, Alan Prior.

Baldock and O'Connell decided to first interview Bert Hamlin Woodage on 19 April 1960, and it was a good choice. Woodage, who was Sir Gordon's second stable jockey, admitted giving a number of stimulants to horses to enable them to win and told the officers that he had obtained the drugs from Rogers.

'Yes', he told the detectives, 'I have given one or two.'

That was sufficient to question Rogers the same day.

'When I searched his cottage', O'Connell told me, 'I found a hypodermic syringe with what later proved to be horse's blood on it, a quantity of caffeine and a bunch of letters from stable lads, including Woodage. There was much reference to horses and dope.'

Taken to Marlborough police station, Rogers made a series of admissions, naming Harry Tuck, a chemist's dispenser from Hednesford, Hertfordshire as his supplier. Edmond Murphy, a 28-year-old stable lad, was brought in and confronted with Rogers who, he eventually admitted, had given him powders. Rogers was released on bail, but the following morning, his lifeless body was found at the back door of his cottage. He had been shot, and although the local coroner recorded a verdict of suicide, there were those who thought there was very much more to the cause of death, suggesting it was something other than self-administered.

Nevertheless, with Rogers' confession and the twenty-five incriminating letters, the Squad men now had a template for other arrests. Two days after Rogers' interview, the officers interviewed Harry Tuck, who admitted sending Rogers caffeine in dosages for the odd horse, then in bulk, over a period of years, knowing precisely what it was going to be used for.

Caffeine is a stimulant, but only if it is injected into the horse between half an hour and two hours before a race. If it is administered six hours or more before a race it becomes a depressant and has the opposite effect, slowing the horse down.

On 26 April, Robert Mason, a stable employee, was interviewed and he admitted obtaining caffeine from Rogers and administering it to five horses, telling the officers, 'Yes. It's no use. I cannot tell a lie.'

Two days later, James Boyce, an unemployed stable lad, was spoken to. His initial response was a complete denial, either of knowing Rogers or of administering powders to horses under his control; but confronted with the incriminating letters he had written, he admitted giving powders to two horses, although it was felt that he had doped more than just two.

To tremendous press coverage, simultaneous arrests were carried out on 5 July 1960, the warrants alleging that the prisoners had conspired with Bertie Rogers and other persons unknown to administer drugs to horses so as to affect their performance in different horse races, and thereby to cheat and defraud owners of horses running in those races and such bookmakers and others that should make bets on the results of those races.

After appearing at Newbury Magistrates' Court, the men were committed to stand trial at Gloucestershire Assizes, commencing on 25 October 1960.

Sir Gordon Richards gave evidence, praising Woodage as 'a first-class worker' and saying he would not have believed it if anyone had told him that Woodage would do anything to harm a horse. Apart from the rumours that had prompted the investigation, he knew nothing of his horses being fed stimulants, telling the court that, 'Good food, good hay and good oats are the things to make a horse go.'

But although the trial Judge, Mr Justice Barry, discharged stable lad Edmond Murphy halfway through the trial, the weight of the evidence against the others was far too heavy, and on 31 October 1960 the four men were found guilty, with the Judge telling them:

> It is indeed a disaster that you have allowed yourselves to become involved in, what I am afraid, was obviously a quite widespread fraudulent scheme to tamper with the racehorses. It is a scheme and a practice which, if it were allowed to go unchecked would undermine, as you all know quite well, the whole integrity and cleanness of the sport, which such a large number of people in this country are interested in. You know quite well that you were running a very grave risk, not only so far as yourselves were concerned but also placing your employers in very considerable jeopardy. It is a most painful thing to impose prison sentences on men such as you, but I have to uphold my duty to the public, and I have to make it clear to all those who might be tempted to indulge in these practices that they cannot go unpunished.

Woodage and Tuck each were sentenced to eighteen months' imprisonment, with the two stable lads, Boyce and Mason, being sentenced to nine and six months, respectively.

Several matters arose out of this. This is one of the very few cases recounted in this book where there was no attempt to bribe or threaten witnesses, or to tamper with the jury. The reason is clear. All of the defendants were of good character and they could not implicate anyone further up the line, simply because they did not know whom to implicate. They had all been tools of 'Bandy' Rogers, and with him dead – and Rogers could certainly have named quite a number of others – the chain was broken. Equally, no pressure was brought to bear by the ringleaders on the jury or witnesses in order to exculpate the four defendants. Why on earth should they? The defendants were disposable; in other words, tough luck.

But Rogers *had* been a threat. So why had he received the beating, one month before his interview by the police? The answer was revealed during the trial. Rogers had distributed his powders to a large number of stable lads, telling them which horses to administer the caffeine to, then had told those further up the chain which horses to back. But a number of the stable lads gave evidence for the prosecution that they had *not* administered the powders; they had thrown them away. However, Rogers and his associates had not known that, and when the horses they had backed at Rogers' suggestion failed to win, they suspected him of treachery or incompetence or both; hence the beating. And following Rogers' one and only interview with the police, that was when his lifeless body was found. Was it suicide – the official verdict by the Berkshire Coroner, Mr N. B. Challenor – or something more sinister? Had someone decided to shut Rogers' garrulous trap for ever?

And who were the glamorous couple whom Rogers had met – especially the seductive French blonde? And who was the mysterious 'Joe' who had been present when Rogers was driven off to become the recipient of a thorough bashing?

Nobody knew, then; but we're just about to find out.

CHAPTER 25

'A Beautiful French Blonde'

In exhibiting great moral courage by bringing the matter right out into the open, Sir Gordon had done the racing industry an enormous favour; it led to the harsh rules which had been set up by the Jockey Club being relaxed. But there was a backlash; now trainers were encouraged to report cases of doping to the Jockey Club, who in turn referred them to the police. There were so many, however, that the police refused to investigate them all.

Therefore the racing industry set up its own research establishment with its own investigator – former Flying Squad officer, ex-Detective Superintendent Bob Anderson – at Newmarket. He wisely arranged for two dope tests to be carried out at each meeting, the horses concerned being chosen by lot; in addition, security at the racecourse stables was intensified.

Stimulants to improve a horse's performance came in several types: a glucose solution could be injected into the horse minutes before a race, or anabolic steroids could be administered. However, given the upsurge in racecourse security, these methods would present difficulties to the dopers.

Therefore, as that door to criminality was closed, another was opened; the dopers decided to target the trainer's own stables prior to the races being run; and like all good conspiracies, these were carried out under cover of darkness.

* * *

A far more sophisticated method to improve a horse's performance was blood doping. Two days before a race, the stables would be infiltrated by the gang and 5–7 pints of the horse's blood would be drawn off. In a few hours, the horse's metabolism would naturally make up the deficiency. But 24 hours before a race, the blood would be re-injected into the horse; its blood count would thus be raised by 5 per cent and the animal would be bursting with energy and able to knock seconds off its performance. It was a clever ruse, especially since no drugs had been administered, but quite obviously, because it required a double intrusion into the stables, not without its risks.

The same hazards applied to the dopers who wished to retard a horse's performance. To administer a depressant involved at least two members of the gang entering the stables at night, one of them calming and pacifying the horse whilst the other inserted the dope into the horse's mouth using a method known as 'balling'. Forcing the horse's mouth open, the doper would grasp the animal's tongue with one gloved hand, twisting it and forcing the tongue between the horse's teeth to protect the doper's hand, in order that the dope might be inserted into the animal's mouth.

The ball – or 'bolus' – consisted of ground-up tablets, one variety being a depressant called Notensil, a quantity of which had been stolen from the West Park Mental Institute, Epsom. It could be used, carefully, under veterinary supervision to calm fractious animals, although it was stipulated that it should not be dispensed to horses within four days of racing. Since those administering the drug were not veterinarians and were directing all their energies to slowing the horse down, that really was not their concern.

With the unfortunate animal's tongue forced between its teeth, the bolus would be inserted into the side of the horse's mouth (and as far back as possible) before being pushed down its throat. If it was not swallowed immediately, water could be offered to the horse as an inducement, and if that failed, a stick would be used to poke the bolus down.

The gang member holding the horse's head would often apply a head collar and try to stop the animal raising its head too high. In order to do so, a piece of string or rope – known as a twitch – was used to divert the horse's attention.

The crumbled tablets were wrapped in tissue paper and bound with sticky tape or rubber bands so that the outer casing of the ball would gradually liquefy in the horse's stomach. The more tissue that was used, the longer the bolus would take to dissolve. It became an art form; over time, gangs were able to judge exactly how much tissue was required for it to dissolve just prior to the commencement of the race. The materials binding the bolus would be assimilated (and disposed of) in the animal's faeces.

The purpose of doping a favourite would be to prevent it winning or being placed, thereby affecting the betting. Large sums would be placed in forecast betting, eliminating the favourite, and at the same time the gang informed dishonest bookmakers, who could then lay off on the favourite.

And this was the method used by the gang which included 'the beautiful French blonde', the man named 'Joe' and a number of other shady characters.

⋆   ⋆   ⋆

The beautiful young woman who introduced herself as Mlle Rosemarie Laumaine was neither French nor a blonde. Her real name was Micheline Emilienne Lugeon, and she was Swiss and a brunette. She arrived at stables in a black Ford Zephyr saloon, exquisitely dressed and having donned a blonde wig, and used her beauty, charisma and captivating accent to charm stable boys into permitting her to inspect the horses in their stables – in the absence of the owners. Mlle Laumaine expressed surprise that the owners were not there (she knew, of course, that they would be absent), but because she was on such friendly, almost intimate terms with the owners, she felt sure that they would not object; and since she seemed to know so much about them, the stable boys felt quite confident in permitting her to inspect the horses as well. The reason given by Mlle Laumaine was that she was a French racehorse owner and she was looking for somewhere to place her horses; stables such as those owned by Lord Rosebery and the Queen Mother's trainer, Major Peter Cazalet.

And as she inspected one horse after another, stroking their muzzles and murmuring compliments in a beguiling accent, while the stable boys, eyes aglow, panted admiringly after her, no one seemed to notice her smartly dressed chauffeur, who dutifully followed in her footsteps making copious notes. Only he wasn't a chauffeur. His name was William John Roper, he was a wealthy bookmaker known as 'Mr Racing', he was as dodgy as they come and despite a 31-year age difference, he was Mlle Lugeon's lover.

As the gleaming black Ford Zephyr drove off, with the seductive French lady saucily waving goodbye, the stable lads could hardly wait for the owner to return and tell them how helpful and accommodating they had been to their employer's 'friend'. Only when the dust had settled from the explosion of rage on the part of the owner, who had never heard of Mlle Laumaine, did they realize, as they clutched their P45s and sought employment elsewhere, that everything had not been as it seemed.

Using this subterfuge, Roper and his mistress visited twenty-one stables in forty-one days and obtained an awful amount of useful information.

From the doping side came Edward 'Teddy' Smith, who worked at a chemist's factory together with Richard McGee; he stole quantities of soporific drugs, including one called Luminal. A jockey, Emmanuel Lipman Leonard 'Darkie' Steward, and his friend, Brian Perry, met Smith; Steward wanted Smith to get drugs to enable a horse to win – which it did.

Two more were introduced into the group: Edward Dyer, a bookmaker, and Joe Lowry – the 'Joe' referred to previously – a distinctly dodgy character and the possessor of twelve previous convictions, including a three-year sentence for officebreaking. It was Lowry's job to befriend susceptible stable boys and jockeys; it was Smith's job to make up the constituent parts of the bolus. Steward administered the 'twitch' to the horse while holding its head; on one occasion, he was not wholly successful and his hand was severely bitten, although by now the number of readers who might feel any sympathy for the injuries inflicted on Steward is probably minimal.

In spite of a string of successes, matters sometimes went awry; on one occasion the bolus was defective (or wasn't administered at all), which resulted in a tremendous loss for the dodgy bookmakers, Albert Dimes included.

A nephew (also a bookmaker) of Edward Dyer similarly got his fingers seriously burned. His name was Charlie Mitchell, he had been involved in doping greyhounds and he was a very dangerous character, who had served periods of Borstal Training and imprisonment. He also possessed a hair-trigger temper. He blamed Steward for the mishap and dished out a savage beating; it's not beyond the bounds of possibility that he was the author of Bandy Rogers' misfortunes.

What brought about the collapse of the gang was a mixture of greed and stupidity.

There were three runners in the last race at Lewes in August 1962: Countess, Lucky Seven and Dear Jac. It was Countess, the favourite, who came in last, by ten lengths, over the mile-and-a-quarter track; Dear Jac (who had never raced before) came second at odds of 20–1; but it was the second favourite, Lucky Seven, who won, by four lengths.

Countess had been well and truly doped the previous night, and Roper and Co had been at the course placing bets for their duped clients on Countess, shortening the odds from 4–6 to 4–11; at the same time, Lucky Seven's odds improved from 7–4 to 11–4. The gang had bet on the forecast as well: Lucky Seven to beat Dear Jac; and Roper and his associates, including Charlie Mitchell and Albert Dimes, had made a mint of money. But the credit offices of some of London's biggest bookmakers discovered that large sums of money had been phoned through just when Lucky

Seven's starting price had reached 11–4, one of which had been from Roper's office.

So that was the greed aspect of their downfall; the stupidity was provided by Teddy Smith. Like the dope-administering Bandy Rogers, he was garrulous and boastful in drink, telling customers in pubs that he was known as 'The Witch Doctor' due to his ability to dope horses. When arrested on 8 August 1962, he was in possession of drugs for horse-doping (including a bolus), and when his home was searched, a quantity of luminal sodium, methyl amphetamine and Tramcopal tablets, sufficient to have stopped 600 horses in their tracks, was discovered.

Steward and McGee were arrested the same day (others in the gang were more difficult to trace) and after appearing at Brighton Magistrates' Court they were committed in custody at the end of November to stand their trial at Brighton Quarter Sessions, on charges of conspiracy to defraud.

The trial was fixed to start on 31 December 1962 and one thing was clear. Smith's verbosity was not confined to the pub; he had sung like a bird, he had implicated everybody he could possibly think of and he was going to turn Queen's Evidence. It would be another ten years before the 'Supergrass' system came into being, but the effect was much the same. By turning Queen's Evidence (or 'QE' as it was more popularly known) and testifying against his contemporaries, Smith was pretty well guaranteed to get a reduced sentence.

That might well have been the case, had Smith not fallen from the prison's top-floor landing, the day before the trial started. 'The Witch Doctor' would never beguile his audience again; forty-two days later, he died of his injuries.

Despite Smith's enforced absence, the trial did go ahead on that New Year's Eve, with Steward pleading not guilty and McGee pleading guilty to five counts of theft of drugs, for which he was sentenced to six months' imprisonment, and eighteen months, consecutive, for conspiracy to cheat and defraud.

Owen Stable, for the prosecution, told the jury of nine men and three women:

> You may have seen in this morning's press something about the man, Edward Smith. I mention that only to invite you to entirely dismiss from your minds anything you may have seen about him in this morning's newspapers and bear in mind that you are solely concerned in this matter with the trial of Stewart.

When Steward appeared in the witness box he did not fare very well. In cross-examination he admitted the names of the people who had paid him for racing tips – all save one. Asked who had paid him £100 for information, Steward twice refused to answer, until he finally, unwillingly, told the court, 'His name was Albert Dimes.'

On 7 January 1963, Steward was found guilty of conspiring with McGee and Smith to procure drugs. Steward's barrister, Mr Montague Sherborne, submitted that 'The villains of the conspiracy are still not in the dock' and added that his client was 'in a very great state of fear, not only for himself but for members of his family'.

The Recorder, Mr Charles Doughty QC, told Steward:

> I accept that you were only a tool in a highly organized business, which is quite capable of threatening and obviously has threatened witnesses. I also accept that there are people – a person or persons – who must be bookmakers, who are behind all this.

Steward was then sentenced to four years' corrective training.[1]

Following the sentence, the court was addressed by a barrister, Mr John Alliot, who stated that he had been instructed by a Mr Albert Dimes, who, he said, 'denies categorically any complicity in this matter at all'.

'What is his occupation?' asked the Recorder and was told that Dimes was a bookmaker.

'I have heard what you have said', replied the Recorder and then, his tongue firmly in his cheek, added, 'Perhaps your client can assist the police. He will, no doubt, be able to help the police in any way he can.'

However, on 30 July 1963, the Court of Criminal Appeal quashed Steward's conviction. So Darkie Steward was free once more – for the time being, at least – but during the intervening period, the same hand of fate that had plucked him from his cell at Wormwood Scrubs had gathered in the rest of the gang.

---

[1] Under the Criminal Justice Act, 1948, if a person over the age of twenty-one was convicted of an offence punishable with two years' imprisonment or more, and having been convicted on two occasions since the age of seventeen, they could be sentenced to corrective training for a period of not less than two years and not more than four.

CHAPTER 26

Intimidation and Retribution

Roper was arrested on 27 May 1963, swiftly followed by Mitchell, Lowry and Dyer; by 24 June, Field and Perry had also been arrested. During the committal proceedings at Brighton Magistrates' Court, Field's girlfriend was accused of interfering with a witness, a claim she hotly denied. The suggestion was that the witness referred to was May Kibble, the partner of the late Edward Smith who had testified that she had seen Roper and Mitchell regularly visit Smith's premises where the horse-doping drugs were kept. On 11 July, the defendants were committed in custody to Sussex Assizes for trial.

Eleven days later, Micheline Lugeon (who had been known to her landlords as 'Mrs Bell') was arrested and taken to Brighton Magistrates' Court, where she was remanded in custody for one week. On 2 October 2019, the trial of William Roper, Charlie Mitchell, Joe Lowry, Jackie Dyer, Alex Field, Brian Perry and Micheline Lugeon, all charged with conspiracy to defraud by administering drugs to racehorses to affect their performance, commenced. The Judge was Mr Justice Melford Stevenson, and once more, Owen Stable was the prosecutor.

It was at the end of the prosecution's case that May Kibble gave evidence, which was in complete contradiction to the testimony she had given at the Magistrates' Court; now, not only could she not identify Charlie Mitchell as being at Smith's house, she was also unable to recognize him.

Joe Lowry denied any knowledge or involvement in horse-doping; indeed, he told the court, 'I don't believe there was any doping going on. It was all sensational paper talk.'

When Stable showed Lowry a piece of paper with Albert Dimes' name written on it and asked if he knew him – this was not shown to the jury, nor was the name mentioned in court – Lowry replied that he did, and added, '"The King of the Underworld" tried to cut him up. He defended himself, got tried and was acquitted.'

There would have been very few jury members who were unaware that the 'King' referred to was Jack Spot or that the name on the paper was that of Albert Dimes.

Micheline Lugeon, cross-examined, was asked if she could explain why horses in different parts of the country – Freshwinds, Irish Honour and Bronze Warrior were mentioned – were found doped after she had visited their stables.

'I would not know', she replied. 'I do not know anything about doping', and added, 'You are trying to cover the dirty work of stable boys and trainers.'

Owen Stable brought up the name of Bronze Warrior again when he cross-examined Bill Roper, asking him if he could account for the fact that one of the prosecution witnesses had seen his co-accused, Lugeon, looking carefully at the horse which had been doped, at Kelso races. To this Roper replied, 'I could not do so.'

Referring to the vast quantity of dope found in Smith's house, Stable asked if it was obvious that he was 'selling dope to dopers?' and Roper replied, 'I would know nothing about it.'

Field denied knowing anything about the doping of horses 'from first to last', and Mitchell said nothing at all, never venturing into the witness box.

Summing up, the Judge told the jury:

> It would not be a surprise if any respect or sympathy you feel
> in this case were strictly confined to the horses . . . There are a
> number of witnesses – using my words carefully – who may not
> have inspired your respect, much less your admiration. You have
> got to form your own assessment of these witnesses.

It was a typical Melford Stevenson address to a jury, and on 30 October, the twentieth day of a trial which had heard testimony from 121 witnesses, the jury retired for four hours before returning verdicts of guilty on all of the defendants. Exempting the jury from further service for the rest of their lives, the Judge sentenced 26-year-old Lugeon to twelve months' imprisonment, telling her:

> I have not any doubt that you lent yourself to this wicked
> conspiracy but you have made use of a generous endowment
> of charm and intelligence which could have been turned to
> account in honest work, to embark on this disgraceful course of
> fraudulent conduct.

Bill Roper received an unwelcome fifty-eighth birthday present when he got the heaviest sentence of three years' imprisonment, the Judge telling him:

> It is perfectly obvious that you were the brains behind this plot.
> You organized all that was done and you were quick to see and
> turn to profit every opportunity that presented itself to you,

to corrupt those who were corruptible and you succeeded in corrupting a very large number of people. You used a strong intelligence to obtain that result and behind it all there was the motive of most unpleasant greed.

Mitchell, Lowry and Dyer were each sentenced to two years' imprisonment, Field got twelve months' imprisonment to run consecutively to a five-year sentence for housebreaking which had been passed on him at Stoke-on-Trent Quarter Sessions in May 1962 and Brian Perry was placed on probation for two years.

As the prisoners were led away to commence their prison terms they failed to hear Mr John Elton, the barrister for Lugeon, tell the Judge, 'I have been instructed by Mr Albert Dimes, the London bookmaker, to make it clear that he is in no way connected to the doping conspiracy.' This announcement was greeted by Melford Stevenson with a silence that was more arctic than frosty.

Before we go on to the next horse-doping case, Charlie Mitchell, who had so little to say in court, should be mentioned again. In February 1964, he successfully appealed his conviction and, like 'Darkie' Steward, became a free man once more. But in August 1965, the Flying Squad began investigating allegations of greyhound doping from December 1964 onwards, and in January 1966 Mitchell was one of six people arrested. The trial at the Old Bailey came to an abrupt halt on 25 April 1966 when a prosecution witness admitted giving perjured evidence, having received £390 'to get Charlie Mitchell off'. On 14 May, two of the defendants were each sentenced to five years' imprisonment, but Mitchell was not one of them; he was one of three defendants who were acquitted.

When the Kray firm was arrested on 8 May 1968, one of their number was Charlie Mitchell, who was charged with five offences of fraudulent transactions. Detective Superintendent Leonard 'Nipper' Read, in charge of the investigation, was not particularly surprised that Mitchell had nothing to say; he was flabbergasted when Mitchell later asked to see him, telling him that the twins had tasked him with gathering together £50,000 to provide payment to a New York contract killer to murder both Read and his No. 1 prosecution witness, Leslie Payne. It sounded rather improbable, but enquiries were made which revealed that what Mitchell had said was absolutely accurate. Unsurprisingly, Mitchell became Read's No. 2 prosecution witness, and 'The Firm's' jaws dropped collectively when the Magistrate at Bow Street Court was informed of this and Mitchell stepped out of the dock and into the witness box.

After the twins were weighed off (by Mr Justice Melford Stevenson) for thirty years, and those who appeared in the dock with them for substantial sentences, Mitchell was provided with an armed minder, Detective Constable Hugh Parker (who told me, 'The six-month period was an education you could not buy'). But by 1971 the protection had lapsed, and when someone blasted a sawn-off shotgun at him from a passing car outside his address at Ellerby Street, Fulham, Mitchell was fortunate to escape with his life. There was a rumour that Ronnie Kray had ordered Mitchell's demise, but whether it was true or not, a little later it must have come as welcome news to Ronnie's rapidly disintegrating mind in Broadmoor that his adversary had come to a violent end, many miles away in Marbella.

So much for Charlie Mitchell; but we've not yet finished with 'Darkie' Steward or Joe Lowry, nor a few other horse doping ne'er-do-wells.

* * *

By 17 September 1965 Terry O'Connell was a detective inspector attached to the Flying Squad, and it was on that night that an observation was carried out at Collingridge stables, Lambourn, West Berkshire.

O'Connell had received reliable information that a horse named Spare Filly, who was entered as the favourite at odds of 6–4 in a five-horse race at Kempton Park the following day, was going to be doped. Three of the other horses in the race were regarded as 'no-hopers', but if Whisky Poker (regarded as a racing certainty if Spare Filly was stopped) won, the gang stood to collect £50,000.

A Flying Squad team staked out the area; at either end of the yard were the east and west gates, with the stables accommodating twenty-two horses, including Spare Filly, but as O'Connell told me:

> We arrived at the stables in the dark, there was little time to make an appraisal and the layout of the buildings and the surrounding neighbourhood was completely strange. The stables were surrounded by a paddock, which made the observation very difficult to keep and the weather that night could not have been worse – rain and a strong gale.

Three hours passed and then, at 2 o'clock in the morning, two cars arrived, a two-tone Ford Zephyr and a blue Hillman, which parked 100 yards from the stables; three men got out. There was some conversation, the man in the Hillman said, 'Half an hour' and the car drove off. The three men climbed over the east gate, and the officers heard the sound of a bolt being drawn and saw the light come on in Spare Filly's stable. The officers crept forward to see 'Darkie' Steward about to put a head collar on the horse. Next to him was a taxi driver named John Barnham, who was holding a stick. Also holding a stick and standing outside the stable was a man named James Cronin; he was carrying a milk bottle filled with water. The Squad men closed in but were spotted. Cronin shouted, 'Hold it – there's someone coming!' and then a terrific fight ensued. Barnham had been a professional featherweight boxer, and although his last bout had been ten years earlier, he had lost none of his pugilistic skills. Unfortunately, his opponents on this occasion included Detective Sergeant Pat Sugrue, a very tough character, and Terry O'Connell, the 6 feet 1½ inch former Royal Marine, whose fighting skills had been honed during wartime service with 45 Commando. The result was that Barnham was well and truly subdued.

Steward lashed out at Detective Sergeant George Garbutt with the horse collar and escaped but he was arrested the following day; he had been living in the same house as the late Edward Smith's paramour, May Kibble.

Cronin dashed off across the fields with Detective Constable Peter Goldworthy in hot pursuit. He caught up with him, hit Cronin on the head with his truncheon, then seized him, but he struggled free. Goldworthy chased him once more and grabbed hold of him but then slipped and fell; Cronin ran off into the darkness and disappeared.

Two packets of dope balls were found at the scene; one contained the equivalent of twenty crushed Notensil tablets, the other, sixty. To slow Spare Filly's performance, only ten would have been needed.

'Don't blame that on me', said Barnham (who had originally told the officers he had gone to the stables 'for a kip') and, asked what he meant by that remark, replied, 'Honestly Guv, I don't know. One of the other fellows brought it with him.'

The observation resumed, and soon the Hillman reappeared. It was being followed by a police car and Detective Sergeant Jack Keane's Squad car, which had been parked on the forecourt of a public house, drove into the road and blocked the Hillman. Inside it, together with two balls containing Notensil, scissors and a rubber hammer was none other than Joe Lowry. The significance of the hammer was that it was used to crush the Notensil tablets; a similar one was found at Barnham's address.

With the best will in the world, 52-year-old Lowry could only be described as a whiner. 'Oh, dear – this is bad', he told Keane. 'It's those bloody trainers and jocks you ought to be after. Those are the people you ought to get your hands on. They have a licence to do what I'm doing. I'm not a murderer. No one gets hurt. I'm getting too old for villainy.'

It is possible that he realized that these protestations were making not the slightest impression on Keane, because now he started grovelling. 'Give me a bit of help if you can, Guv', he begged. 'Don't be too hard, will you?'

Since Lowry had only been released from his two-year sentence thirteen months previously, he needed all the help he could get. He was rapidly being transformed into a tragic figure; en route to Newbury police station, Barnham asked, 'How many of us have you got?' and when he was told that Lowry had been arrested, he sorrowfully replied, 'Poor old Joe, the poor old fellow.'

Not, however, as tragic as all that; charged with conspiring to administer drugs to racehorses, at one of the remands at Newbury Magistrates' Court, Mr W. J. Wood from the Director of Public Prosecutions office told the bench that threats had been made against the police officers, adding, 'I do not know whether it was on the instruction of the accused, or not' – and that was pretty well guaranteed to keep them in custody until their trial at Berkshire Assizes which commenced on 31 January 1966 and at which the three men all pleaded not guilty.

The night before their arrest, Barnham stated, he and Lowry were in the notorious Log Cabin Club in Wardour Street, where they were chatting to the flyweight boxing champion, Terry Spinks. A friend of the Kray twins, Spinks would be of assistance when, later that year, Frank 'The Mad Axeman' Mitchell was murdered. Among those said to be responsible was one Ronnie Olliffe, but that couldn't be true, said Spinks, because they had been drinking together in the Log Cabin at the time of the murder. Despite Spinks' diminutive size, it's what's known as having high friends in low places.

Lowry denied making the incriminating statements and said they had been set up by someone wanting to claim the £500 reward that the Jockey Club had offered for dopers. But on 8 February, the jury of ten men and two women took two hours to find the men guilty and Mr Justice Veale told them:

> You three men have all been convicted on the clearest possible evidence. Each of you has told a pack of lies on dope and you have instructed your counsel to attack the police. Of course,

I do not sentence you for the perjury you have committed but the nature of your defence does not encourage leniency. This kind of offence is becoming too common. It is a serious matter and it must be stopped. Not only you but others who are minded to behave as you have behaved must be made to realize that severe punishment will follow.

Joe Lowry (whose convictions dated back to 1930) received a five-year sentence, with Barnham and Steward each being sentenced to four years' imprisonment.

Cronin escaped to Eire but a few years later, he injudiciously returned to visit a West End club, where he was recognized by O'Connell, and at Oxfordshire Assizes on 19 November 1969 he pleaded guilty to conspiracy to cheat and defraud and received a two-year suspended sentence.

As for Spare Filly, who ran as planned and drug-free at Kempton Park the day after the arrests, she was beaten fairly and squarely into second place by Whisky Poker.

And on the night of the observation, Terry O'Connell had hoped that, when the gang turned up, one of them would be Charlie Mitchell, who was known to be deeply involved in the plot; but why would he need to, when he had a bunch of mugs – albeit talented ones in the realm of horse-doping – to do the dirty work for him?

★   ★   ★

It's now time to return to the more conventional racetrack gangs; and in particular, Albert Dimes.

CHAPTER 27

The Fall and Rise of Dimes

C hain-smoking Albert Dimes was a fixer. He organized bare-knuckle fights in a field at Epsom between gypsies and his own men; he also had under his control a venal doctor who for a fee could get young men exempted from the necessity of performing National Service. Those who wanted to work on the docks needed 'a docker's ticket' – Dimes supplied them with that commodity and also fenced gear which had been stolen before it passed through customs.

Spot had for some time paid £300 for pitches at racecourses, keeping one for himself and letting out the others for a fee to various bookmakers. This was not acceptable to Dimes, who had sided with Hill and who told him, 'This is your final warning – I don't want you to go away racing any more!'

Trouble had been brewing since the summer of 1955. Although Spot and Billy Hill, the self-proclaimed 'Boss of Britain's Under-world', had been in partnership for ten years, there had been a falling-out and Hill was seen at the Derby in company with Dimes, Bert Marsh, Johnny Ricco and Tommy Falco. It was simply so that Hill could show his solidarity with Dimes.

Jack Spot was there, too, and he had hired the Kray twins, Reg and Ron, in case of trouble. But if there had been all-out gang warfare, it would have led to police intervention. Spot wanted to avoid trouble, and the twins sensed this and quickly came to despise him. In fact, they transferred their allegiance to Billy Hill, whom they all but worshipped.

In undermining Spot's authority and credibility, Hill put the word about that Spot was a grass (which might well have been true), but Eddie Chapman, the wartime secret agent who had aligned himself with Hill during a larcenous trip to Tangier, went too far when he suggested that a venal cop had showed them Spot's file from the Yard and that his informing 'was for all to see'. This was nonsense. Informants' true identities were never recorded on their criminal record files, or anywhere else at the Yard. It was simply a boast to credulous listeners that (a) they had a crooked cop in their pockets and (b) this was proof positive that Spot was a grass.

At the August Epsom meeting when the Apprentices' Derby was run, Dimes moved one of his bookmakers on to the pitch belonging to Spot, who moved him off it. It was Bert Marsh who demanded that Spot hand over control of the pitches, and the police intervened, but it was only postponing the inevitable. In fact, Bert Marsh was in charge of the Italian faction, and it was suggested that he had wound up Dimes to provoke a confrontation with Spot. If that was the case, it was successful.

There was a fight between Dimes and Spot in Frith Street, Soho on 11 August 1955; both were badly injured, with Spot suffering facial wounds, over his left eye and to his left cheek, ear and neck, as well as four cuts to his arm, plus two to his chest, one of which penetrated a lung. Dimes was equally badly damaged: the six-inch wound to his forehead had penetrated to the bone and required twenty stitches, and he received two stab wounds, one to his stomach, the other to his thigh, as well as lacerations to his chin and thumb.

Both were prosecuted for causing an affray and were remanded in custody.

After two trials, both Spot and Dimes were found not guilty. Spot rather illogically feared reprisals from Hill and Dimes; but there was no need. Dimes had been acquitted and now he and Bert Marsh had control of the racetracks, whilst Hill had his clubs and, with two enormous heists of a few years previously, had no further financial problems. Therefore, it was the height of foolishness at Christmas 1955 for Spot to contract his bodyguard, Joe Cannon, and two others to shoot Hill and Dimes. The plot fizzled out, but Hill and Dimes heard about it and decided such *lèse-majesté* could not go unpunished. It led to a savage attack on Jack Spot, in the presence of his wife, and although Hill and Dimes were identified by Spot's wife as being two of the attackers, they were impressively alibied and were never charged. Although Spot refused to give evidence, his wife was made of sterner stuff, and several of Spot's assailants were successfully prosecuted. In revenge, Spot was framed, in a very amateurish way, for cutting Tommy Falco, who was backed up by Johnny Ricco. It was not one of Hill's better thought-out plans; he and Dimes were called by the prosecution to the Old Bailey to deny that they had directed that Falco should be wounded so that Spot could be blamed ('Was it likely that they would come forward and say there *was* a frame-up?' asked Spot's barrister), and Spot quite rightly was acquitted. Nevertheless, he continued to slide, and when he failed to pay the £732 in costs and damages demanded by the High Court after Duncan Webb successfully sued Spot for attacking him, bankruptcy proceedings were instituted. Spot provided a statement of his affairs which showed liabilities of £1,321 and assets of £125, and although most of what he said was disproved by the Official Receiver, he was declared bankrupt.

It seemed that Spot was going the same way as had Darby Sabini; he and his wife were evicted from their flat in Hyde Park Mansions, and when the couple tried to visit his wife's relatives in Canada, Spot was refused entry. His wife opened the Highball Club in Bayswater in June 1958; one month later, they received a visit from twenty thugs armed with crowbars who wrecked the place, and one month after that, the club was burnt to the ground. Reggie Kray later claimed responsibility for the arson attack whilst he was serving his thirty-year sentence (so it was extremely unlikely that he would have received a consecutive sentence for it, had he been charged – he wasn't, so he didn't), and Spot and family moved to Ireland. He returned to seek semi-official employment, although that, too, came to an end when in 1962 he was fined £12 at West London Magistrates' Court for stealing meat from his employer. His wife died in 1988 and Spot followed her to the grave in 1995; he had been living, impoverished, in a residential home.[1]

⋆   ⋆   ⋆

Billy Hill's star was now in the ascendancy and, because of their strong association, so was that of Albert Dimes; at least in the world of criminality.

Unfortunately, he was attracting publicity for all of the wrong reasons. Following the fight with Spot, there was newspaper coverage after Dimes was awarded £666 for a back injury involving a taxi and a van; it was suggested that the real cause of the injuries was the fight with Spot. In a separate case, it transpired that he had not paid tax since 1951, and he later agreed to pay a refund of £135 in respect of National Insurance contributions.

After the trials involving Spot, on 21 June 1956, Anthony Greenwood, Labour MP for Rossendale, raised the matter of gang warfare in the House of Commons (as did Lieutenant Colonel Marcus Lipton, Labour MP for Brixton). 'Yesterday, there was a further case of razor-slashing in the West End and in three recent cases at the Old Bailey there has been blatant perjury', said

---

[1] For a very full and detailed account of the breakdown in the Spot/Hill/Dimes relationship, see *London's Gangs at War*, Pen & Sword Books, 2017.

Greenwood. 'How long have the public to wait before the activities of these squalid, cowardly small-time hoodlums like Comer, Dimes and Hill are effectively curbed?'

Although nobody was aware of it, the answer was 'never', although it was sufficient for Dimes (probably smarting from being labelled 'small-time') to go to the House of Commons the following day and demand that his name be cleared from the 'unfounded allegations'; Greenwood refused to meet him so the result was, it wasn't.

In 1961, Dimes' and Hill's names were mentioned in frauds-man Charles Da Silva's trial; it was said that they had obtained £8,000 of the money gained in one of his scams. This was hotly denied by Dimes, who didn't go to prison; Da Silva did, for six years.

The following year, when a man named Harvey Holford was accused of shooting dead his wife, he needed a reason for carrying a gun since he already had a conviction for the selfsame offence. The excuse he gave was that it was for protection from Billy Hill and Albert Dimes, following an argument with a man who had connections with these two. It was an echo of those who, a few years previously, had used the Sabini name to justify their actions or provide an excuse for their own transgressions.

Whenever Dimes' name was mentioned unfavourably, as by a Member of Parliament or in any number of court trials, his response was to hit back immediately and volubly, resulting in a great deal of publicity. Some might have thought that he 'doth protest too much', as said by Queen Gertrude of an insincere character in Shakespeare's *Hamlet*, but it was clear that these protestations only added to Dimes' persona.

CHAPTER 28

Dimes Triumphant?

The racetrack gang wars had pretty well ended with the confrontation between Spot and Dimes in Frith Street in 1955; after that, the Betting and Gaming Act 1960 was passed, which came into force on 1 January 1961. It permitted betting shops to open, and within nine months there were 8,780 operating in Britain; one year later, there were almost 20,000. Albert Dimes was one of the applicants, and he needed a licence to be granted by Magistrates. With a background and reputation such as his, this was not going to be easy, but Westminster Magistrates were persuaded to issue a licence in the name of Al Burnett, the owner of the Pigalle night club and a chum of Dimes.

Dimes was a financier as well as a fixer. If anyone had any problems, they'd go to his betting shop in Frith Street, where disputes would be sorted out. Not all, though; Dimes fell out with Captain Soames, secretary of the East Essex point to point meetings. Soames had asked Dimes to collect 'voluntary contributions' from bookmakers for the Hunt funds because, as Soames said, 'It would have been impossible for a local man to collect from a Londoner.' So Dimes obliged him; then kept the money. Since such a collection was contrary to National Hunt rules, there wasn't a lot Soames could do about it, except to declare that Dimes 'wasn't a gentleman'. That was probably also the opinion of the secretaries of the Cambridge Harriers and the East Sussex point to point meetings – Dimes collected for them, too. Harry White – now affiliated to Dimes since the White family's falling out with Spot – sprang to his defence: 'Albert took over, just to keep the peace', he said.

When Billy Hill's autobiography, heavily ghosted by Duncan Webb, *Boss of Britain's Underworld*, was published, Dimes was introduced at the book launch to one of the more gullible guests, Lady Docker, as 'Chief Inspector Dimes' – and it was true, like Hill he had courted the friendship of a number of senior officers.

The late Commander Terry O'Connell QPM told me that whilst he was serving at West End Central police station (which policed Soho), Albert Dimes approached him to claim that Detective

Sergeant Harry Challenor MM had attempted to extort £1,000 from him.

This was almost certainly untrue. Challenor had been the terror of the club owners, gangsters and racketeers who infested Soho, and they had never met a police officer quite like him. He could not be frightened or bought, so it was decided to frame him. The word was that £1,000 was on offer to anyone (without any previous convictions) who could lure Challenor into a compromising position, probably on the promise of providing information, before handing over £1,000 in marked notes; this was to coincide with the press photographing the entire transaction and would result in Challenor being nabbed by 'rubber-heelers' – police officers tasked to investigate such sordid matters.

The result of such a scenario being successfully accomplished would be this: Challenor would be investigated and almost certainly suspended from duty. If charges, either criminal or disciplinary, were brought, all well and good. But even if such charges were dismissed, it would inevitably lead to Challenor being transferred to somewhere other than Soho; and the gangsters' problems would be solved.

O'Connell told Dimes to keep him up to speed with any possible developments in the matter; but since Challenor had never approached Dimes in the first place, no further information was forthcoming. In fact, gangland saved themselves £1,000; Challenor's downfall came after he planted offensive weapons once too often on entirely innocent members of the public, and an unpleasant little anarchist provided the evidence for Challenor's demise, for free.[1]

Any underworld gossip came to Dimes first, and he was an unofficial banker to those serving prison terms. He was a charismatic figure as he drove around in his large white convertible; he backed Eddie Richardson and Frankie Fraser in their fruit machine business and also suggested they sort out the problems at Mr Smith and the Witchdoctor's club, in Catford, South London. But the Kray twins were making inroads into London's West End. Could Dimes stop them? Not very likely; they were as dismissive of Dimes as they had once been of Jack Spot. 'Albert can't fight for fuck', they said, and given their combined ferocity and a twenty-year age gap between them and Dimes, now in his fifties, it could well be they were right.

---

[1] For more on this extraordinary cop, see *The Scourge of Soho: The Controversial Career of SAS Hero, Detective Sergeant Harry Challenor MM*, Pen & Sword Books, 2013.

Then fate intervened; Dimes, having suggested that Richardson and Fraser 'sort out' the problems at Mr Smith's Club, matters were sorted out in rather an extravagant way with a full-blooded affray, after which Fraser was charged with the murder of Dickie Hart, who had himself been armed with a .45 Colt automatic.

That got the Krays' adversaries, Fraser and Richardson, out of the way (plus quite a few of their associates), so there really was nobody to stop the Krays' inroads into the West End – except for Ronnie Kray himself. Two nights after the Mr Smith's Club affray, Ronnie shot dead the Richardson brothers' associate George Cornell in the Blind Beggar public house. This, in itself, led to a rather odd situation.

Ronnie taunted Reg that he had killed a man but that Reg was incapable of doing so; it led to near-lunatic arguments, undoubtedly fuelled by drink, one of which culminated in Reg demanding a gun from anyone who possessed one, so that he could demonstrate to his equally deranged brother that he was just as capable of homicide – and to prove it, he would shoot Albert Dimes. Fortunately, no one in the gathering possessed such a weapon – at least, they said they didn't.

But matters were rectified by the twins jointly murdering 'Jack the Hat' McVitie, after which they had other more pressing matters to deal with rather than actively pursuing an incursion into London's West End.

By now, Billy Hill had more or less faded from the scene. He was spending more and more time in the South of France and Tangier; he died in 1984, one year before the demise of his old adversary, Spot. The latter died penniless. The same applied to Hill – or did it? There were conflicting rumours; perhaps he died as rich as Croesus (which was far more likely).

In early December 1966, Angelo Bruno of the Mafia family in Philadelphia plus the notorious Meyer Lansky came to London on a gambling junket; the following year, Dimes visited Bruno on his home territory (almost certainly using a false passport) to discuss installing gaming machines in clubs. His longtime friend Bert Marsh also assisted the New York-based Giotti family with the same venture.

In 1970 there had been a gang-related fight involving Ronnie Knight's brother, David. In turn, at the Latin Quarter Club in Wardour Street, David was stabbed to death by the doorman Alfredo Zomparelli who, possibly coincidentally, was employed by Albert Dimes.

To all intents and purposes, Dimes had retired from violent crime; he acted as an advisor on Joseph Losey's 1960 film *The*

Criminal, starring his friend, Stanley Baker, who played a character named Johnny Banion, said to be based on Dimes himself.

He was not only liked and admired by the criminal fraternity; in the world of celebrities, as well as being a companion of Stanley Baker, Dimes always attended the big boxing matches, including the one where (the then) Cassius Clay defeated Henry Cooper. The following day, Clay's hugely disputed torn boxing glove and its twin turned up in the window of Dimes' Frith Street betting shop. Then they mysteriously disappeared. Reg Kray later said that Dimes presented the gloves to him as a gift, but then Reg Kray was a stranger to the truth.

Dimes ran his bookmaking business until his death from cancer at his home at Oakland Avenue, Beckenham in November 1972. The funeral at Beckenham was attended by some 200 mourners, and the Kray twins (by then serving thirty-year sentences, and with Reg forgetting his homicidal thoughts regarding Dimes) sent a wreath with the words, 'To a fine gentleman'. That in itself was a gracious tribute, except that the twins added 'From Ron and Reg Kray' and the wreath was destroyed by the family, saying it brought disrespect to Albert's memory.

But whatever else Dimes may have left as a legacy, there was one matter that raised a question mark. It was said that on his deathbed Dimes ordered that the police be told the truth concerning the murder of 'Scotch Jack' Buggy.

CHAPTER 29

A Question of Murder

John James Buggy was born in the United States and had moved to Glasgow, hence becoming known as 'Scotch Jack' Buggy. He gained the reputation of being a hardman and was certainly a disagreeable sort of fellow. Having moved to London, 27-year-old Buggy, together with another man, went to the Pigalle Restaurant on the evening of 24 September 1960. His intention was to try to persuade Shirley Bassey, who was appearing in cabaret there, to accompany them back to a West End flat where a party was being held, so that she might entertain the guests. Unsurprisingly, Miss Bassey's manager told them she was not available, but the men persisted in hanging around, until a fight broke out which culminated in Buggy shooting one of the club's diners; and on 30 January 1961 at the Old Bailey, he was convicted of causing grievous bodily harm and sentenced to nine years' imprisonment.

Following a failed escape attempt, he was released from prison in December 1966, but in May 1967, 'Nipper' Read, then a detective chief inspector at West End Central, was asked to call and see a regular informant. Read was told that Buggy had been murdered at the Mount Street Bridge Club a few nights previously and that 'his body has been done away with. Apparently, he was making a right nuisance of himself. Albert was called in at the end.'

So that, it appeared, was the connection with Albert Dimes. There was a further connection: the manager of the club was Franny Daniels, who had been sent down for three years with Billy Hill for a smash and grab in 1940. He had been one of those who escaped from 'The Battle of Heathrow' and he, Hill and Dimes had been present when Patrick Marrinan (Hill's venal barrister) was sent to Eire to try to prevent the extradition of two of Jack Spot's attackers, as were all three when the plot was formed to frame Jack Spot for cutting Tommy Falco.

Buggy's girlfriend reported him missing to the police, and rumours abounded: that Buggy had been involved in protection rackets, that he was to meet some businessmen from Manchester and that he had been warned that he would be shot unless he settled gambling debts of – the amounts varied – between £20,000 and £30,000. A further rumour was that he had been asked by Roy James to track down the man who had been entrusted with looking after James' share of the loot from the Great Train Robbery. The night before Buggy's disappearance, a bomb had gone off in the hallway of the Mount Street club. Buggy had been a member of the US armed forces; did knowledge of explosives stem from that service? It was said that Buggy was 'making a right nuisance of himself'. To whom – Albert Dimes? Because another rumour was that it was a Mafia-backed killing, and Dimes was involved with the Mafia.

Buggy's decomposing body was discovered floating by two off-duty police officers who were fishing at Seaford, Sussex on Monday, 5 June 1967. He had been shot twice and kicked; he was gagged, and his body was wrapped in wire.

One of the people whom the police wished to interview was Charles 'Waggy' Whitnall, the nephew of Franny Daniels, who was an associate of both Billy Hill and Buggy. Apparently there had been a thorough disagreement over a matter of £20,000 which Hill had handed to Whitnall, who had allegedly invested the money in circumstances which were not immediately known to the other stakeholders. On the day of his disappearance, at the Mount Street club Buggy had denounced Whitnall's transactions and had been invited into his office. It was later said that three shots then rang out and Whitnall emerged from the office and told everyone to go home for the day. The police wanted to question Whitnall, who was not immediately available; traced to Vienna, he eventually agreed to be interviewed in the presence of a London solicitor, which took the case no further forward at all.

Then five years later, Albert Dimes made his deathbed assertion; and that took the matter no further forward either.

But something else did. Duggie Wardle was an Australian and a professional blackmailer who was serving a nine-year sentence for that offence. He came forward to say that Franny Daniels had confessed involvement in the murder to him, five months after the event, telling him, 'What happened in the Mount Street club was done in temper. For doing what I have done, I could cut off my right arm.' It was not a direct confession to murder, but the words suggested some deep involvement in the matter.

Franny Daniels was sixty-three years of age when he stood trial at the Old Bailey, seven years after the murder, in 1974. Charged with Buggy's murder, his companion in the dock was Abraham 'Pinky' Lewis, a 65-year-old minicab driver, who was also charged, together with Daniels, with harbouring the murderer, attempting to pervert justice by destroying evidence and making false statements; but on 4 November, both men were acquitted of all charges.

So why was it that Dimes uttered his deathbed insistence that the police should be told of the truth surrounding Buggy's death? He obviously believed that the finger of suspicion would be pointed at his close associate Franny Daniels and his nephew. Did he believe them to be innocent? And if he did, it follows that he must have known who the guilty parties were. A staunch Catholic, perhaps he felt that expiating his conscience in insisting that the police be given the details of Buggy's killer(s) would pave the way for the pearly gates to be well and truly opened to him. The suspects and the motives were plentiful; and now it seems unlikely that the truth will never be known.

All through his criminal life, Dimes had been associated with murders, although he was never actually charged with any of them: the death in 1938 of Michael McCausland, the pre-war murder of 'Chick' Lawrence, the wartime murder of 'Little Hubby' Distleman, Edward 'The Witch Doctor' Smith's fall from the prison landing, the killing of David Knight by Dimes' doorman Zomparelli and then the murder of Buggy. Certainly, his life was surrounded by serious violence, whether actually participating in it or actively planning it. Murderer – or blemished good guy?

Epilogue

It was said that it was Dimes' close friend Bert Marsh (he had helped Dimes into a taxi following the bloody confrontation with Jack Spot and gave evidence for Dimes) who was the true driving force behind the Italian fraternity in Clerkenwell. Although he had a considerable input into criminality in Soho (which, I was assured, 'he kept going until his death'), much of his time was spent in Clerkenwell. Four years after his friend Albert Dimes' death, Marsh died on 3 October 1976, leaving – according to official records, at least – just £1,503. Even though he had been convicted of killing a man and assaulting others, he was hugely respected in the area – in his later years, he was a quiet, courteous man but one whose word was law – and a large wake was held for him in 'Little Italy'.

It was his reputation, his persona that kept the local tearaways in check. It was what my friend Maria meant when she told me that it was Bert Marsh who kept the streets safe; and so we come full circle. It was Marsh who kicked off this book and it's he who finishes it.

Now that police seldom patrol the streets of Clerkenwell (or anywhere else for that matter), now that violent crime has spiralled out of control, what precisely do members of the public want, to ensure their safety? A community service order issued to some recalcitrant, cocky yob who, rather than carry out the community work, would be more likely to nick the orange hi-vis jacket he'd been handed than wear it?

Or would they prefer the likes of Bert Marsh to administer a good hiding, to stop that anti-social piece of garbage right in his tracks?

Me? I'm out of it.

You? Let me know.

Bibliography

Adamson, Iain	*The Great Detective*	Frederick Muller Ltd., 1966
Bunker, John	*From Rattle to Radio*	Brewin Books, 1988
Chinn, Carl	*The Real Peaky Blinders*	Brewin Books, 2017
Cornish, G. W.	*Cornish of the Yard*	The Bodley Head, 1935
Darbyshire, Neil and Hilliard, Brian	*The Flying Squad*	Headline, 1993
Davidson, Earl	*Joey Pyle. Notorious: The Changing Face of Organized Crime*	Virgin Books Ltd., 2003
Divall, Tom	*Scoundrels and Scallywags (and Some Honest Men)*	Ernest Benn, 1929
Edwards, Robert	*Henry Cooper: The Authorised Biography of Britain's Greatest Boxing Hero*	BBC Books, 2002
Fido, Martin	*The Krays: Unfinished Business*	Carlton Books, 1999
Fraser, David, Fraser, Patrick and Marsh, Beezy	*Mad Frank & Sons*	Sidgwick & Jackson, 2016
Fraser, Frankie as told to Morton, James	*Mad Frank*	Warner Books, 1994
Frost, George 'Jack'	*Flying Squad*	Rockliff, 1948
Goodwin, John C.	*Sidelights on Criminal Matters*	Hutchinson & Co. 1923

Greeno, Edward	*War on the Underworld*	John Long, 1960
Hart, Edward T.	*Britain's Godfather*	True Crime Library, 1993
Higgins, Robert	*In the Name of the Law*	John Long, 1958
Hill, Justin and Hunt, John	*Billy Hill, Gyp & Me*	Billy Hill Family Ltd., 2012
Huggins, Mike	*Horseracing and the British: 1919–1939*	Manchester University Press, 2003
Johnson, W. H.	*Surrey Villains*	Countryside Books, 2004
Kirby, Dick	*The Guv'nors: Ten of Scotland Yard's Greatest Detectives*	Pen & Sword Books, 2010
Kirby, Dick	*The Sweeney: The First Sixty Years of Scotland Yard's Crimebusting Flying Squad 1919–1978*	Pen & Sword Books, 2011
Kirby, Dick	*The Brave Blue Line: 100 Years of Metropolitan Police Gallantry*	Pen & Sword Books, 2011
Kirby, Dick	*Death on the Beat: Police Officers Killed in the Line of Duty*	Pen & Sword Books, 2012
Kirby, Dick	*The Scourge of Soho: The Controversial Career of SAS Hero Detective Sergeant Harry Challenor MM*	Pen & Sword Books, 2013
Kirby, Dick	*Whitechapel's Sherlock Holmes: The Casebook of Fred Wensley OBE, KPM, Victorian Crime Buster*	Pen & Sword Books, 2014
Kirby, Dick	*London's Gangs at War*	Pen & Sword Books, 2017

Kirby, Dick	*Scotland Yard's Flying Squad: 100 Years of Crime Fighting*	Pen & Sword Books, 2019
Kray, Reg	*Villains we have Known*	Arrow Books, 1996
Lucas, Norman and Scarlett, Bernard	*The Flying Squad*	Arthur Barker 1968
Lucas, Norman	*Britain's Gangland*	Pan Books, 1969
Magee, Bryan	*Clouds of Glory: A Hoxton Childhood*	Jonathan Cape, 2003
McDonald, Brian	*Gangs of London: 100 Years of Mob Warfare*	Milo Books Ltd., 2010
Morton, James	*Gangland: Volumes 1 & 2*	Time Warner, 2001
Morton, James	*East End Gangland*	Time Warner 2003
Morton, James	*Gangland: The Lawyers*	Virgin Books, 2003
Morton, James and Parker, Gerry	*Gangland Bosses: The Lives of Jack Spot and Billy Hill*	Time Warner 2005
Morton, James	*Gangland Soho*	Piatkus, 2010
Murphy, Robert	*Smash and Grab*	Faber & Faber 1993
Narborough, Fred	*Murder on my Mind*	Allan Wingate, 1959
Nesbitt, Michael	*The Sabini Gang and the Racecourse Wars of the 1920s*	Privately published, 2018
Parker, Robert	*Rough Justice*	Fontana, 1981
Pearson, John	*The Profession of Violence*	Panther Books, 1977
Rawlings, William	*A Case for the Yard*	John Long, 1961
Read, Leonard with Morton, James	*Nipper*	Macdonald, 1991

Read, Piers Paul	*The Train Robbers*	W. H. Allen & Co., 1978
Reid, Jamie	*Doped*	Racing Post Books, 2013
Sharpe, F. D.	*Sharpe of the Flying Squad*	John Long, 1938
Shore, Heather	*London's Criminal Underworlds, c.1720–c.1930: A Social and Cultural History*	Palgrave Macmillan, 2015
Thomas, Donald	*An Underworld at War*	John Murray, 2003
Thomas, Donald	*Villains' Paradise*	John Murray, 2005
Thorp, Arthur	*Calling Scotland Yard*	Allan Wingate Publishers, 1954
Vanstone, Charles	*A Man in Plain Clothes*	John Long, 1961
Wilson, Pamela Sydney	*Home was a Grand Hotel: Tales of a Brighton Belle*	Book Guild Ltd., 2008

Index

Abelson, Mick 74–8
Ackroyd, Tommy 55
Allard, John 32–4
Allen, Mr G. 80
Alliot, John (Barrister) 186
Alzapiede, Mr 59–60
Amadio, Antonio 105
Anderson, John – *see* Papa, P.
Anderson, Sir John (Home
    Secretary) 40–4
Anderson, ex-D/Supt.
    Robert 181
Andibert, Raymond 74
Appleby, DS 46
Archer, PC 48
Armstrong, Thomas Samuel
    John 20–1, 84
Avory, Mr Justice 67

Baker, Arnold (Lawyer) 59–61
Baker, George 42–4
Baker, Mrs 42
Baker, Sir Stanley 201–2
Baldock, D/Supt. William,
    BEM 176–80
Banks, Edward 33–4
Barker, Mr (Lawyer) 23
Barkley, William 156
Barnett, Sam 30–4
Barnham, John 191–3
Barrett, Lionel 82
Barry, Dr Geraldine 58
Barry, Mr Justice 179
Barton, Henry Richard 96–8
Barzo, Antonio 11–12
Bayliss, William 33–4

Beckitt, Dr 71
Beland, William 43
'Mrs Bell' – *see* Lugeon, M.E.
Bennett, Arthur 'Porky' 161–5
Bennis, Stephen Patrick
    127–35
Bennis, Timothy 127–35
Bennyworth, Tommy aka
    'Monkey' &
    'The Trimmer' 14, 80–2, 162
Beresford, Walter, 22, 39
Berman, Jack 34
Berrett, DDI James 31–4, 146
Best, Joseph 24–5
Beveridge, DCS Peter
    Henderson,
    MBE 163
Bigham, AC(C) Sir Trevor,
    CB 101
Bild, Charles 35–7
'Bill Sheldon's Unknown' –
    see Langham, G.
Bingley, Mr (Magistrate) 45
Birkett, Sir Norman, KC
    118–22
Biron, Sir Chartres
    (Magistrate) 19, 82, 83
Blencowe, Mr J. I. (Magistrate)
    128–9
Blitz, Albert 123–35
Blitz, Barnett 73–8, 81, 123–35
Boffa, Paul 48–53
Bogard, Isaac 147–8
Bond, Harry 126–35
Bonniface, Arthur 132–5
Boothey, DI William 48–8

Boyce, James 178–80
Boyd, Mr (Magistrate) 88
Bray, George 6
Brett, Fred 46–56
Bros, Mr (Magistrate) 16, 23
Brown, D/Supt. 44, 54–5,
    64–7, 93, 101–103, 146
Bruno, Angelo 201
Buggy, John James,
    'Scotch Jack' 202–5
Buonocore, Sidney
    103–105, 109
Burman, Jack 102–3
Burnett, Al 163, 199
Byfield, Henry 10
Byrne, Mr L.A. (Barrister)
    119–22
Byrne, Mr Justice 172

Cadman, PC 6
Caldecote, LCJ Lord 156
Camp, James 51–6
Cann, James 42–3
Cannon, Joe 196
Capocci, Harry 150–7
Carpenter, John 25–6
Cassella, Tomasso 12
Cassels, Mr J.D. (Barrister) 44,
    53–6, 129–35
Cazalet, Major Peter 183
Challenor, DS Harold Gordon,
    MM 199–200
Challenor, Mr N.B.
    (Coroner) 180
Chapman, Eddie 195
Charles, Mr E.B. (Lawyer) 89
Charles, Gomer, 170–4
Churchill, George 127–35
Churchill, Winston, PC, MP 87
Cimini, Louisa 117
Clark, PC Robert 48
Clarke, Percival (Lawyer)
    50–6, 59–61, 77–78
Clayton, Douglas 132

Coburn, Walter 5
Cohen, Harry 41, 59–61
Cohen, Israel 34
Cohen, Joseph 30–4
Cohen, Solomon 41
Cole, PC 61
Coleman, Ellen 149–50
Collette, Joseph 150–7
Collins, PC Leonard 85
Collyer, DS Walter 125–35, 147
Comer, Jack – see Spot, J.
Comacho, Jacob – see Spot, J.
'Conky' 123–35
Connelly, Bert 150
Conway, Thomas 32–4
Cook, William Barney 25–6
Cooper, Wilfred Jerome 70
Copley, DS 56
Copple, Morris 104
Corbett, DDI, Henry Arthur
    Finbar,
'Chesty' 99, 146–7
Cornell, George 201
Cortesi, Augustus xiv, 57–61
Cortesi, George xiv, 57–61
Cortesi, Harry, 'Enrico'
    xiv, 57–61
Cortesi, Paul xiv, 57–61
Cory, DS, Herbert 43–4,
    107–9
Costognetti, Angelo 97–8
Crawford, Alexander 39–40
Crocker, Detective 81
Croke, Albert Henry 81–2
Cronin, James 191–3
Crowley, Patrick 154
Curtis, King 'Rough House'
    160–1
Cutler, Albert 116–22

Dance, DDI Alf 112
Daniels, Francis 'Franny' 164,
    203–5
Darby, William 29

'Darkie the Coon' –
    see Bogard, I.
Darling, Mr Justice 23, 46,
    60–1
Dasher, Joseph 45–6
Da Silva, Charles 198
Davidson, James 169
Davies, Mr 24
Davis, John Arthur (Solicitor)
    41–2,
  50, 112–113, 116–122
Dawkins, Detective 39–40, 145
Dawson, PS 110 'V' Joseph
    31–4
Defries, Simon 15–16
Delew, Jack 47–56
Desmond, Joseph 149–50
D'Eynecourt, Mr (Magistrate)
    13, 35
Deyong, Moss 24
Dickinson, Mr – see Jackson,
    John
Dido, George 71–72
Differary, John McCarthy
    107–9
Differary, Queenie 107–9
Dill, Lt. Col. Victor Robert
    Colquhoun, M. C., 169–74
Dimeo, Alberto –
    see Dimes, A.G.
Dimes, Albert George 150–7,
    165, 184, 186, 187–93,
    195–207
Dimes, Victor 152
Distleman, Harry 150–7, 205
Divall, DCI Tom 24, 91–2
Dodson, Sir Gerald (Recorder
    of London) 156–157
Doralli, Antonio 57
Doralli, Louisa 57–61
Dorrie, Bernie 101–2
Doughty, Charles,
    QC (Recorder) 186
Douglas, Archie 40

Drake, George 63–7
Driscoll, William 96
Duby, Detective 74
Du Cann, Mr G.L. (Barrister)
    76–8
Dummett, Mr (Magistrate) 98
Duncan, DCI, Alec 112–13
Dunne, Sir Lawrence
    (Magistrate) 173
Dutchen, Barnet 15–16
Dyer, Edward 184–6, 187–93

Edis, George 83
Edwards, William 42–4
Eggeman, John 117
Eivers, Thomas 31–4
Elboz, Isaiah 84
Eliot, Lord, DL, JP 170–4
Elton, John (Barrister) 189
Emanuel, Eddie 14, 21, 39, 56,
    73–8, 92–3
Emanuel, Philip 39
Emden, Buck – see Blitz, B.
Evans, Gertrude 107–9

Fagioli, George 43–4, 55
'Fair–haired Eddie' – see
    Fletcher, E.
Falco, Tommy 195–6, 203
Farquhar, DS 163
Fellows, Harry 79–80
Fenton, Horace
    (Barrister) 108
Field, Alex 187–93
Fireman, Maurice 34, 71–2, 79
Fleisher, Eddie –
    see Fletcher, E.
Fletcher, Eddie 149–57
Flowers, John, KC 118–22,
    129–35
Ford, Harry 94–5
Ford, James 34, 41–4, 80,
    91–2, 94–5
Forman, Maurice 20–1

Fowles, Billy 34–5
Foy, James 34–5
Francasal 167–74
Franklin, Charles 29
Fraser, Francis Davidson,
    'Mad Frank' 144, 173,
    200–1
Fraser, John Mathison,
    JP 142–3
Frater, Mark 125–35
Fright, Matthew 63–7
Frost, PC 305 'CO' George,
    'Jack' 124
Fuller, Mr E. Newton
    (Magistrates' Clerk) 37
Fulton, Mr (Barrister) 54–6

Gale, William 34–5
Gatford, PC, William 84–5
Garbutt, DS George 191
Gardiner, George 127–35
Gianicoli, Angelo –
    see Langham, G.
Gibbon, DI 24
Gilbert, Fred xiv, 21–2,
    39, 40, 42–4, 45, 46–56,
    57, 93
Gilbert, John 55
Gilder, George 131–5
Giles, Walter 30–4
Gill, Mr (Magistrate) 46
Gill, Norman 34–5
Gillan, DI John 65–7
Giotti family 201
Glynn, William 84
Godfrey, David 104–5
Godley, ex–DCI 141
Goldworthy, DC Peter 191
Goller, 'Big Bill' 163–4
Gooch, DCI Dan 94, 124
Goodwillie, DDI David 15–16,
    43–4, 47, 145
Gorsch, Morris – see Lewis, J.
Goulding, William 32–4

Graham–Campbell, Sir Rollo
    (Magistrate) 104–105
Graham, William, 'Cockney
    Bill' 33
Green, Lazarus 30–4
Greeno, DCS Edward,
    MBE 95–6, 124, 138–44,
    168–74
Greenwood, Anthony,
    MP 197–8
Gregory, Recorder of London,
    Sir Holman 108–9
Griffey, DI 108–9, 141
Griffin, Steve 64–7, 83
Grosse, DDI, Albert 25–6, 40,
    49, 58–61, 146
Groves, PC William 127–35

Hain, Leslie Edward 128–35
Hall, Mr Clarke (Magistrate)
    162
Hall, Sir Edward Marshall,
    KC 75–8
Hambrook, D/Supt. Walter 51,
    77–8, 146
Hamilton, Mr Justice 10
Harding, Arthur 93–4, 98,
    148, 162
Hardy, Mr G.L. (Lawyer) 81–2
Harper, James 65–7
Harris, Gurchen 92–3
'Harry Frenchie' –
    see Cortesi, H.
Hart, Mr 115
Hart, Dickie 201
Harvey, Robert 22
Hatter, Samuel 34
Hayden, William 33–4
Hayes, Alfred 162–3
Hayes, Timmy 96–8
Heath, Neville 168
Heaps, Insp. 21
Heath, Frank 35–7
Henry, DDI John 117–122

Hepworth, Lt. Col.
    (Magistrate) 40
Hermann, Marie 75–6
Hewitt, PC, George 5
Higgins, D/Supt Robert
    Mold 99
Hilbery, Mr Justice 129–35
Hill, William Charles,
    'Billy' 98, 157, 159–65,
    195–202, 203
Hill, Mr C.V. (Lawyer) 19
Hill, Maggie 159
Hirschowitz, Samuel 20
Hobbs, William Cooper
    (Solicitor) 52–3
Hodge, D/Supt. Frederick
    George 169–74
Holford, Harvey 198
Homer, William 65–7, 73
Hornett, PC 5
Horrickey, Charlie 162
Horwell, CC(CID) John 98
Horwood, Commissioner,
    Brigadier-General Sir
    William, GBE, KCB,
    DSO 87–8
Hosford, Dr 36
Hughes, Ernest 32–4
Hooper, Sub-Div. Insp. 31
Humphreys,
    Mr Travers (Lawyer)
    (later Mr Justice) 60–1,
    139–44
Hunter, PC 24
Hutton, Dick 123–35
Hyams, Isidore 75–8

Illingworth, Michael 127–35
Isaacs, David 90
Isow, Jack Aaron 103–5
'Italian Albert' – see Dimes, A.G.

Jackson, John 81–2
Jackson, Joseph 42–4, 54–6

Jacobs, Aaron 39–40
Jacobs, Philip (aka Phil Oker)
    20–1, 84
Jacobs, Mrs
    (Widow of Philip) 20
James, Roy 204
Janes, DS Stanley George
    125–35, 147
Jeacock, Thomas 150
Jeffrey, DI 154
Jenner, Detective 79–80
Joel, Abraham 20–7
Johnson, William – see Sage, G.
Jones, George –
    see Churchill, G.
Joyce, Edward 37
Joyce, Thomas 24–5
Joynson-Hicks, Sir William,
    Bt., PC, DL, 'Jix' 87–8, 98

Kateley, Harry 169–74
Kassel, Max 147
Kay, Violet 154
Keane, DCI Jack 191–2
Keeves, Mr (Lawyer) 24
Kemp, Amy 48–56
Kibble, May 187–93
Kilby, Joseph John 126–35
Kimber, Anna 18–19
Kimber, Billy xiv, 9–11, 14,
    18–20, 21–5, 35–7, 46, 59,
    92, 143
Kimber, Joe 19–20
Kimber, Maude 18
Kimberley, Charles 83
Kimberley, Isaac 83
Kimberley, Moses 83
Kimberley, William 64–7, 83
King, Alfred George 111
'King of the Upton Park
    Gypsies' – see Skurry, A.E.
Klosowski, Severin 49
Knight, Mr (Lawyer) 25
Knight, David 201, 205

Knight, Ronnie 201
Kray, Reg 96, 143, 159, 162, 189, 192, 195, 197, 200–1
Kray, Ron 143, 159, 189, 192, 195, 200–1, 202

Lander, DS 70
Lane, Frank 33
Langham, George 41–4, 59, 80
Lansky, Meyer 201
Laumaine, Rosemarie –
see Lugeon, M.E.
Lawrence, Charles Edward, 'Chick' 150–1, 205
Lawrip, Mr A.J., KC (Deputy Chairman) 85
Le Chevalier 70
Lederman, Sammy 151, 161
Lee, John 32–4
Lee, Phil 148
Lee, Tancy – see Homer W.
Leon, Joe 150–2
Leonardo, Signor 12
Less, Herbert 34
Lester, Montague 94
Levene, Jack – see Fireman, M.
Levison, Solomon 30–4
Levy, David 26–7, 29
Levy, Moey 19, 21, 26–7, 29, 80–1, 161–5
Lewis, Abraham, 'Pinky' 204–5
Lewis, Isaac 30–4
Lewis, Jack 96–8
Lewis, Harry 34
Lewis, Michael 30–4
Lewis, Ted 'Kid' 63
'Lightning Bookmakers' 7
Lipton, Lt. Col., Marcus, MP 197–8
'Little Hubby' –
see Distleman, H.
Lowry, Joe 184–93
Ludlow, Ernest Frederick 64–7

Lugeon, Michelline Emilienne 183–93
Luper, Mr 101–3
Lynch, PC James 127–35

MacCormac, Dr William 116
Machin, Teddy 161–5
Mack, Ernest 29, 34
Mack, Thomas 34, 48–56, 60, 79–80, 103–5, 109, 127–35, 151–7
Mancini, Antonio Alfred 'Babe' 79–80, 103, 151–7, 161
Mancini, Tony 154
Mansfield, Harry 73–8
Manson, George 111–13
Margolis, Harry 46–56
'Maria' xiii–xv, 207
Marrinan, Patrick 203
Marshfield, DI 37
Martin, Antonio 'Anthony' 24–5
Martin, Master 30
Martin, Mr 30
Martin, Mrs 30
Martin, Stephen 81
Mason, Robert 178–80
Mazzarda, Silvio, 'Shonk' 112–13
McCausland, Matt 9–10, 18, 65–7
McCausland, Mike 9–10, 18, 150, 205
McDonald, Charles 'Wag' 9, 131
McDonough, Thomas 83
McGee, Richard 183–6
McKay, Peter Carl –
see Monolulu
McNaughton, Mr Justice 120–2, 155–7
McVitie, Jack 'Jack the Hat' 201
McNeil, Peter 51–6
Melville, John 84

Merritt, PS 63 'V' 31–4
Milandi, Ugo 12
Milburn, Edith 97
Mitchell, Charlie 184–3
Mitchell, Frank 'The Mad
    Axeman' 192
Mitchell, Leonard 34–5
Modebodze, Georges 70
Monololu, Ras Prince 3
Monte-Colombo, Ada 118
Monte-Colombo, Anesio 117
Monte-Colombo, Camillo
    115–22
Monte-Colombo,
    Leonelli 116
Monte-Colombo, Massimino
  Francesco Antonio 115–22
Monte-Colombo, Nestor
    115–22
Moore, George 55
Moore, James 70–1
Morris, Jack 30–4
Morrison, Herbert
    (Home Secretary) 141
Mosley, Sir Oswald 160–1
Moss, George aka 'Mad
    Mossy' 25–6
Moss, Harry 73–8
'Mr Racing' – see Roper, W.J.
Mullins, Claude
    (Magistrate) 120
Mullins, John, 'Jack' aka
    'Dodger' 14, 31, 71, 81–2,
    96–8, 101– 3, 123, 162
Murphy, Edmond 178–80
Murray – see Wilkins, H.
Myers, Harry (Lawyer)
    50–1, 52

Narborough, D/Supt. Fred 147
Neil, D/Supt., Arthur
    'Drooper' 49
Newman, Charles 85
Newman, Joseph 85

Newman, Thomas 'Wassle'
    162–3
Nunn, Detective 74
Nyberg, Simon 48–56

O'Brien, John 112–13
O'Brien, William 33–4
O'Connell, Commander
    Terrence John, QPM
    176–80, 190–3, 199–200
Oliver, Ronald (Barrister)
    59–61, 76–8
Olliffe, Ronnie 192
O'Rourke, Sgt. Maj. Michael,
    VC, MM 71–2

Papa, Pasqualino 'Bert Marsh'
    xiv, 45–6, 60, 79–80, 113,
    114–22, 157, 195–202
Parker, DC Hugh 190
Paul, Gilbert (Recorder) 142
Paul, James 94–5
Payne, Prison Officer 121–2
Payne, Leslie 189
Payne, Sidney 84
Penfold, Robert William 88
Periglione, Giovanni 69–70
Perry, Brian 184–93
Pessieto, Georges 45
Phillips, Arthur 42–4, 79–80
Phillips, John Thomas 40–4,
    79–80
Phillips, Leonard 170–1
Pierrepoint, Albert 156
Pinnock, DS 19
Pobjoy, Arthur 46
Poole, Major, MC 69
Potter, Bill 144
Potter, Rosie 144
Presswell, William Thomas
    79–80
Pride, DI George 101
Prior, Alan 177
Purchas, Mr (Barrister) 162

Raczynski, Casimir 149–50
Raczynski, Nicholas aka
    Roberts 149–50
Raimo, Eddie 150–1, 161–5
Read, ACC Leonard 'Nipper',
    QPM 189, 203
Reynaud, Gaston 69–70
Reynolds, Jackie 161–5
Ricco, Johnny 195–6
Rice, Sandy aka Alex Tomaso
    22, 57–61
Richards, Sir Gordon
    176–80, 181
Richardson, Eddie 200–1
Ricketts, Mr (Lawyer) 80
Ricketts, Charles 94–5
Riley, George 36
Roach, Mr Justice 53–6
Robbins, PC 10
Robbins, PC, Harry 85
Robinson, Mr 98
Robinson, David 30–4
Roche, William Fred 149–50
Rogers, Bertie 'Bandy' 183–6,
    187–93
Roper, William John 183–93
Roseberry, Lord 183
Rosenberg, John 104–5
Rosenberg, Myer 115–22
Roux, Mme 69–70
Rowlatt, Mr Justice 32–4
Rowlett, William 84–5
Russell, Earl 93
Rutherford, Detective John
    Alec, KPM 42–4, 94. 145–6

Sabatini, James 103–5, 109
Sabini, née Potter (also
    Porter), Annie Emma
    (wife of Darby) 14, 143
Sabini, Darby aka Ottavio
    Handley, Octavius Sabini,
    Charles Sabini, Fred
    Sabini, Fred Handley,

Frank Handley, Charles
    Sullivan, Dan Cope xiv,
    11–14, 21–5, 33, 35, 39, 40,
    41, 42–4, 45, 57–61, 69,
    71–2, 76, 80–1, 88–91, 103,
    137–44, 197
Sabini, née Handley, Elizabeth
    Eliza (wife of Octavio)
    12–13
Sabini, Fred (elder brother of
    Darby) 12
Sabini, George (brother of
    Darby) 13, 64
Sabini, Harry 'Harryboy' aka
    Harry Handley (brother of
    Darby) 13, 39, 40–1, 50–6,
    57–61, 71–2, 79–80, 89,
    103, 111–13, 135–44
Sabini, Fl. Sgt. Harry
    (son of Darby) 143
Sabini, Joseph (brother of
    Darby) 13, 21, 48–56,
    60, 93
Sabini, Mary
    (sister of Darby) 13
Sabini, Octavio, (father of
    Darby) aka Octavia, Ottavio,
    Joseph, Charles 11–12
Sage, Ellen 52–6
Sage, George, 'Brummie' xiv,
    9, 21–2, 25, 40, 46–56, 87,
    88, 92, 93
Salter, Mr Justice 78
Samnel, Charles 75–8
Samuels, Samuel 47–56
Sangers, Jack 96–8
'Scarface' – see Distleman, H.
Scholz, Laura 111–13
Schroder, Sir Walter
    (Coroner) 75
Schwarz, Charles 'Woolf' 30–4
Selby, DS 25–6, 145
Selby, PC 218 'G' Walter 12
Sellers, Mr Justice 171

Sharman, Charles Crank (Solicitor) 36–7, 49–56
Sharp, PC, George 95
Sharpe, DCI Frederick Dew 'Nutty' 94–5, 124, 147–8
Shearman, Mr Justice 25
Sherborne, Montague (Barrister) 186
Shobrook, Ernest Westaway 19
Shoesmith, PC 31–4
Shortt, Edward, KC 87, 92
Shuman, DI 71–2
Skurry, Arthur Edward 161–5
Slade, Mr G.O. (Barrister) 140–4
Smith, Edward 'Teddy' 183–6, 187–93, 205
'Smith, John' 5–6
Smith, Joseph 55
Smith, Sidney Thomas 143–4
Smith, DDI William 23, 145
Soames, Captain 199
Solomon, Alf xiv, 14, 21, 23–4, 35–7, 40–1, 56, 65–7, 73–8, 81, 82, 101–3, 123–35
Solomon, Henry 36–7, 40–1
Sparks, DCS Herbert William 'The Iron Man' 173
'Spinkey' – see Spinks, J.
Spinks, James 125–35
Spinks, Terry 192
Spooner, D/Commander Reginald William Lockerby 168–74
Spot, Jack 67, 79, 135, 157, 159–65, 187, 195–202, 203
Spring, Charles 126–35
Stable, Owen (Barrister) 185–93
Stachini, Giulio O. 11–12
Steadman, Charles 96–8
Steadman, George 96–8
Steele, DI 74–5
Stevens, DDI 29–33, 82
Stevens, Mr – see Mancini, A.A.

Stevens, PC 36
Stevenson, Mr Justice Melford 187–93
Steward, Emmanuel Lipman Leonard 'Darkie' 184–193
Straney, Ernest 69
Stringer, William 32–4
Stripp, Insp. Harry 126–35
Sugrue, DCS Patrick 191
Sullivan, Dan 13
Sullivan, Michael 40, 47
Sundock, Frank 34
Swaine, John 169–74
Swanland, Cecil 113–14
Swanland, Margaret 113–14
Swannell, PS 41
Swift, Mr Justice 67
Symmons, Mr (Magistrate) 49–52, 65–7
Symons, Colin 107–9

Tatum, Walter 87
Taylor, Supt., F. 138
Taylor, Harry – see Newman, J.
Taylor, Joseph 79–80
Thomas, Mr 71
Thomas, Philip 36–7
Thorp, DCS Arthur 152–7
Tiano, Michael 1035, 109, 149–50
Timewell, James 93
Tobin, Lawrence – see Baker, G.
Tongue, DS 25–6
Trinder, Edward William George 73–8
Tuck, Harry 178–80
Tuckey, Edward 32–4
Tuckey, Henry 31–4
Tuckey, Thomas 32–4
Tyler, John 131–5

Vallance, Dr Herbert 128–9
Valli, Marzielli 12

Veale, Mr Justice 192–3
Vincent, Arthur 32–4
Vine, Mr Laurence (Lawyer) 94–5

Waghorn, Supt. 128–35
Wakeling, DS 104
Waldron, DS 34–5
Wallace, Mr (Lawyer) 82
Wardle, Duggie 204–5
Watmore, PC, William 50–1
Watts, Ernest 81
Watts, George 81–2
Webb, Duncan 165, 196–7
Webber, DI 20
Welton, Thomas Mayhew 84
Wensley, CC (CID) Frederick Porter, OBE, KPM 17–18, 94, 145
West, George 48–56, 93
Weston, Harry 41
Weston, William 83
White, Alf (Jr.) 107–9
White, Alf (Sr.) 9, 11, 14, 21, 39, 40–41, 42–4, 47–56, 63–7, 81–2, 90, 93, 96, 105, 106–9, 137, 149
White, Harry 149–50, 163, 199
White, William 107–9
Whitehouse, William 83

Whiteley, Herbert 30–4
Whitnall, Charles 'Waggy' 204–5
Whittaker, Mr C.J.M. (Solicitor) 84
Whitton, Joseph 32–4
Wicks, Jim 117
Wiggins, Edward 69
Wiggins, George 69
Wild, Sir Ernest, KC 163
Wilkins, Detective 15–16
Wilkins, Harry 125–35
Wilkins, Herbert 116–22, 123
Williams, Tommy 148
Williams, William – see Kimberley, W.
Williams, William Maurice 167–74
Wilson, Thomas 15–16
Winter, Leonard 81–2
'The Witch Doctor' – see Smith, E.
Wood, George 163
Wood, Ken 144
Wood, Mr W.J. (Lawyer) 192
Woodage, Bert Hamlin 177–80
Wooder, Jimmy 161
Woods, DS 45
Wye, William 53–6

Zomparelli, Alfredo 201, 205